# AA

# BRITAIN
## *for*
# FREE

*Over 1000
places to visit*

ALL ADMISSION · FREE · ALL ADMISSION · ALL ADMISSION

Produced by the Publishing Division
of the Automobile Association.

**Cover:** Kim Ludlow
**Typeset by:** Servis Filmsetting
Limited, Manchester
**Printed by:** BPCC Hazells Ltd
Member of BPCC Ltd

Every effort is made to ensure
accuracy, but the Publishers do not
hold themselves responsible for any
consequences that may arise from
errors or omissions. Whilst the
contents are believed correct at the
time of going to press, changes may
have occurred since that time or will
occur during the currency of this
book.

A CIP catalogue record for this book is
available from the British Library.

**ISBN 0 7495 0424 2**

Published by The Automobile
Association, Fanum House,
Basingstoke, Hampshire RG21 2EA.

# CONTENTS

# USEFUL INFORMATION

## ANCIENT MONUMENTS

These are identified in the directory with (AM), or (CADW) in the case of Welsh Ancient Monuments, at the end of the entry. Further information can be obtained from the following:

ENGLAND
*English Heritage, P O Box 43, Ruislip, Middlesex HA4 0XW.*

SCOTLAND
*Scottish Development Department, 20 Brandon Street, Edinburgh EH3 5RA.*

WALES
*CADW, Brunel House, Fitzalan Road, Cardiff CF2 1UY.*

At properties marked 'Keykeeper', the key must be obtained from a place nearby and details are usually displayed at the property itself.

## THE NATIONAL TRUSTS

(NT) at the end of a directory entry indicates that the property is in the care of the National Trust; (NTS) means National Trust for Scotland. Only those properties which are free of admission charges are included in this book, but many more National Trust properties are free of admission charge to Trust members.

Further information can be obtained from:

ENGLAND AND WALES:
*National Trust for Places of Historic Interest or Natural Beauty, 42 Queen Anne's Gate, London SW1H 9AS.*

SCOTLAND:
*National Trust for Scotland, 5 Charlotte Square, Edinburgh EH2 4DU*

## THE NATIONAL GARDENS SCHEME

Some of the gardens in the directory make reference to the charity known as The National Gardens Scheme. In some cases, any voluntary donations which visitors like to make will be forwarded to this charity; in others there may be a specific day or days during the year when an admission fee is charged to raise money for the charity. The abbreviation NGS in an entry signifies a connection with the charity.

## SYMBOLS AND ABBREVIATIONS

In addition to those detailed above, certain symbols and abbreviations have been used in the book in order to make the best use of the space available.

| | |
|---|---|
| ✆ | Telephone number |
| ♿ | Accessible to visitors in wheelchairs |
| ⊡ | Refreshments are available |
| ⏶ | Picnic area |
| 🐕 | No dogs |
| → | entry continued overleaf |
| BH | Bank Holiday |
| PH | Public Holiday |
| Etr | Easter |
| ex | except |

Months of the year and days of the week have been abbreviated to their first three letters.

# ABOUT THIS BOOK

The directory is arranged in alphabetical order of towns and entries within towns are also in alphabetical order. As far as possible, places in remote locations are listed under the nearest town or village, but in some cases the distance involved is too great for this to be sensible. In those cases the establishments are listed under their own name.

If you are looking for a particular place and are unsure about which town it might be located under, a comprehensive index, by establishment name, can be found at the back of the book. There is also a County List for easy reference to all the places in a particular area.

## ISLANDS

A number of Britain's offshore islands are included in the directory and the establishments on those islands are listed under the island name, eg Man, Skye or Wight. Under the main island heading, towns on the island are listed in alphabetical order. The Channel Islands are grouped together under a Channel Islands heading, then listed under Guernsey or Jersey as appropriate.

## OPENING DATES

All the dates quoted in the directory are inclusive, so that Apr – Oct means that the establishment is open from the beginning of April to the end of October.

## TELEPHONE NUMBERS

Unless otherwise stated, the telephone exchange will be that of the town under which the establishment is listed. Where this is not the case, we include the exchange name, but in every case the number we give includes the full STD code. The exchange name would only be necessary if you telephone from within the local area, when a local code should be used in place of the STD code.

Please note that telephone numbers are always subject to change. If you have any difficulty in obtaining a number, check with the operator.

## DONATIONS AND CHARITY BOXES

Some of the places listed in the directory are administered by Charities, Trusts and Associations. While they do not charge an admission fee, donations are very much appreciated to help with the cost of restoration work and any administration necessary to open the establishment to the public. Some may operate a system of voluntary contributions and others may have donation boxes available.

## CATHEDRALS

A few cathedrals are listed in the guide, but we have been cautious about listing any more because, although they are, strictly speaking, free of admission charges, many are now making very strong requests for donations. For some time now the most famous and historic cathedrals have charged an entrance fee to see particular sections such as towers, crypts, chained libraries etc. The fact is that the fabric of these ancient and beautiful buildings is crumbling and huge amounts of money are necessary to keep them in proper order. Bearing that in mind, few of us would expect to have the opportunity of looking round without making some contribution towards the upkeep, but that does put most of the major cathedrals outside the scope of this book.

## CARE OF THE COUNTRYSIDE

There are many entries in the directory for countryside sites and nature reserves. Many have public footpaths or waymarked trails leading through them, and visitors should always stick to the marked paths. The object of the reserves is that these areas should remain undisturbed, and irreparable damage can be done to them by those who, perhaps quite innocently, wander over them at will. Nature reserves and bird reserves are more likely to have restricted areas than country parks, which have been developed specifically to give public access to the countryside.

## ABERBARGOED
Mid Glamorgan

**STUART CRYSTAL**
Pengam Glassworks
On a self-conducted factory tour
visitors can see the manufacture of
crystal glassware at close hand,
from glassmaking to decorating.

Open: factory Mon–Fri 9–3.30; shop
daily 9–5, incl most BH.
Shop.

## ABERDARE
Mid Glamorgan

**DARE VALLEY COUNTRY PARK**
Country park and visitor centre.
Land Rover trips during summer
months (charge).

℘ 0685 874672/883099.
Open: park at all times, Visitor Centre
Etr–Sep daily 9–5 (10–6 weekends);
winter weekdays 10–5
🖵 (times as Visitor Centre) 🚻
🔥 toilets for the disabled.

## ABERDEEN
Grampian

**ABERDEEN ART GALLERY**
Schoolhill
Aberdeen Art Gallery, built in 1884
in neo-classical style, houses one of
the most important provincial art
collections in Great Britain ranging
from 18th-century portraits by
Raeburn, Hogarth, Ramsay and
Reynolds to 20th-century works by
Paul Nash, Ben Nicholson and
Francis Bacon. There are also
paintings by Impressionists such as
Monet, Pissaro, Sisley and Bonnard.
In addition, a significant collection
of Scottish domestic silver and
other decorative arts is normally on
show. The Art Gallery also presents
a lively and diverse programme of
special exhibitions and events.

℘ 0224 646333.
Open: Mon–Sat 10–5 (8pm Thu) Sun
2–5. (Closed Xmas and 1–2 Jan.)
🖵 🔥 Shop 🐾 (ex guide dogs).

**CRUICKSHANK BOTANIC GARDEN
(UNIVERSITY OF ABERDEEN)**
St Machar's Drive
Developed at the end of the 19th
century, the 10 acres include rock
and water gardens, collections of
spring bulbs, gentians and Alpine
plants. There is also an extensive
collection of trees and shrubs.

℘ 0224 272704.
Open: all year Mon–Fri 9–4.30; also
Sat & Sun May–Sep 2–5. Guided tours
on request. Donations welcome. 🔥

**DUTHIE PARK & WINTER GARDENS**
Polmuir Road/Riverside Drive
Beautifully laid out 50-acre park
with floral displays in all seasons,
including a 'rose mountain'.
Children's play areas and many
interesting sculptures and
monuments. The modern
conservatories, known as the
Winter Gardens, feature exotic
plants, flowers, birds, fish and
turtles. There is also a cactus
house, with some 600 species and
varieties of cacti and succulents,
and a Japanese garden designed in
traditional style. The most recent
additions to the Winter Gardens is a
three-house conservatory with a
major collection of ferns, plus
shrubs, alpine plants and water and
sculpture features. Sunday morning
and afternoon music in the Winter
Gardens all year round (this
extends to Sun evgs and Sat pms
Jun–Aug). Major free annual
events.

℘ 0224 583155.
Open: Daily 10–half hour before dusk.
🖵 🔥 toilets for the disabled, manual
& battery-operated wheelchair loan.
Shop 10–5 or later.
(🐾 in Winter Gardens).

**JAMES DUN'S HOUSE**
61 Schoolhill
18th-century building which
underwent an award-winning
renovation in 1975 and now houses
a varied and changing programme
of special exhibitions.

℘ 0224 646333.
Open: Mon–Sat 10–5. (Closed Xmas

and 1–2 Jan.)
🐾 (ex guide dogs).

**KINGS COLLEGE**
High Street
The college was founded in 1494,
but its crown tower was a 17th-
century addition. The chapel, with
its richly carved woodwork, dates
from the 16th century.

℘ 0224 272000 Ext 2579.
Open: Mon–Fri 9–5, Sat 9–12.30 (may
be closed Sat for wedding).
🔥 (ramp) 🐾

**MARISCHAL COLLEGE**
Broad Street
The college was founded in 1593
but the present building dates from
1844. Forming part of Aberdeen
University, it is said to be one of the
finest granite buildings in the world
with its 233ft-high Mitchell Tower.
The College houses the University
Anthropological Museum, the
Henderson Collection of classical
vases, the Grant-Bey Egyptian
Collection, a collection of Chinese
art (with bronzes of the Shang Yin
period). Tang Dynasty horses, and
carved jade of the Ming Dynasty.

℘ 0224 272000 Ext 3133.
Open: Term time Mon–Thu 9am–
10pm; Fri & Sat 9–5; Sun 2–5.
Vacation periods Mon–Fri 9–5.
🐾

**MARITIME MUSEUM**
Provost Ross's House, Shiprow.
This award winning museum,
housed in the city's oldest surviving
building, reflects the many aspects
of Aberdeen's important maritime
history. Subjects explored include
the development of the harbour,
whaling, fishing, ship-building,
wrecks and rescues and the North
Sea oil and gas industries. The
house, a National Trust for Scotland
property, takes its name from an
18th-century merchant.

℘ 0224 585788. For group bookings
0224 646333.
Open: Mon–Sat 10–5. (Closed Xmas
and 1–2 Jan.) NTS Visitor Centre
May– Sep & 1–19 Dec, Mon–Sat 10–4

(5pm, Jun, Jul–Aug).
&. (ground floor only) Shop
🐕 (ex guide dogs).

**PROVOST SKENE'S HOUSE**
Guestrow, off Broad Street
An outstanding example of Scottish
17th century domestic architecture.
The house is named after its most
notable owner, Sir George Skene, a
rich merchant engaged in trade with
the Baltic States, and Provost of the
city from 1676 to 1685. Room
settings range from Cromwellian
times to the Victorian era. The
chapel contains one of the most
important cycles of religious
painting in Scotland. The top floor
of the building houses a museum of
civic and domestic history.

☏ 0224 641086.
Open: Mon–Sat 10–5. (Closed Xmas
and 1–2 Jan.)
🖵 &. (ground floor only) Shop
🐕 (ex guide dogs).

**ST MACHAR'S CATHEDRAL**
Chanonry, Old Aberdeen
The Cathedral is Church of
Scotland, although the appellation
is historic rather than descriptive.
The partly castellated building is a
magnificent granite structure of
simple, austere grandeur mainly
dating from the 15th century. The
Heraldic Ceiling of 1520 is of oak
and is painted with emblems of
spiritual and temporal monarchs.
The West Front has two squat west
towers surmounted by spires.
There is stained glass of distinction.

☏ 0224 485988.
Open: daily 9–5. Donations.
Guided tours available on application
to the Church Secretary, St Machar's
Cathedral.
&. (ground floor only).

# ABERFELDY
Tayside

**ABERFELDY DISTILLERY**
Scotch whisky distillery and
woodland garden with specimen
trees and Himalayan plants.

☏ 0887 20330.
Open: Etr–Oct Mon–Fri 10–4.
Coach parties by prior arrangement
🐕

# ABERYSTWYTH
Dyfed

**NATIONAL LIBRARY OF WALES**
Penglais Hill
One of Britain's six copyright
libraries, housed in imposing
building of 1911–16, with later
additions. Large number of books
in all languages, musical
publications, prints, drawings and
old deeds; specialises in Welsh and
Celtic literature. Exhibitions of
pictures.

☏ 0970 623816.
Open: Mon–Fri 9.30–6, Sat until 5pm.
(Closed BH & 1st week of Oct.)
🖵 &. Shop 🐕

**YR HEN GAPEL**
Tre'r'ddôl
(On the main A487 road 9m
from Aberystwyth and
Machynlleth)
This museum of 19th-century
religious life in Wales reflects those
activities which had such far-
reaching effects on the social life of
both rural and industrial Wales.
Displays based on Mr. R. J.
Thomas's collection of local
bygones in a chapel. Run jointly by
Ceredigion District Council and the
Welsh Folk Museum, St. Fagans.
Tourist Information Centre in
museum.

☏ 0970 86407.
Open: Apr–mid Sep Mon–Sat
9.30–4.45.
&. (part) 🐕

# ACHILTIBUIE
Highland

**THE SMOKEHOUSE**
(3m NW)
Viewing windows, story boards and
leaflets enable visitors to see and
learn how smoked salmon and
other speciality products are
prepared.

☏ 085482 353.
Open: Etr–Oct Mon–Sat 9–5; Oct–Etr
Mon–Fri.
Shop.

# ACTON BURNELL
Shropshire

**ACTON BURNELL CASTLE**
Ruined 13th-century fortified manor
house built by Robert Burnell,
Bishop of Bath and Wells.

Open: at all reasonable times.
&. (AM)

# ALDERSHOT
Hampshire

**QUEEN ALEXANDRA'S ROYAL ARMY
NURSING CORPS MUSEUM**
Royal Pavilion, Farnborough
Road
A small military museum with a
pictorial history of army nursing
from the Crimea to the Falklands
Campaign.

☏ 0252 24431 Ext 4301.
Open: all year Tue–Wed 9–12.30 & 2–
4.30; Thu 9–12.30. Other times by
appointment. Donations welcomed.
Guided tours for small groups by prior
arrangement.
Shop.

**ROYAL ARMY DENTAL CORPS
HISTORICAL MUSEUM**
Evelyn Woods Road
Next door to the Aldershot Military
Museum, with many exhibits
illustrating the connection between
dentistry and the Army from 1600 to
the present.

☏ 0252 24431 Ext 2782.
Open: all year Mon–Fri 10–12, 2–4.
Guided tours available. Cars checked
by military police.
Shop.

**ROYAL CORPS OF TRANSPORT
MUSEUM**
Buller Barracks
Uniforms and badges of Royal
Corps of Transport and
predecessors. In addition models
and photographs of vehicles used
from 1795 to present day.          →

☏ 0252 348837.
Open: Mon–Fri 9–12, 2–4. (Closed
BH.) Voluntary donations.
&. Shop ✿ Parking area 200 yds.

## ALLEN BANKS
Northumberland
(1.5m SE of Bardon Mill off A69)
Covering 185 acres, Allen Banks is
located in the deep valley of the
River Allen shortly before it flows
into the River South Tyne. The
valley is noted for its deciduous
woodland of mature beech and oak
inhabited by roe deer and the rare
red squirrel. There are attractive
riverside trails and in Moralee
Wood on the Eastern side of the
river, a steep climb gives rewarding
views.

☏ Scots' Gap 067 074 691.
Open: all year during daylight hours.
Donation box. Occasional guided
walks, ☏ 0434 344218 at a
reasonable time for details.
禾 &. (some); toilets for the disabled
(National Key Scheme) ✿ (ex on
lead)
(NT)

## ALTON
Hampshire

**CURTIS MUSEUM & ALLEN GALLERY**
High St
The 19th-century museum building
has recently undergone a complete
reorganisation and shows the
fascinating history of the area, from
fossils to brewing – an important
local industry. The Allen Gallery
150yd from the museum on the
other side of the High Street,
consists of a group of 16th and
18th-century buildings. It displays a
wide range of travelling exhibitions,
a selection of silver, and a superb
display of pottery.

☏ 0420 82802.
Open: Tue–Sat 10–5. Parties by
appointment. Tours by arrangement.
禾 &. (ground floor only) Shop ✿

## AMBLESIDE
Cumbria

**HAYES GARDEN WORLD**
(0.5m S on A591)
Beautiful landscaped nursery
gardens display an abundance of
plants, shrubs and trees, while
fascinating tropical plants thrive in
the Crystal Palace plant house.

☏ 05394 33434.
Open: daily, 9–6 (or dusk). (Closed
25–26 Dec, 1 Jan.) Parties by
appointment. Guided tours for parties
by arrangement.
&. (wheelchairs on loan) ⬚ 禾
Shop.

## AMPTHILL
Bedfordshire

**HOUGHTON HOUSE**
(1m NE off A418)
Ruined early 17th-century mansion
built for Mary, Countess of
Pembroke, sister of Sir Philip
Sidney, and with work attributed to
Inigo Jones. Often identified with
the 'House Beautiful' in Bunyan's
'Pilgrim's Progress'.

Open: at all reasonable times.
&. (ground floor & gardens only).
(AM)

## ANDOVER
Hampshire

**ANDOVER MUSEUM**
Church Close
The museum, housed in a fine
Georgian building, has collections
relating to the area's natural history
and geology, history and
archaeology. English glass and iron
foundry displays. The Art Gallery
exhibits are varied, and changed
monthly.

☏ 0264 66283.
Open: Tue–Sat 10–5 (Etr–Sep Sun 2–
5). Parties by appointment.
&. (limited) Shop ✿

## ARBORFIELD
Berkshire

**ROYAL ELECTRICAL AND
MECHANICAL ENGINEERS' MUSEUM**
Isaac Newton Road
The museum records the history of
the REME – the Army's major repair
and maintenance corps – using
displays, photographs, models and
life-size tableaux.

☏ Arborfield Cross 0734 760421 Ext
2567.
Open: Mon–Fri 9–12.30 & 2–4.30 (4
on Fri). (Closed BH.) Donations
welcome. Guided tours available.
Parties over 15 must give 2 weeks'
notice. Cars may be searched before
parking.
&. ✿ Shop.

## ARBOR LOW
Derbyshire

**ARBOR LOW HENGE**
(Off unclass road 0.75m E of
A515 at Parsley Hay)
A particularly fine example of a
henge monument with two
entrances in the containing bank
which is 6ft high and has a diameter
of 250ft. There are some 50 stones
many of which are standing. There
is also a later Bronze Age barrow on
the site.

Open: accessible at all reasonable
times.
(AM)

## ARMATHWAITE
Cumbria

**EDEN VALLEY WOOLLEN MILL**
Tour of working mill to see weaving
in progress. Courses in weaving,
spinning and dying including
workshop for children in the
handweaving studio.

☏ 06992 457.
Open: Etr–Oct daily, Nov–Dec Mon–
Sat, Jan–Etr Sat 9.30–5.30. Coach
parties by arrangement.
&. Shop.

## ARROWE PARK
Merseyside

**IVY FARM VISITOR CENTRE**
(0.5m from Junction 3 of M53)
Arrowe Park is The Wirral's largest
park, consisting of 400 acres with a
golf course, lake and woodlands.
The Visitor Centre provides
information on all the parks in The
Wirral. There is also a butterfly farm
of native British species (summer
only) and an observation beehive.

✆ 051 678 4200.
Open: all year daily 11–3.
Guided walks by prior arrangement.
&. Shop.

## ASHBOURNE
Derbyshire

**DERWENT CRYSTAL**
Shawcroft
Glass blowing and decorating
demonstrations.

✆ 0335 45219.
Open: all year (ex Xmas–New Year)
Mon–Sat, Factory 9–10 & 10.30–12.30;
Shop 9–5. Guided tours for 25 or
more by prior arrangement.

## ASHBURTON
Devon

**ASHBURTON MUSEUM**
1 West Street
Exhibits include local history,
Dartmoor artefacts, local geology,
documents and records, and the
Paul Endacott North American
Collection.

✆ 0364 53278 (hon. curator).
Open: mid May–Sep, Tue, Thu, Fri,
Sat 2.30–5. Donations welcome.
Guided tours available for pre-
arranged groups. ✍

## ASHFORD
Kent

**INTELLIGENCE CORPS MUSEUM**
Templer Barracks
Items concerning the Corps from
the two World Wars and other
articles up to the present day.

✆ 0233 657208.

Open: Tue, Thu 9–1, 2–5.
Parties by appointment.
&. Shop ✍

## ASHTON-UNDER-LYNE
Greater Manchester

**MUSEUM OF THE MANCHESTERS**
Market Place
Museum illustrating the history of
the Manchester Regiment and its
integral relationship with the local
community from the Boer War to
National Service.

✆ 061 344 3078.
Open: all year Mon–Sat (ex Christmas
week & BH) 10–4.
&. Shop.

**PORTLAND BASIN INDUSTRIAL
HERITAGE CENTRE**
Portland Place, Portland Street
South
Tameside's social and industrial
history over the last 200 years. The
story is told in several sections
starting with pre-Industrial
Revolution. On to the Industrial
Revolution and its effect on the lives
of the people, how the factory
system determined that adults and
children were expected to work
long hours in bad conditions for
little pay. Other sections deal with
the growth of political awareness
and the importance of religious
movements for spiritual,
recreational and educational needs.

✆ 061 308 3374.
Open: all year, summer Tue–Sat 10–6
Sun 12–6; winter Tue–Sat 10–4, Sun
12–4. Parties by advance
arrangement.
责 &. (lift/ramps) Shop.

## ASH VALE
Surrey

**RAMC HISTORICAL MUSEUM**
Keogh Barracks
A well-lit and highly organised
collection of some 2,500 items,
mainly of military interest but with
many unusual items of general
interest. Some working models;

medal displays. Exhibits include a
horse-drawn ambulance and a 1942
Austin K2 ambulance. There are
three cases of items relating to the
Falklands War and a display of a
patient on an operating table.

✆ Aldershot 0252 340212.
Open: Mon–Fri 8.30–4. (Closed Xmas,
New Year & BH). Weekends &
evenings by appointment only.
Donation box. Guided tours by
arrangement.
&. toilets for the disabled. Shop ✍

## ASTON ROWANT
Oxfordshire

**NATURE RESERVE**
(1.5m W of Stokenchurch on
unclass road off A40)
The Nature Reserve commands an
excellent view over the Oxfordshire
Plain and is located on the scarp
slope of the Chiltern Hills. There
are extensive beech woodlands, and
scattered areas of juniper scrub
among chalk grasslands. In
summer, warblers, nightingales,
kestrels and sparrowhawks can be
seen. Violet helleborine, large white
helleborine and wood barley are
some of the unusual plants found in
the wooded areas.

✆ Ickford 0844 339719.
Open: daily, dawn to dusk.
Parties by appointment. Guided tours
available for educational groups by
arrangement. No picknicking. Visitors
are requested not to park along
approach road. Dogs on leads only.

## AULDEARN
Highland

**BOATH DOOCOT**
(Off A96 in Auldearn, 2m E of
Nairn)
A 17th-century dovecote on the site
of an ancient castle where, on 9 May
1645, Montrose flew the standard of
Charles I and defeated an army of
Covenanters. The plan of the battle
is on display.

Open: accessible at all reasonable
times.
(NTS)

## AVEBURY
Wiltshire

**STONE CIRCLE**
The largest stone circle in Europe, measuring 1,400ft across, consists of 100 sarsen stones, some of them about 20ft high. Within the main circle there are traces of a smaller one. There is an enclosing bank of chalk, 20ft high in places, and a chalk ditch. Leading away to the south east is an avenue of stones.

Open: accessible at all reasonable times.
(AM)

## AVELEY
Essex

**BELHUS WOODS COUNTRY PARK**
(Access from Romford Road)
Woodlands and open areas for walking, picnicking and fishing. Three lakes – two for fishing, one for birdwatching. There is also a visitor centre and programme of special activities.

✆ 0708 865628.
Open: all year daily 8–dusk. Visitor Centre Sat 2–5, Sun & BH 10–5, Wed 1–4. Parking charge Sun & BH Etr–Oct Guided tours available.
🍽 (times as Visitor Centre) 🪑
🚻 (most).

## AVIEMORE
Highland

**CRAIGELLACHIE NATIONAL NATURE RESERVE**
(Follow signs within Aviemore Centre to underpass below A9 trunk road)
Lying on the western edge of Aviemore, this 642-acre nature reserve rises to over 1,700ft. It takes its name from a crag whose name translates from Gaelic as 'rock of the stony place'. One third of the reserve is covered by birch woodlands, the remainder is moorland. The starting point of the mile-long nature trail is close to Loch Puladdern and from the trail there are impressive views. The birch trees support several species

of moth including the great brocade and the angle-striped sallow. Over 160 species of beetle have been recorded and there are interesting plant, bird and animal communities. There are three areas of open water – Loch Puladdern, Lochan Dubh and the old Aviemore reservoir.

Open: all year, dawn–dusk.

## AXBRIDGE
Somerset

**KING JOHN'S HUNTING LODGE**
The Square
Restored early Tudor house with exhibits covering history of River Axe valley from the Stone Age. Old photographs, town stocks and constables' staves also on show.

✆ 0934 732012.
Open: Apr–Sep, daily 2–5. Parties by appointment.
(NT)

## AXMINSTER
Devon

**AXMINSTER CARPETS LTD**
Gamberlake
Visitors can see the manufacture of fine Axminster carpets from winding the bobbins, weaving, to adding the latex backing to the finished product and view the qualities and designs produced in the Showroom.

✆ 0297 32244.
Open: Mon–Fri 9.30–12, 2–5. Parties by appointment only. Guided tours available for pre-booked parties
🚫

## AYLESBURY
Buckinghamshire

**BUCKINGHAMSHIRE COUNTY MUSEUM**
Church Street
Housed in former grammar school built in 1720 and two 15th-century houses, which were completely altered in the mid 18th century. Currently being refurbished, but the Aylesbury Gallery, telling the history of the town, and the Special Exhibitions Gallery remain open.

*Carved detail on King John's Hunting Lodge, Axbridge*

✆ 0296 88849.
Open: Mon–Sat and BHs, 10–1.30, 2–5.
🚻 Shop 🚫

## AYLESFORD
Kent

**KIT'S COTY HOUSE**
(1.5m NE off unclass road)
The best-preserved Neolithic burial chamber in Kent, dating from about 3,500 BC. Three upright stones are capped by a fourth. The covering mound of earth has long since disappeared.

Open: accessible at all reasonable times. (AM)

## AYR
Strathclyde

**MACLAURIN ART GALLERY & ROZELLE HOUSE**
Rozelle, Monument Road
Contemporary and traditional art decorative and applied. Nature trail in surrounding park with open-air sculpture; work by Henry Moore on display. Art exhibitions based on permanent collections in mansion house. Small military museum.

✆ Alloway 0292 43708 or 45447.
Open: Mon–Sat 10–5, Sun (Mar–Oct only) 2–5. (Closed Xmas & New Year period.) Donation box.
🍴 ✻ ⓧ ♿ (ground floor only).

## AYSGARTH
North Yorkshire

**YORKSHIRE DALES NATIONAL PARK CENTRE**
Visitor centre with interpretative display, maps, guides and local information available.

✆ 0969 663424.
Open: Apr–Oct daily 9.30–5, plus some winter weekends.
♿ Parking charge.

## BACONSTHORPE
Norfolk

**BACONSTHORPE CASTLE**
(0.75m N off unclass road)
A late 15th-century moated and semi-fortified house, incorporating a gate-house, a range of curtain walls and towers.

Open: at all reasonable times.
(AM)

## BADBURY RINGS
Dorset

(Off B3082 4m NW of Wimborne Minster)
A massive Iron Age hill fort comprising three concentric rings, the centre of which is thickly wooded. Four Roman roads lead from the fort to Dorchester, Old Sarum, Poole Harbour and Bath. Also of interest is the Roman posting station of Vindogladia which lies just outside the fort.

Open: accessible at all reasonable times.

## BALLOCH
Strathclyde

**BALLOCH CASTLE COUNTRY PARK**
Situated on the shore of the loch, with large area of grassland suitable for picnics and surrounded by extensive woodlands. Views of the loch from the castle terrace (c1808). Walled garden. History trail, tree trail. Countryside ranger service.

✆ Alexandria 0389 58216.
Open: Visitor Centre; Etr–Sep 10–6.
Country Park daily, dawn–dusk.
Parties by arrangement.
⚞ ♿ (part) toilets & parking for the disabled.

## BALMERINO
Fife

**BALMERINO ABBEY**
(Off A914 5m SW of Newport-on-Tay)
Visitors may view the abbey ruins from the grounds but may not enter the buildings which are in a dangerous state. Restoration work is being undertaken as funds allow.

Open: grounds are open at all times.
⚞

## BAMBURGH
Northumberland

**GRACE DARLING MUSEUM**
Radcliffe Road
Pictures, documents and various relics of the heroine, including boat in which she and her father, keeper of Longstone Lighthouse, Farne Islands, rescued nine survivors from the wrecked SS *Forfarshire* in 1838.

✆ Seahouses 0665 720037.
Open: daily, Etr–mid Oct 11–6.
Donations gratefully received. Large parties by appointment.
♿ Shop ✻

## BAMFORD
Derbyshire

**HIGH PEAK GARDEN CENTRE**
(On the A625 midway between Hope and Hathersage)
Well-established garden centre in the Peak District supplying all the usual garden needs. Also outdoor activities and aquatic centres, mountain bike hire, paintings and prints.

✆ Hope Valley 0433 51484.
Open: daily 10–6.
🍴 (Apr–Nov) ♿ Shop ✻

*Bamburgh's museum to local heroine, Grace Darling*

## BANBURY
Oxfordshire

**BANBURY MUSEUM**
8 Horsefair
This small museum exhibits items of local history, archaeology and photography. Changing programme of temporary exhibitions and of local artists' work. Tourist Information Centre.

✆ 0295 259855.
Open: Oct–Mar, Tue–Sat 10–4.30; Apr–Sep, Mon–Sat 10–5. Donation box. Parties by appointment. Guided tours by arrangement.
⌗ ♿ (chair lift to first floor) parking, entrance and toilets for the disabled. Shop ✖

## BANCHORY
Grampian

**BANCHORY MUSEUM**
Council Chambers
Exhibition of local history and bygone days.

✆ Peterhead 0779 77778.
Open: Jun–Sep daily (ex Thu) 2–5.20. Donation box.
Shop ✖ (ex guide dogs).

## BANFF
Grampian

**BANFF MUSEUM**
High Street
Exhibition of British birds. Local history and armour also on show.

✆ Peterhead 0779 77778.
Open: Jun–Sep, daily (ex Thu) 2–5.20 (donation box).
♿ (ground floor only) Shop ✖ (ex guide dogs).

## BANGOR
Gwynedd

**BANGOR MUSEUM & ART GALLERY**
Old Canonry, Ffordd Gwynedd
The museum portrays local history, collections of 17th–19th century furniture, crafts, costumes and textiles, maps, ceramics, and prehistoric, Roman and Dark Age antiquities. The Art Gallery stages exhibitions of sculpture, crafts and

paintings each year changing at approximately monthly intervals.

✆ 0248 353368.
Open: Tue–Sat. Art Gallery open 10.30–4.30 during exhibitions. Museum open 12–4.30. Donation box.
♿ (ground floor only – Art Gallery) Shop exhibits works of art. ✖

## BARNARD CASTLE
Co Durham

**EGGLESTONE ABBEY**
(1m S on minor rd of B6277)
Picturesque remains of Premonstratensian Abbey, including a substantial part of the church and some of the claustral buildings, on right bank of River Tees.

Open: at all reasonable times.
♿
(AM)

## BARNSLEY
South Yorkshire

**COOPER GALLERY**
Church Street
The former grammar school, founded in 1660, bought by Samuel Cooper in 1912 to display his collection of mainly Dutch, French and Italian paintings. The permanent collection has been augmented by loans and donations, and there is a fine group of English watercolours and drawings. The gallery has a programme of temporary exhibitions and related activities.

✆ 0226 242905.
Open: all year Tue 1–5.30, Wed–Sat 10–5.30. (Closed Sun).
♿ (ground floor) car parking for the disabled to rear of gallery by prior arrangement. Shop.

## BARNSTAPLE
Devon

**ST ANNE'S CHAPEL & OLD GRAMMAR SCHOOL MUSEUM**
St Anne's Chapel is a 14th-century building which was used as a grammar school from 1549 until 1910. It retains many features of

great architectural and historical interest, including a recently restored 17th-century schoolroom with the original school furniture. Crypt contains new museum of schooling.

✆ 0271 78709/46747.
Open: May–Oct Tue–Sat 10–1 & 2–5. Other times by arrangement.
Shop ✖

## BASILDON
Essex

**LANGDON HILLS COUNTRY PARK**
One Tree Hill and Westleigh Heights
Former farmland and woods with a variety of wildlife habitats and panoramic views of south Essex. There is an information room and an AA viewpoint.

✆ 0268 42066.
Open: all year daily 8–dusk. Guided tours and coach parties by arrangement.
⌗ ♿ (part) toilets for the disabled.

## BASINGSTOKE
Hampshire

**VIABLES CRAFT CENTRE**
Harrow Way, Viables
Craft workshops in converted farm buildings with resident craftsmen and women. There are miniature railway rides (charge) on the first Sunday of the month May to October. Craft fairs May Day BH weekend and last weekend in November.

✆ 0256 473634.
Open: Tue–Fri 1–4, Sat & Sun 2–5 (Closed 25 Dec for 2 weeks).
⌗ (wine bar: Tue–Sun 12–3, lincensed restaurant: Tue–Fri 12–2, Tue–Sat from 7pm; Tearoom Tue–Fri, 12–4, Sat & Sun 2–5). ⌗ ♿ (limited) toilets for the disabled. Shop.

**WILLIS MUSEUM AND ART GALLERY**
Old Town Hall, Market Square
The ground floor houses a Tourist Information Centre, a temporary exhibition gallery and natural

history displays. Upper floors tell the story of the town from prehistoric times to the present day and house a magnificent display of clocks, watches, embroideries toys and dolls.

✆ 0256 465902.
Open: Tue–Fri, 10–5, Sat 10–4. Parties by arrangement.
Shop ✖

## BATH
Avon

### BOTANIC GARDENS (ROYAL VICTORIA PARK)
Avenues of cherry trees (which blossom in spring) are only one of the thousands of different varieties of plants, trees and shrubs here. They come from all parts of the world, demonstrating what can be grown on local soil. Rock gardens, stream garden, pools, heather garden and herb garden. The Gardens form part of some 50 acres of Royal Victoria Park, which offers good views of the Royal Crescent.

✆ 0225 61111.
Open: daily, 8–sunset.
❏ &

### VICTORIA ART GALLERY
Bridge Street
The museum contains a varied collection of 18th- to 20th-century British paintings, watercolours and drawings with the European Old Masters well represented. Also on display is the Carr collection of English glass and watches from the 18th and 19th centuries. There is a mixed programme of temporary exhibitions.

✆ 0225 461111 Ext 2772.
Open: Mon–Fri 10–5.30, Sat 10–5.
(Closed BH.) Occasional lunchtime tours or lectures.
✖

## BATLEY
West Yorkshire

### ART GALLERY
Market Place
Permanent collection of British oil paintings, water colours, drawings and sculpture from mid 19th century onwards. A permanent exhibition of the local history of Batley. Temporary loan and special exhibitions throughout the year.

✆ 0924 473141.
Open: Mon–Fri 10–6, Sat 10–4.
(Closed Sun & BH, Good Fri, 25–26 Dec.)
✖

### BAGSHAW MUSEUM
Wilton Park (Best approached from Upper Batley Lane.)
An eccentric late-Victorian mansion housing collections of local history, archaeology, geology, ethnography, oriental arts, natural history and folk life.New galleries are entitled 'Divine Creatures', 'Mythical Beasts' and 'The Kingdom of Osiris' and there is a wide range of activities and temporary exhibitions.

✆ 0924 472514.
Open: Mar–Oct Mon–Fri 10–5, Sat & Sun 12–5, Nov-Feb daily 12–5 (subject to revision). (Closed Good Fri, 25–26 Dec.)
& (ground floor and gardens only)
Shop ✖

## BEACON FELL
Lancashire

### BEACON FELL COUNTRY PARK
(2.5m NE of Inglewhite)
The Beacon Fell Country Park covers a wooded hilltop to the south-west of the Forest of Bowland. Around the perimeter there are a number of car parks and many woodland paths lead to the summit (873 ft) which commands a good view across the Lancashire coastal plain. The wooded slopes are mostly coniferous and a home for many small mammals and a variety of birds. About half a mile south-east is the Carwags Information Centre which contains a small exhibition.

✆ Chipping 09956 235 or Preston 0772 263896.
Open: Country Park accessible at any reasonable time; Information Centre open by Ranger request & weekends.
无 ❏ (most days, pm only).

## BEARSDEN
Strathclyde

### ROMAN BATH HOUSE
Roman Road
Considered to be the best surviving visible Roman building in Scotland, the bath-house was discovered in 1973 during excavations for a construction site. It was originally built for use by the Roman garrison at Bearsden Fort, part of the Antonine Wall defences.

Open: Apr–Sep Mon–Fri 9.30–6, Sun 2–6.
(AM)

## BEDALE
North Yorkshire

### BEDALE MUSEUM
Bedale Hall (On A684, 1.5m W of A1 at Leeming Bar)
Grade I listed building with one of the most spectacular rooms of its period in the North of England, with stucco work by Cortese and the original floor. There is also a charming museum of local history containing archive material from the 17th century, Victoriana, costume and early toys. Tourist Information Centre.

✆ 0677 424604 or 422037.
Open: Etr–Oct, Mon Sat 10–4; Nov–Mar, Tue only 10–4. Other times for parties by appointment. Guided tours available by appointment. Parties by prior arrangement.
& ✖ (ex guide dogs).

## BEDFORD
Bedfordshire

### BEDFORD MUSEUM
Castle Lane
A local history and natural history museum with 19th-century room sets, displays on agriculture. Bedfordshire geology, archaeology, birds and mammals, fossils and minerals. Also a programme of temporary exhibitions.

✆ 0234 353323.
Open: all year, Tue–Sat 11–5, Sun &
BH Mon 2–5 (Closed Mon ex BH,
Good Fri & Xmas.) Donation box.
& (lift available on request) toilets
for the disabled. Shop ✿

**CECIL HIGGINS ART GALLERY AND
MUSEUM**
Castle Close
Award-winning recreated Victorian
mansion. Rooms are displayed as
though the house were still lived in
to give an authentic atmosphere.
The adjoining gallery has an
outstanding collection of ceramics,
glass and watercolours, and is set
in gardens leading down to the river
embankment.

✆ 0234 211222.
Open: all year Tue–Fri & BH Mon
12.30–5, Sat 11–5, Sun 2–5. (Closed
Mon, Good Fri, 25–26 Dec.) Donation
box (National Art Collections Fund).
Guided tours & coach parties by prior
arrangement.
& (lift to upstairs galleries; ramp &
handrails to entrance). Shop ☒

**BEDWYN, GREAT**
Wiltshire

**BEDWYN STONE MUSEUM**
Back Lane
An open air museum that explains
the ancient secrets of the
freemason and how the carvings
trace the behaviour of man. Finest
known sequence of carvings is to be
found in the church adjacent.

✆ Marlborough 0672 870043.
Guided tour of museum and church
available by prior arrangement.
Open: all year.
& toilets for the disabled.

**BEMBRIDGE**
*See Wight, Isle of*

**BERKELEY**
Gloucestershire

**BERKELEY NUCLEAR POWER
STATION**

✆ 0453 810431.

Open: all year, tours at 10, 2 and 7
Mon–Sat (ex Sat evening). Visitors
must book in advance.

**BERKHAMSTED**
Hertfordshire

**BERKHAMSTED CASTLE**
Remains of an 11th-century motte
and bailey castle with later circular
Keep. Former home of Black Prince
and one-time prison of King John of
France.

Open: at all reasonable times.
&
(AM)

**BERWICK-UPON-
TWEED**
Northumberland

**CASTLE AND TOWN WALLS**
Remains of 12th-century stronghold
incorporating three towers and west
wall. Medieval town walls
reconstructed during Elizabethan
period

Open: at all reasonable times.
(AM)

**LINDISFARNE WINE & SPIRIT
MUSEUM**
Palace Winery, Palace Green
An exhibition of beautiful artefacts
from the wine and spirit industry
with a free sample of Lindisfarne
Mead.

✆ 0289 305153.
Open: Etr–Oct Mon–Sat 10–5.
Pot shop and perfumery.
&

**BEVERLEY**
Humberside

**ART GALLERY & MUSEUM**
The Hall, Lairgate
Local antiquities, Victorian bygones
and china, pictures by F W Elwell of
Beverley and others, and bust of Sir
Winston Churchill by Bryant Baker
of New York. Various solo Art
Exhibitions.

✆ Hull 0482 882255.
Open: Mon–Sat 10–5 (Thu 10–12.30
only).
☒ Shop ✿

**BEXLEY**
Greater London

**BEXLEY MUSEUM**
Hall Place, Bourne Road
Local history museum housed in
Tudor and Jacobean mansion.
Grade I listed building and ancient
monument with contrasting
elevations of chequered flint and
brick. Magnificent grounds and
gardens with topiary in form of
'Queen's Beasts', roses, rock,
water, herb, peat gardens,
conservatory houses and recreation
facilities. Special exhibitions.

✆ Crayford 0322 526574 Ext 221.
Open: House, all year, Mon–Sat 10–5;
Sun 2–6 (summer only); Gardens:
Mon–Fri 7.30–dusk, Sat & Sun 9–dusk.
⌂ (summer only) & (ground floor
only) Shop ✿

**BIDDENDEN**
Kent

**BABY CARRIAGE COLLECTION**
Bettenham Manor
A unique collection of 450 baby
carriages (prams) of a bygone era.
Exhibits portray the history of the
pram up to the present day and
include 18th-century stickwagons,
perambulators and mailcarts,
Edwardian bassinettes, Victorias
and large coachbuilt prams of the
twenties. The museum, in a Kentish
oast house, adjoins a 15th-century
moated manor house of historical
and architectural interest and is set
in a 15-acre garden.

✆ 0580 291343.
Open: all year (ex Xmas Day) by
appointment only. Guided tours
available by arrangement. Donations
welcome.
& (ground floor & garden only) ✿

**BIDDENDEN VINEYARDS**
Little Whatmans (1.5m S off
A262)

Locks at Bingley

## BINGLEY
West Yorkshire

**BINGLEY FIVE RISE LOCKS**
(0.5m N of Bingley on canal towpath)
One of the wonders of the waterways. The lock staircase is situated on the Leeds and Liverpool Canal and was designed and built by John Longbotham of Halifax during the 1770s.

Open: Towpath accessible at all reasonable times.

## BINHAM
Norfolk

**BINHAM PRIORY**
The Priory, or at least its extensive ruins, dates from the 12th century. The main fragment to survive intact is the western end of the monastic church which is now used as the parish church. Inside, there is a perpendicular, seven-sacrament font and the stalls have misericords.

Open: accessible at all reasonable times.
&
(AM)

## BIRDLIP
Gloucestershire

**CRICKLEY HILL COUNTRY PARK**
(Off A436)
On the extreme edge of the Cotswold scarp, 143 acres of grassland and old beech woodlands, the steep grassy slopes rich in flowers and butterflies. From the edge of the hill there are views to the Malverns, Forest of Dean, mountains of South Wales and the Severn Valley. Site of archaeological interest. Visitor Information Centre with displays; sales point sells trail leaflets.

℘ Gloucester 0452 863170.
Open: Apr–Sep Sat pm & Sun 10–5.30. Will also open weekdays if enough demand – please telephone in advance. Coaches by appointment. →

Kent's oldest commercial vineyard. Visitors may walk through 22 acres of vines, visit the winery and shop, containing a 17th-century cider press, and sample the wines, ciders and apple juices produced here.

℘ 0580 291726.
Open: all year daily, except 24 Dec–1 Jan and Suns in Jan & Feb. Coaches welcome.
Shop.

## BILLERICAY
Essex

**CATER MUSEUM**
74 High Street
A folk museum of bygones, mainly of a rural nature, housed in an 18th-century building. Room displays of a Victorian bedroom and sitting-room. Early photographs. Model fire engines dating from earliest times to the 1950s.

℘ 0277 622023.
Open: Mon–Sat 2–5.

## BILLINGHAY
Lincolnshire

**OLD VICARAGE MUSEUM AND CRAFT WORKSHOP**
Church Street
The Old Vicarage, dating from the mid 1600s, is a cottage made of 'mud and stud'. Blacksmith Ian Cauldwell is in residence creating items which are both practical and sculptural. The display area to the side of the forge shows examples of his work, material about the cottage and a collection of old village photographs.

℘ 0526 861179.
Open: Etr–Oct Tue–Sun & B H, Nov–Etr Thu–Sat ex BH, 10–1 & 2–5.
& (ground floor).

&. (picnic table & viewpoint accessible to persons in wheelchairs; subject to ground conditions). ⊼

## BIRKENHEAD
Merseyside

**BIRKENHEAD PRIORY**
Priory St
Founded in 1150, the Priory provided accommodation for a prior and 16 Benedictine monks. Most of the buildings were neglected after the Dissolution. The church tower of St Mary's has recently been renovated. An interpretation centre traces the history and development of the site.

℘ 051 666 1249.
Open: Tue–Sat 10.30–1.30 & 2–5, Sun 2–5. (Closed Xmas and Mon, but open BH Mons.) St Mary's tower open Tue–Sun 2–5 pm for guided tour. &. (ground floor only).

**TAM O'SHANTER WIRRAL URBAN FARM**
Boundary Rd, Bidston (4m NW off A553)
The Tam O'Shanter Cottage, around which the urban farm is based, is about 300 years old. In 1837, a stonemason living in it carved the Tam O'Shanter Stone, showing a scene from the Burns poem, which is mounted in the end wall of the cottage. Visitors can see livestock such as poultry, geese and ducks, pigs, sheep and goats. Educational materials. Dogs must be kept on a short lead.

℘ 051 653 9332.
Open: daily 10–4. Donation box. Guided tours available by prior appointment. Two weeks advance notice required for group visits. &. (widened paths) toilets for the disabled. Shop ⊼

**WILLIAMSON ART GALLERY & MUSEUM**
Slatey Road
Exhibits include a major collection of work by English water-colourists and Liverpool school of painters; sculpture; decorative arts; ceramics (English, Continental, Oriental

wares); glass, silver and furniture. Also a large collection of paintings by P Wilson Steer, as well as approximately 25 special exhibitions throughout the year. A local history and maritime museum containing model ships is adjacent.

℘ 051 652 4177.
Open: Mon–Sat, 10–5; Thu, 10–9; Sun 2–5. (Closed 25–26 Dec & Etr Mon.) &. toilets for the disabled should be available by Autumn 1991. Shop ⊗ (ex guide dogs).

## BIRMINGHAM
West Midlands

**ASTON HALL**
Trinity Road, Aston
Built between 1618 and 1635, Aston Hall was one of the last great Jacobean country houses to be built in England. Despite being sacked by Parliamentarian soldiers, much decorative work survives, particularly moulded plasterwork, and the noted great staircase and long gallery. Fine paintings, furniture, silver and ceramics from the Birmingham Museums and Art Gallery collections are displayed.

℘ 021 327 0062.
Open: late Mar–Oct daily 2–5. Donations. Guided tours evenings only, charged according to circumstances.
⊡ (2–4.45) &. (ground floor only) braille guide available.

**BIRMINGHAM NATURE CENTRE**
Pershore Road, Edgbaston
A six-acre site with past and present British wildlife in naturalistic enclosures, including otter, lynx, beaver, wild cat, fox and snowy owl. There is a unique indoor display of rodents, reptiles and fish. Insect exhibits include an observation beehive and apiary and a wood ants' nest. Special events include sheep shearing and woolcrafts and a craft fair.

℘ 021 427 7775.
Open: Mar–Oct daily 10–5, weekends Oct–Mar. Donation requested. Guided tours charged according to

circumstances.
⊡ (10–4.30) &. toilets for the disabled 'Green' gift shop.

**BLAKESLEY HALL**
Blakesley Road
Birmingham's finest Elizabethan building, an attractive timber-framed farmhouse recently restored. A dozen rooms have been furnished as they were in 1684 when an inventory of the house's contents was drawn up. Reproduction soft furnishings and textiles have been introduced to enhance the 17th-century feel of the Hall, and staff greet visitors in period costume. Even the food and drink in the kitchen is appropriate to the time. Pushchairs and stilleto heels are not permitted in the house.

℘ 021 783 2193.
Open: mid Mar–Oct every day 2–5. Donation welcome. Coach parties by prior arrangement.
&. (ground floor) Shop.

**CITY MUSEUM & ART GALLERY**
Chamberlain Square
Fine and applied arts, Natural History, archaeology and social history exhibits. There is a fine collection of paintings from the 14th century to the present day, including a most important collection of Pre-Raphaelite paintings. Applied arts include costume, silver, ceramics and textiles; there are social history and archaeological exhibits, prehistoric, Egyptian, Greek and Roman antiquities, an important coin collection and the famous Pinto Collection of wooden items. There are frequent lectures, temporary exhibitions (charge made for some), demonstrations and holiday activities for children.

℘ 021 235 2834.
Open: Mon–Sat 9.30–5, Sun 2–5. (Closed Xmas & New Year's Day.) Guided tours available Wed & Sat 2.30 pm. Parties by arrangement. ⊡ (9.30–4.30) &. (most floors accessible; lift). Shop ⊗ (ex guide dogs).

**MUSEUM OF SCIENCE & INDUSTRY**
Newhall Street (close to Post Office Tower)
Displays from the Industrial Revolution up to the present including a new 'hands-on' Gallery of Light and Science. Engineering hall was formerly a Victorian plating works and contains machine tools, electrical equipment, working steam, gas and hot air engines. Locomotive hall. Transport section. Science section. Pen room. Music room. In the aircraft section World War II Spitfire and Hurricane, and collection of aircraft engines. James Watt building contains oldest working steam engine in the world, dated 1779. Steam weekends.

℘ 021 236 1022.
Open: Mon–Sat 9.30–5, Sun 2–5. (Closed Xmas & New Year's Day.) Parties by prior arrangement with Schools Liaison Officer.
toilets for the disabled. Shop (ex guide dogs).

**SAREHOLE MILL**
Cole Bank Road, Hall Green (5m SE of city centre on Stratford Road, A34)
Birmingham's last working watermill with one of the two waterwheels regularly operated according to the availability of water in the millpond. A miller is in residence on the first Sunday of the month and there are displays on local agricultural and rural life.

℘ 021 777 6612.
Open: Mar–Oct daily 2–5. Donations. Guided tours available to specialist groups only by prior arrangement.
(ground floor only) Shop.

**SELLY MANOR MUSEUM & MINWORTH GREAVES EXHIBITION HALL**
Corner of Maple Road and Sycamore Road, Bournville
A 14th/16th-century half-timbered house re-erected in Bournville. Collection of old furniture, etc. and herb garden. Exhibitions.

℘ 021 472 0199.
Open: mid Jan–mid Dec, Tue–Fri

10–5. Parties & guided tours by arrangement.
(ground floor only) Shop

**WEOLEY CASTLE**
Alwold Road (Off A38 Bristol rd)
Ruined 13th-century moated manor house with a small museum displaying objects found during excavations of the site in the 1930s and 1950s.

℘ 021 427 4270.
Open: Mar–Oct Tue–Fri 2–5. Donation.

**BIRSAY**
*See Orkney*

**BIRSTALL**
West Yorkshire

**OAKWELL HALL AND COUNTRY PARK**
Nova Lane, near Birstall Smithes (6m SE of Bradford)
Elizabethan moated manor house (1583), with Civil War and Brontë connections. It was 'Fieldhead', in Charlotte Brontë's novel *Shirley*. There is an extensive Country Park, formal gardens, visitor centres and shop. Full programme of summer events.

℘ Batley 0924 474926.
Open: all year Mon–Sat 10–5, Sun 1–5. (Closed 25–26 Dec, 1 Jan & Good Fri.) Please telephone to confirm opening times. There is a charge for the Hall only from Mar–Oct.
(Mon–Fri 12–4, Sat & Sun 1–4)
(ground floor & grounds) toilets for the disabled. Shop (ex guide dogs).

**BLACKBOYS**
East Sussex

**BROWNINGS FARM**
A 350-acre farm on the edge of the High Weald area of outstanding natural beauty. A farm trail guides visitors through farmland and woodland to converted Sussex barns now used as craft workshops.

℘ 0825 890338.
Open: all year, every day 9–sunset. Guided tours (charge) by prior arrangement. Coach parties by appointment.
Shop

**BLACKBURN**
Lancashire

**LEWIS MUSEUM OF TEXTILE MACHINERY**
Noted for series of period rooms portraying continuous development of textile industry from 18th century onwards. The gallery on the first floor has changing exhibitions.

℘ 0254 667130.
Open: Tue–Sat 10–5. (Closed Mon, Sun, Good Fri, Xmas, New Year's Day & some BHs.) (Booking 3 weeks in advance will enable a party to see machinery in operation.)
Shop (ex guide dogs).

**MUSEUM & ART GALLERY**
Museum Street
Local history, militaria, coins, ceramics, fine books and manuscripts, paintings, icons, watercolours and Japanese prints. Children's corner.

℘ 0254 667130 or 680603.
Open: Tue–Sat 10–5. (Closed Mon, Sun, Good Fri, Xmas, New Year's Day & some BHs.)
(ground floor only) Shop (ex guide dogs).

**BLACKPOOL**
Lancashire

**CORONATION ROCK COMPANY**
11 Cherry Tree Road North, Marton
Manufacturers and retailers of sugar confectionery.

℘ 0253 62366.
Open: all year Mon–Fri (ex BH) 9–3.30 (Fri 9–2). Guided tours are available. Coach parties must pre-book.
(ramp to viewing gallery) Shop.

## GRUNDY ART GALLERY
Queen Street
Established 1911, this gallery
exhibits a permanent collection of
paintings by 19th- and 20th-century
artists. Also touring exhibitions,
one man shows, group exhibitions
and classical concerts in winter and
spring.

℘ 0253 751701.
Open: Mon–Sat 10–5. (Closed BH.)
Tours by appointment.
✵ᕟ (ground floor only).

## BLACKTOFT
North Humberside

### SOUTH FARM CRAFT GALLERY
Saddlethorpe Lane. (Follow
signs from B1230 at
Gilberdyke.)
See a potter and other craftspeople
at work. There are five workshops,
a gallery shop and tea room. Craft
weekends with live music a feature.

℘ Howden 0430 441082.
Open: all year Wed–Sat 10–5, Sun
11–5 (Jan–Mar 10–4). Pre-booked
group guided tours evening only Tue–
Sun (charge).
ᕟᕟ (ground floor; ramps & wide
doors) toilets accessible with
assistance.

## BLADNOCH
Dumfries & Galloway

### BLADNOCH DISTILLERY
(Just S of Wigtown on A714)
Scotland's most southerly distillery,
producing 8-year-old single lowland
malt.

℘ 09884 2235/2236.
Open: all year Mon–Fri 10–4. Guided
tours are available. Parties accepted
with min 24 hrs notice.
ᕟ (shop only) Shop.

## BLANDFORD FORUM
Dorset

### ROYAL SIGNALS MUSEUM
Blandford Camp
Museum of history of army radio

and line communications; paintings,
uniforms, medals and badges.

℘ 0258 482248.
Open: Mon–Fri 10–5. Wknds (Jun–
Sep), 10–4. (Closed BH and 10 days
Xmas.) Small groups can be given
tour by prior appointment.
✵

## BOLTON
Gt Manchester

### TONGE MOOR TEXTILE MUSEUM
Tonge Moor Library, Tonge
Moor Road
Includes Arkwright's waterframe
(1768), Crompton's spinning mule
(1779) and Hargreave's spinning
jenny.

℘ 0204 21394.
Open: Mon & Thu 2–7.30, Tue & Fri
9.30–5.30, Sat 9.30–12.30. (Closed
Sun & Wed.)
ᕟ ✵

### WARBURTONS
Hereford Street
Tour of bread bakery.

℘ 0204 23551.
Open: Tue & Thu afternoons, Tue–
Thu evenings 2.30 & 7.30. Guided
tours only. Coach parties max 25
persons.

## BO'NESS
Central

### KINNEIL MUSEUM & ROMAN FORTLET
Kinneil Estate
Situated in the renovated 17th-
century stable block of Kinneil
House. The ground floor illustrates
aspects of the history of Bo'ness, in
particular its pottery. On the upper
floor, the exhibition '2000 Years of
History' tells the story of Kinneil
Estate from the Roman period to
the present. The Emperor
Antoninus Pius, St. Serf, Mary
Queen of Scots, and James Watt are
among the many historical
characters associated with the
Estate. Kinneil Roman fortlet is
open for viewing near the museum.

℘ 0506 824318.
Open: Apr–Sep, Mon–Sat 10–5
(Closed 12.30–1.30 Mon–Fri); Oct–
Mar, Sat only 10–5.
ᕟ (ground floor only) Shop ✵

## BORTH
Dyfed

### BRYNLLYS FARM
(Take the B4353 (Borth road)
off the A487 Aberystwyth-
Machynlleth road. After 1.5
miles turn right into Dôl y
Bont just after railway bridge.
Take first left after humpback
bridge and Brynllys is 400 yds
on the right.)
A working organic farm for four
generations. There are three farm
trails of one, two and three miles
and superb views.

℘ 0970 871 489.
Open: Mar–Nov every day 10–6 for
family visits (max 6). Group visits
(max 25) book by post only to
Centre of Alternative Technology,
Machynlleth, Powys (charge).
ᕟ Shop. Coach access difficult.

## BOURNEMOUTH
Dorset

### THE SHELLEY ROOMS
Beechwood Av, Boscombe
The rooms and library
commemorate the life and work of
Percy Byshe Shelley and his artistic
circle.

℘ 0202 551009.
Open: all year Mon–Sat 2–5. Coach
parties welcome if arranged in
advance.
ᕟ

## BOWES
Co Durham

### BOWES CASTLE
(0.25m W on A66)
Massive Norman keep dating from
c1170, set within the earthworks of
the Roman fort of 'Lavatrae'

Open: at any reasonable time.
(AM)

## BRADFORD
West Yorkshire

**BOLLING HALL**
Bowling Hall Road
A Yorkshire manor house which
dates from the 15th century and
contains fine furnishings, including
a rare Chippendale bed, heraldic
glass and 'ghost room'. Special
events programme.

℘ 0274 723057.
Open: Apr–Oct, Tue–Sun & BH Mon
10–6; Nov–Mar, Tue–Sun 10–5.
(Closed Good Fri, Xmas Day &
Boxing Day.)
& (ground floor only). Braille labels.
Shop ⊗ (ex guide dogs).

**CARTWRIGHT HALL ART GALLERY**
Lister Park
Contains permanent collections of
European and British paintings,
sculpture, drawings, modern prints
and ceramics. Also includes varied
exhibitions and special events.

℘ 0274 493313.
Open: Apr–Sep, Tue–Sun & BH Mon
10–6; Oct–Mar, Tue–Sun 10–5.
(Closed Mon ex BH.)
⊟ 禾 & toilets for the disabled. Shop
⊗ (ex guide dogs).

**INDUSTRIAL MUSEUM**
Moorside Mills, Moorside Road
Where better to house a museum in
Bradford than a former spinning
mill? Features include the growth of
the woollen and worsted textile
industry, transport and motive
power galleries, and the restored
mill owner's house. New in 1991 is
'Horses at Work' with rides and
demonstrations of harness-making,
shoeing etc.

℘ 0274 631756.
Open: Tue–Sun & BH Mon 10–5.
(Closed Mon ex BH.) Parties by
arrangement. Guided tours available
for groups by appointment.
⊟ & Shop ⊗ (ex guide dogs).

**NATIONAL MUSEUM OF
PHOTOGRAPHY, FILM & TELEVISION**
Prince's View

Incorporates displays, models and
galleries that explore photography
in all its many forms including
press, medical/scientific, moving
pictures, exhibitions and studios.
Displays and talk-over tapes make
for realism and visitor participation.
A new addition is the Kodak
Museum, where interractive and
theatrical displays tell the story of
photography from earliest days to
the launch of the first snapshot
camera. IMAX cinema (charge).

℘ 0274 727488.
Open: Tue–Sun 10.30–6. (Closed
Mon ex BH.)
⊟ (licensed) 禾 & (lifts) toilets for
the disabled. Shop
⊗ (ex guide dogs).

## BRAMBER
West Sussex

**BRAMBER CASTLE**
Former home of the Dukes of
Norfolk, this ruined Norman
stronghold lies on a South Downs
ridge with good views.

Open daily.
(NT)

## BRANDESTON
Suffolk

**THE SUFFOLK CIDER COMPANY**
The Cider House, Friday Street
Watch apples being crushed in the
traditional way, hear a short talk on
cider-making and sample a range of
apple juices and ciders. Daytime
tours are free, but there is a charge
for evening tours.

℘ 072 882 537/538.
Open: May–Sep, Mon–Fri, 9–1 &
2–4.30. Apple pressing starts in Aug.
Coach parties by appointment only.
Shop.

## BRANSBY
Lincolnshire

**BRANSBY HOME OF REST FOR
HORSES**
A hundred acres of paddocks where
over 140 rescued horses, ponies
and donkeys are cared for.

℘ 0427 788464.
Open: all year, daily 8–4. Guided
tours available. Light refreshments
can be served to pre-booked parties
by arrangement. All parties by prior
appointment.
& Shop 禾

## BRANSGORE
Hampshire

**MACPENNY'S**
Burley Road
One-time gravel pits have been
converted into this large woodland
garden and nurseries, with rare
trees, shrubs, rhododendrons,
azaleas, camellias and heathers and
a large herbaceous section.

℘ 0425 72348.
Open: Mon–Sat 9–5; Sun 2–5 (ex
Xmas and New Year). (Donation
box: proceeds to National Gardens
Scheme). Coaches by prior
arrangement.
禾 (NGS)

## BRECON
Powys

**BRECKNOCK MUSEUM**
Captain's Walk
Archaeological and local historical
exhibits, folk life, decorative arts
and natural history. Unique 19th-
century assize court. Regularly
changing temporary exhibitions.

℘ 0874 4121.
Open: Mon–Sat (incl BH) 10–1 &
2–5.
& (ground floor only, but access to
all by prior arrangement) Shop ⊗

## BRENTWOOD
Essex

**THORNDEN COUNTRY PARK
(NORTH AND SOUTH )**
Old parkland, lake and woods with a
new visitor centre at Thornden
North. For horse-riding at
Thornden contact Parks Office
(0277) 216297. Day fishing permits
(charge).

℘ 0277 211250 North, 0277 811379
South. →

Open: all year, daily 8–dusk. Parking charge Sun & BH in summer only (ex OAP, disabled, motorbikes). Guided tours by appointment. Parties by prior arrangement. ⅊ (part) toilets for the disabled. Shop ⌒

## WEALD COUNTRY PARK
South Weald
Old parkland, lake and woods. For fishing and horseriding permits contact Parks Office 0277 216297. Day fishing permits (charge).

℘ 0277 216297.
Open: all year, daily 8–dusk. Parking charge Sun & BH in summer (ex OAP, disabled, motorbikes). Guided tours by appointment. Parties by prior arrangement. ⅊ (part) toilets for the disabled. Shop ⌒

## BRIDGEND
Mid Glamorgan

### NEWCASTLE
Small ruined 12th-century and later stronghold, with rectangular tower, richly carved Norman gateway to south side and massive curtain walls enclosing polygonal courtyard.

Keys available locally. (CADW)

## BRIDGWATER
Somerset

### ADMIRAL BLAKE MUSEUM
Blake Street
The Museum is housed in the birthplace of Admiral Robert Blake (1587–1657). Exhibits include an audio-visual of the Battle of Sedgemoor, industrial history of Bridgwater and its docks and the Archaeology of Bridgwater and District. In the Blake Room there is a diorama of the Battle of Santa Cruz, Blake's greatest victory over the Spaniards. Several of Blake's personal belongings are also on show.

℘ 0278 456127.
Open: daily, Mon–Sat 11–5; Sun 2–5.

Donations welcome. Parties of more than 12 by appointment. ⅊ Shop ⌒

## BRIDLINGTON
Humberside

### PARK ROSE POTTERY AND LEISURE PARK
Carnaby Court Lane
Pottery Walkabout to see how pottery is created by mould-making, glazing and firing. Children's Fun Park with slides, swings and adventure play area.

℘ 0262 602823/4.
Open: all year, daily 10–5. ⌸ (licensed) ⅊ toilets for the disabled. Shop.

## BRIERLEY
West Yorkshire

### HOWELL WOOD COUNTRY PARK
(12m NW of Doncaster)
Country park with a wide variety of woodland trails. An old ice house beside a pond is of historical interest.

℘ 0226 711280.
Open: daily dawn–dusk. Guided tours available.

⅊ (specially surfaced woodland trail)

## BRIERLEY HILL
West Midlands

### ROYAL BRIERLEY CRYSTAL
North Street
The company was founded in 1847 and every piece of its crystal is made and cut by hand. The 1½ hour factory tour shows the production of hand-made crystal and includes a visit to the site museum which contains some unique pieces.

℘ 0384 70161.
Open: Factory tours by appointment only, Mon–Fri 11, 12 & 1. Shop Mon–Fri 10–6, Sat 9–5, Sun 10–4.20. ⌸ (Mon–Fri 9–4.45) ⅊ (foundry demo studio & video in coffee shop accessible). Shop.

## BRIGHOUSE
West Yorkshire

### BRIGHOUSE ART GALLERY
Halifax Road
Temporary exhibitions throughout the year of local artists' work and of other modern works of interest.

*Museum at Bridgwater*

✆ 0484 719222.
Open: Mon–Sat 10–5, Sun 2.30–5.
(Closed Sun, Oct–Mar; Xmas & New
Year's Day.) ♿ (ground floor only).
🐾

## BRIGHTON
East Sussex

**BOOTH MUSEUM OF NATURAL
HISTORY**
194 Dyke Road
Contains British birds mounted in
natural settings, butterfly gallery,
also whale and dinosaur bones,
environmental display. Temporary
exhibitions.

✆ 0273 552586.
Open: Mon–Sat (ex Thu) 10–5, Sun
2–5. (Closed Good Fri, 25–26 Dec &
New Year's Day.) Parties by
appointment.
♿ Shop 🐾

**MUSEUM & ART GALLERY**
Church Street
The collections include Old Master
paintings, watercolours, Sussex
archaeology, folklife and local
history, ethnography and musical
instruments. Also the Willett
Collection of pottery and porcelain,
and display of 20th-century fine and
applied art, including Art Nouveau,
Art Deco and 19th & 20th-century
costume. Also various special
exhibitions.

✆ 0273 603005.
Open: Tue–Sat 10–5.45, Sun 2–5.
(Closed Good Fri, 25–26 Dec, New
Year's Day and Mon, but open BH
Mons.) Charge made for entry into
some of the larger temporary
exhibitions. Parties by arrangement.
Educational tours to British schools
free by appointment.
🚗 (closed Sun) ♿ (ground floor
only) tactile tours by pre-
arrangement. Shop 🐾

## BRIGSTOCK
Northamptonshire

**BRIGSTOCK COUNTRY PARK**
(S of village off A6116 Brigstock
bypass)

The Park has been developed on
the site of a former sandpit and
covers about 37 acres with picnic
meadows, ponds and varied natural
habitats. Special dog walk. A
number of events are run at the
Park as part of the County Council's
Countryside Events Programme.

✆ 91273 625.
Open: all year, summer 9.30–6, winter
9.30–dusk. Guided tours available to
parties by prior arrangement. Coach
parties by appointment only.
♿ (part) toilets, parking & nature
trail for disabled. Shop 🚻

## BRISTOL
Avon

**ASHTON COURT ESTATE**
Long Ashton
Nature trail, woodland walks,
orienteering, deer park, formal
gardens and varied events. The
Visitor Centre, housed in the stable
block of the old mansion, hosts
changing displays about the
woodlands, wildlife, art and local
history. Other facilities (charge)
include golf courses, model railway
and grass ski slope (Sun & BHs).

✆ 0272 223856.
Open: daily 8.30–dusk.
Admission charge for some shows.
Visitor Centre Open: Sat & Sun & BHs,
Spring–Autumn, 10–5.
🚗♿ (part) toilets for the disabled.
🚻

**AVON GORGE AND LEIGH WOODS**
(Situated on the left bank of
the River Avon, by the Clifton
Suspension Bridge, NE of
A369)
159 acres of woodland, including
Nightingale Valley and the Iron Age
promontory fort of Stokeleigh.
Leigh Woods is a National Nature
Reserve, managed by English
Nature, offering many delightful
walks through deciduous woodland
containing a wide variety of birds.
The Avon Gorge, nearby, is two
miles long and its fossil-rich
limestone cliffs rise to 300 ft. The
soil here suits some rare plants and
the area is an attraction to

botanists. In fact, the rare Bristol
Whitebeam, found here, grows
nowhere else in the world. The
Avon Walkway is a recreational path
which follows the southern bank of
the River Avon through the Gorge.

Open: accessible at all reasonable
times.
NT (part)

**BLAISE CASTLE ESTATE**
Henbury (4m NW of city, off
B4057)
18th-century mansion, now social
history museum with displays on
West Country life from 1750 to the
present. Extensive grounds include
woodland, pond, meadow and
lawns, bisected by the River Trym.
There is a waymarked trail around
the estate.

✆ 0272 223856.
Open: all year daily, dawn to dusk.
♿ (part) toilets for the disabled.
Shop 🐾

**BRISTOL INDUSTRIAL MUSEUM**
Prince's Wharf, Prince Street
A converted dockside transit shed
in the heart of Bristol, 400 yards
from SS *Great Britain*. Display of
vehicles, horse-drawn and motorised
from the Bristol area, locally built
aircraft, aero-engines; railway exhibits
include full-size industrial locomotive
*Henbury*, steamed at least once a
month. Various kinds of machinery
illustrating local trade and
manufacturing. Display of history of
the Port of Bristol. Steam tug trips
(charge).

✆ 0272 251470.
Open: Sat–Wed 10–1 & 2–5. (Closed
25–27 Dec & New Year's Day.)
♿ Shop 🐾

**CITY MUSEUM & ART GALLERY**
Queen's Road
Regional and world-wide
collections, representing ancient
history, natural sciences, fine and
applied arts.

✆ 0272 223571.
Open: daily, 10–5. (Closed Good Fri,
May Day, Spring BH Mon, 25–27 Dec →

& New Year's Day.)
🖵 (licensed) ♿ Shop ✖

**MARITIME HERITAGE CENTRE**
Gas Ferry Road
The Centre introduces the theme of 200 years of Bristol shipbuilding with particular reference to Charles Hill & Son and their predecessor, James Hilhouse.

✆ 0272 251470.
Open daily (ex 24 & 25 Dec), 10–5 (winter); 10–6 (summer). Tokens may be purchased for entry to SS *Great Britain*.
♿ ✖

**OLDBURY COURT ESTATE**
Oldbury Court Rd, Fishponds
Nature trail, river walk, children's playground, cricket and football pitches.

✆ 0272 223856.
Open: daily 8.30–dusk. Coach parties not accepted.
♿ 🚻

**RED LODGE**
Park Row.
16th-century house altered in the early 18th century, with exceptional oak carvings and furnishings of both periods.

✆ 0272 211360.
Open: Mon–Sat 10–1, 2–5. (Closed Good Fri, May Day, Spring BH Mon & 25–27 Dec & New Year's Day.)
✖

**ST NICHOLAS CHURCH MUSEUM**
St Nicholas Street.
The history of Bristol from its beginning until the Reformation including Bristol church art and silver. Changing art exhibitions showing topographical features of the city mainly during the 18th and 19th century and the Hogarth altarpiece originally painted for St Mary Redcliffe. Brass rubbing centre.

✆ 0272 211365.
Open: Mon–Sat 10–5. (Closed Good Fri, May Day, Spring BH Mon & 25–27 Dec & New Year's Day.)

♿ toilets for the disabled.
✖ (ex guide dogs).

**THE GEORGIAN HOUSE**
7 Great George St.
Late 18th-century townhouse with contemporary furniture and fittings. Features include the kitchen, housekeeper's room, cold-water plunge bath and superb furniture.

✆ 0272 211362.
Open: Mon–Sat 10–1 & 2–5. (Closed Good Fri, May Day, Spring BH Mon & 25–27 Dec & New Year's Day.)
✖

**UNIVERSITY BOTANIC GARDEN**
North Road
The Garden contains over 4,000 species laid out in an informal setting. Many of the plants are tropical and include collections from New Zealand and South Africa. There is a small collection of British regional fauna. An arrowed route shows the way around the garden. Its location allows excellent walks and views of the Avon Gorge.

✆ 0272 733682.
Open: Mon–Fri 9–5. Donation box. Guided tours available to groups and parties by prior arrangement in writing with The Curator, University Botanic Garden, Bracken Hill, North Road, Leigh Woods, Bristol BS8 3PF.
♿ most ✖

## BRIXHAM
Devon

**BERRY HEAD COUNTRY PARK**
Gillard Road
Occupying an exposed limestone promontory at the southern end of Tor Bay, the Country Park is rich in limestone-loving wild flowers such as rockrose and orchids. On the cliffs there is a wide variety of sea birds including guillemots, kittiwakes, shags, cormorants and several species of gull. Part of the area has been designated a nature reserve. There are slight traces of an Iron Age promontory fort and in the past centuries a large area has been quarried. Information Centre.

✆ Torquay 0803 882619.
Open: accessible at all reasonable times. Guided tours available.
🖵 (Apr–Sep daily 11–6) ♿ (café & parts of grounds) toilets for the disabled. Parking charge summer season.

## BROADLEY COMMON
Essex

**ADA COLE MEMORIAL STABLES**
Broadlands
A sanctuary for rescued horses, ponies, donkeys and mules saved from distressed conditions or threat of unjustifiable slaughter. Annual open day and fête, carols in the barn with the animals at Christmas.

✆ 099 289 2133.
Open: all year, daily (ex Xmas Day). Donations. Guided tours are available.
♿ (concrete yard). 🚻

## BROADSTAIRS
Kent

**NORTH FORELAND LIGHTHOUSE**
North Foreland Road
Operational lighthouse on the main road between Broadstairs and Margate with a view across the Channel to the French coast on clear days.

✆ 0843 61869.
Open: Apr–Sep daily 10–till 1 hour before sunset. Guided tours available.

## BROADWINDSOR
Dorset

**BROADWINDSOR CRAFT CENTRE**
Redlands Farm (On B3163 2m W of Beaminster)
Craft workshops with working craftspeople producing pottery, fine woodwork and wood turning.

✆ 0308 68362.
Open: April–24 Dec daily 10–5. Coach parties by arrangement.
🖵 ♿ (ground floor). Shop.

Also **EARTHWORKS**
Museum of minerals, crystals and fossils adjacent to gemstone shop.

℘ 0308 68911.
Open: Feb–Dec, daily 10–5. Talks on
fossils and minerals by prior
arrangement.
💺 Shop.

## BROMBOROUGH
Merseyside

**DIBBINSDALE LOCAL NATURE
RESERVE**
Signposted from A41 at
Bromborough
Ancient woodland, wetland and
meadow.

℘ 051 334 9851.
Open: at all times. Guided tours by
prior arrangement. Coaches not
permitted.
💺 (part) circular trail around
Woodslee Pond, fishing platform for
the disabled. 🚻

## BROOK
Kent

**WYE COLLEGE MUSEUM OF
AGRICULTURE**
(4m ENE of Ashford on unclass
road)
An exhibition of old farm
implements and machinery housed
in a fine 14th-century tithe barn.
Display of hop cultivation in old
oast house.

℘ Wye 0233 812401.
Open: May–Sep, Wed 2–5, Sat in Aug.
Parties by arrangement in writing to:
Hon. Curator, Museum, Wye College,
Wye, Ashford, Kent TN25 5AH.
💺 (ground floor only) 🍴

## BROUGHTON
Borders

**BROUGHTON GALLERY**
Broughton Place (Just N of
Broughton village on A701)
Art Gallery on ground floor of house
designed by Sir Basil Spence in
1938 in the style of a 17th-century
Scottish castle. Paintings, prints
and crafts by leading British artists
for sale. The gardens afford fine
views of the Tweeddale hills.

℘ 08994 234.

Gallery open: mid Mar–end Sep daily
10.30–6 (ex Wed). Donation for
garden.
💺 Shop 🍴

## BRUAR
Tayside

**CLAN DONNACHAIDH MUSEUM**
Robes, Jacobite relics, weapons,
silver, glass, books and pictures
associated with the Clan whose
Chief is Robertson of Struan and
whose principal septs are Duncans
and Reids. Clan gathering 3rd Sat of
Jun.

℘ Calvine 079683 264.
Open: Apr–Oct, Mon–Sat (ex Tue)
10–1 & 2–5, Sun 2–5. Donation box.
💺 Shop 🍴

## BRYN-CELLI-DDU
Gwynedd

**BRYN-CELLI-DDU BURIAL CHAMBER**
(3m W of Menai Bridge off
A4080)
Excavated in 1865, and again 1925–
29, prehistoric circular cairn
covering passage grave with
polygonal chamber.

Open: accessible at all reasonable
times.
(CADW)

## BUCKDEN
Cambridgeshire

**BUCKDEN PALACE**
Also known as Buckden Towers, the
palace is mentioned in the
Domesday Book. From the 12th
century it was the residence of the
Bishops of Lincoln, though most of
the buildings date from Tudor
times. It is now the home of
Claretian Missionaries. The Church
and courtyard are open to visitors.

℘ 0480 810344.
Open: all year, daily 9–dusk.
Donation box. Guided tours of Tudor
buildings by prior arrangement (max
20). Parties by previous appointment.
💺

## BUCKIE
Grampian

**BUCKIE MARITIME MUSEUM**
Displays relating to the fishing
industry including exhibits on
coopering, navigation, life-boats
and fishing methods. Selections
from the Peter Anson watercolour
collection of fishing vessels are on
display.

℘ Forres 0309 73701.
Open: all year Mon–Fri 10–8, Sat
10–12.
💺 Shop 🍴

## BURGH CASTLE
Norfolk

**THE CASTLE**
(Far W end Breydon Water on
unclass rd)
Massive walls from former 3rd-
century Roman fort, guarded by six
pear-shaped bastions.

Open: accessible at any reasonable
time.
(AM)

## BURGHEAD
Grampian

**BURGHEAD MUSEUM**
Grant Street
Local history and temporary
exhibitions. Window display on the
Picts.

℘ Forres 0309 73701.
Open: Tue 1.30–5, Thu 5–8.30, Sat
10–noon.
💺 🍴

## BURNLEY
Lancashire

**TOWNELEY HALL ART GALLERY
& MUSEUMS**
14th-century house with later
modifications. Collection of oil
paintings, early English water
colours, period furniture, militaria,
18th-century glassware,
archaeology and natural history.
Nature trails. Loan exhibitions
Apr–Sep.                          →

✆ 0282 24213.
Open: Mon–Fri 10–5, Sun 12–5.
(Closed Sat.) Tours available for
educational groups by prior
arrangement.
⌨ (Apr–Sep) ♿ (ground floor only;
staff will assist) toilets for the
disabled. 🏮 Shop.

## BURNTISLAND
Fife

**BURNTISLAND EDWARDIAN FAIR
MUSEUM**
102 High Street
The museum reconstructs the
sights and sounds of Burntisland's
fairground in 1910, as captured by
local artist, Andrew Young. There is
also a small gallery telling the story
of Burntisland.

✆ 0592 260732.
Open: all year Mon–Sat 10–1 & 2–5
(closed PH). Coach parties welcome.

## BURSTON
Norfolk

**BURSTON STRIKE SCHOOL**
Church Green
In 1914 the reforming zeal of the
teachers at Burston lead to their
dismissal by the local
establishment. In protest, pupils
refused to attend the school, and in
1917 the Strike School was
established by the villages and the
teachers reinstated. Today a
permanent exhibition tells the story
of 'the longest strike in history'.

Open: Aug 9.30–6, open days, BH (ex
Xmas) and key available for access
c/o M. L. Welch Chairman of
Trustees. ✆ 0379 741565. Donation
welcome. Annual Burston Rally
celebrating the beginning of the
strike.

## BURTON AGNES
Humberside

**BURTON AGNES MANOR HOUSE**
Rare Norman house altered and
encased in brick in the 17th and
18th centuries.

Open: all year.
(AM)

## BURWARDSLEY
Cheshire
**CHESHIRE CANDLE WORKSHOPS
LTD**
(Tourist Board signs from
Tarporley or Tattenhall)
Candle workshops with
demonstrations of candle sculpture
and glass artist. There is a
children's play area, an aviary and
candle-dipping where children can
have a go.

✆ Tattenhall 0829 70401.
Open: all year Mon–Fri 10–4. Guided
tours. Coach parties welcome.
⌨ (licensed 10–4.30) 🏮♿ (ground
floor; all entry areas ramped) toilets
for the disabled. Shop.

## BURY
Gt Manchester

**BURY ART GALLERY & MUSEUM**
Moss Street
Contains a fine collection of 19th-
century British paintings including
works by Turner, Constable and
Landseer. The museum outlines the
social history of the town.
Temporary exhibitions.

✆ 061–705 5878.
Open: Mon–Fri 10–6, Sat 10–5.
(Closed Sun & BH.)
♿ (lift) toilet for the disabled. 🐕

## BURY ST EDMUNDS
Suffolk

**ABBEY GARDENS & RUINS**
Angel Hill
Beautifully laid-out formal gardens
form the centrepiece of the Abbey
grounds and lead down to the 13th-
century Abbots Bridge. A riverside
path leads past a hexagonal
dovecote to the ruins. Apart from
the Norman Gate (12th-century
campanile) and the decorated
Abbey Gate, little remains of the
great Abbey which was once an
important place of pilgrimage and
held the Shrine of St Edmund.
Stripped of its facing stone after the
Dissolution of the Monasteries,
there are Tudor, Georgian and
Victorian houses built into it, giving
it the appearance of a folly.

*Bury St Edmunds:*
*Abbey Gate*

✆ 0284 64667 (Tourist Information
Centre). Open: Mon–Sat 7.30–dusk,
Sun 9–dusk.
♿ (gardens).

**THE CLOCK MUSEUM**
Angel Hill
Queen Anne house containing fine
Gershom-Parkington collection of
clocks and watches.

✆ 0284 757072.
Open: Mon–Sat 10–1, 2–5 (Closed .
Good Fri, May BH, Xmas & New
Year.) Donation.
�֍
(NT)

**MOYSE'S HALL MUSEUM**
Cornhill
Built around 1180, Moyse's Hall is
one of the best preserved examples
of a 12th-century townhouse in
England. The museum features
local material ranging from fine      .
Anglo-Saxon remains from West
Stow to relics of the Red Barn
murder.

✆ 0284 757071.
Open: all year, daily (ex winter BH)
10–5 (Sun 2–5). Guided tours by
prior arrangement. Parties max 50.
♿ (ground floor) Shop.

**SUFFOLK REGIMENT MUSEUM**
The Keep, Gibraltar Barracks
Exhibits include uniforms, weapons,
medals, campaign souvenirs,
documents and photographs.

✆ 0284 752394.
Open: all year (except PHs), Mon–Fri
10–12 & 2–4.
♿ (ground floor only). Shop ✖

**BUTE,
ISLE OF**

**ROTHESAY**
Bute

**ARDENCRAIG**
High Craigmore
Developed by Sir John Reid between
1919 and 1923, this garden
produces plants for floral displays
throughout the Isle of Bute. It is
particularly noted for its display of

bushes, its aviaries and its
ornamental ponds.

✆ 0700 504225/504644.
Open: May–Sep daily 9–dusk.
Coaches welcome.
♿ (part only) 🍴 Garden centre.

**BUXTON**
Derbyshire

**GRIN LOW/BUXTON COUNTRY PARK**
Grin Low with its superb vantage
point and picnic area crowned by
Solomon's temple has been
reclaimed from dereliction arising
from many years of quarrying and
lime burning, and connected to the
Buxton Country Park. Additional
attractions are Poole's Cavern, Grin
Low Woods and the Visitor Centre.

✆ 0298 72541.
Open: at all times.
♿ (part) toilets for the disabled.

**PAVILION GARDENS**
St Johns Road
Twenty-three acres of landscaped
park, woodland and two ornamental
lakes. Children's playpark and crazy
golf course.

✆ 0298 3114.
Open: all year, daily (Sat & Sun only
Jan–Feb 10–5.30), Apr–Oct 10–5.30,
Nov–Dec & Mar 10–3.
🍴 (licensed) ♿ (ground floor) toilet
for the disabled. Shop ⛱

**CAERNARFON**
Gwynedd

**SEGONTIUM ROMAN FORT AND
MUSEUM**
Branch archaeological gallery of the
National Museum of Wales. Remains
of Roman fort of *Segontium* and
museum of excavated relics.

✆ 0286 5625.
Open: Mar–Oct Mon–Sat 9.30–6, Sun
2–6; Nov–Feb 9.30–4, Sun 2–4.
(Closed 24–26 Dec, 1 Jan, Good Fri &
May Day.)
Shop ✖
(CADW.)

**CAERWENT**
Gwent

**ROMAN TOWN**
(Beside A48)
Complete circuit of town wall,
together with excavated areas of
houses, shops and temple (in use
from 1st to 4th centuries).

Open: accessible at any time.
(AM)

**CAISTER-ON-SEA**
Norfolk

**CAISTER ROMAN SITE**
Remains, possibly of a fort,
including south gateway, part of a
defensive wall and buildings along a
main street.

Open: at all reasonable times.
♿
(AM)

**CALLANDER**
Central

**KILMAHOG WOOLLEN MILL**
(1m W on A85)
Original working water mill in
operation, together with a charming
mill shop selling Scottish
merchandise – woollens, tweeds,
tartans etc, and a Clan History
Centre.

✆ 0877 30268.
Open: all year daily, May Oct, Mon–
Sat, 9–5.30, Sun 10–5.30; Nov–Apr,
Mon–Sat, 10–4.30, Sun 11–4.30.
(Closed 25 & 26 Dec & 1 Jan).
Coaches welcome.
♿ (partial) toilets for the disabled.
Shop.

**CALLANISH**
*See Lewis, Isle of*

**CALVERTON**
Nottinghamshire

**PATCHINGS FARM ART CENTRE**
Oxton road
The art centre comprises an
exhibition gallery and working    →

studios featuring art, pottery, batik and tapestry. Art materials are stocked and a framing service is provided. There is an antique shop and a restaurant serving home-made food. Lecture tours, demonstrations and courses are available by prior arrangement, and special events include monthly exhibitions and farming attractions.

℘ 0602 653479.
Open: all year, daily (ex 25–26 Dec) 9am–10pm. Guided tours and demonstrations (min 20) charged for. Parties by prior arrangement only. ☐ (licensed) ♿ toilets for the disabled.

## CAMBRIDGE
Cambridgeshire

Ancient university city on the River Cam. Many of the colleges line the east bank overlooking the Backs; sweeping lawns set with willow trees, on the opposite side of the river transformed from rough marshland by Richard Bently (Master of Trinity College from 1669 to 1734). The colleges are open to the public on most days during daylight though there are some restrictions during term time and most colleges are closed from mid-April to mid-June during University examination period.

(All free except Queens College, for which there is a small admission charge.)

**FITZWILLIAM MUSEUM**
Trumpington Street
Houses an extensive art and archaeological collection including Egyptian, Greek and Roman antiquities. European paintings, manuscripts and armour. European & Oriental decorative art. Special exhibitions throughout year.

℘ 0223 332900.
Open: Tue–Sat 10–5, Sun 2.15–5 plus Etr Mon, Spring & Summer BH. (Closed Good Fri, May Day & 24 Dec–1 Jan.) Guided tours Sat & Sun at 2.30 pm; other times for groups by arrangement. Donations welcome.

☐ (licensed, closed Sun) ♿ (please give advance warning of visit) Shop ✇ (ex guide dogs).

**KINGS COLLEGE CHAPEL**
One of the finest Gothic churches in England, the stained glass windows show the story of the New Testament beginning in the north-west corner and ending in the south-west corner. They are the most complete set of Renaissance windows to survive in this country. The intricately-carved screen and choir stalls are fine examples of Renaissance craftsmanship.

Open: term time weekdays 9.30–3.45; Sun 2–3 & 4.30–5.45 (5.15 in winter). University holiday weekdays 9.30–5.45; Sun 10.30–5.45 (5.15 in winter). The chapel may be closed at certain times.

**SCOTT POLAR RESEARCH INSTITUTE**
Lensfield Road
Contains relics and equipment relating to arctic and antarctic expeditions with special emphasis on those of Captain Scott. Includes Eskimo and general polar art collections and information on current scientific exploration.

℘ 0223 336540.
Open: Mon–Sat 2.30–4. (Closed some public & university hols.) Shop ✇

**SEDGEWICK MUSEUM OF GEOLOGY**
Downing Street
Opened in 1904, the museum is part of the unified Department of Earth Sciences, University of Cambridge. There are about a million paleontological specimens including several hundred fossil collections associated with named collectors. The bulk of the collection is fully catalogued with rapid computer access to data, and specimens are readily available for physical examination. Special children's days.

℘ 0223 333437.
Open: all year (ex Xmas & Etr) Mon–Fri 9–1 & 2–5, Sat 10–1 (or by

arrangement with curator). Donation box. Guided tours by prior arrangement. No coaches on University site without prior permission.
♿ (lift). Shop.

**UNIVERSITY MUSEUM OF ARCHAEOLOGY & ANTHROPOLOGY**
Downing Street
Archaeology gallery covering man's development from the earliest times to civilisation throughout the world, and local archaeology up to the 19th century. New anthropology gallery illustrates cultures of Africa, the Pacific and the Americas. Also special exhibitions.

℘ 0223 333516.
Open: Mon–Fri 2–4, Sat 10–12.30. (Closed 24 Dec–2 Jan & 1 wk Etr.) Voluntary donations welcome. Parties by arrangement.
♿ (lifts) Shop ✇

**UNIVERSITY BOTANIC GARDEN**
Cory Lodge, Bateman Street
Originally founded in 1762 and now covering 40 acres with fine botanical collections.

℘ 0223 336265.
Open: Mon–Sat 8–6 (4pm winter). Sun, ticket-holders only. Glasshouses 11–12.30 & 2–4. (For ticket holders – telephone for information.) Donations requested from groups and organisations. ♿ toilets for the disabled. Shop ✇ (ex guide dogs).

## CAMPSALL
South Yorkshire

**CAMPSALL COUNTRY PARK**
(1m from A19, 6m N of Doncaster)
A very natural park, with 3 lakes, grassland and a variety of woodlands.

℘ 0302 873401.
Open: daily dawn–dusk. Guided tours available.
♿ (good wheelchair access throughout).

## CANTERBURY
Kent

**ROYAL MUSEUM & ART GALLERY**
High Street
The city's art museum with a gallery for temporary exhibitions. Other galleries include local artist Thomas Sidney Cooper RA, and the local regiment The Buffs. Also displays of fine porcelain, glass, clocks and watches, paintings; and east Kent archaeology with important Roman and Anglo-Saxon glass jewellery. Canterbury Festival exhibition Oct.

✆ 0227 452747.
Open: Mon–Sat 10–5. Donation box. Parties by arrangement.
Shop ✖

## CANVEY ISLAND
Essex

**DUTCH COTTAGE MUSEUM**
3 Oakfield Road
A 17th-century thatched cottage built for one of Vermuyden's workmen while reclaiming local marshes. There are small collections of furniture, corn dollies, agricultural implements and other artefacts in the cottage and adjoining annexe.

✆ 0268 794005.
Open: Spring BH–Sep Wed, Sun & BH. Wed & Sun 2.30–5 (BH 10.30–1 & 2.30–5). Guided tours.
✿ (ground floor).

## CAPEL DEWI
Dyfed

**Y FELIN WLAN (ROCK MILLS)**
This is one of the few remaining working water-wheels in Wales. Built in 1890 by the great-grandfather of the present owner, it has been in continuous operation since then. The water is supplied from the River Clettwr, a tributary of the Teifi.

✆ Llandysul 0559 362356.
Open: all year Mon–Fri 9–5; also Sat 9–5 Etr–Sep. Guided tours of woollen mill (charge) for groups by appointment only. Parties accepted –

children must be accompanied by a suitable number of adults.
✿ (ground floor areas only: mill shop & weaving can be viewed) Shop ㅈ

## CAPTON
Devon

**PREHISTORIC HILL SETTLEMENT MUSEUM**
Dittisham Fruit Farm
A museum recording 10,000 years of continuous human habitation on the site. There is a collection of flint tools and a reconstructed Stone Age roundhouse with sound and light shows. Pick-your-own and ready-picked fruit and vegetables are available with pure fruit liqueurs from the farm shop.

✆ 080 421 452.
Open: Mar–Nov daily 10–5. Donations. Talks, conducted tours and coach parties (max 20) by prior arrangement only.
Farm shop.

## CARLISLE
Cumbria

**GUILDHALL**
Greenmarket
Renovated, half-timbered early 15th-century Guildhall with exposed timberwork and wattle and daub walls. Once the meeting place of Carlisle's eight trade guilds and retains much of the atmosphere of the period. Displays feature many items relating to these guilds, and other reminders of life in medieval Carlisle.

✆ 0228 23411 Ext. 205.
Open: Tue–Sun 11–4. Parties by arrangement.
Shop ✖ (ex guide dogs).

## CARLOWAY
*See Isle of Lewis*

## CARNASSERIE CASTLE
Strathclyde
2m N of Kilmartin off A816)
Built in the 16th century by John Carswell, first Protestant Bishop of

the Isles. It was taken and partly destroyed in Argyll's rebellion of 1685, and consists of a towerhouse with a courtyard built on to it.

Open: Apr–Sep Mon–Fri 9.30–6, Sun 2–6.
(AM)

## CARRAWBURGH
Northumberland

**TEMPLE OF MITHRAS**
(3.75m W of Chollerford on B6318)
Remains of Mithraic temple dating from 3rd century but with later alterations. On line of Roman Wall near fort of *Procolitia*.

Open: at all reasonable times.
(AM)

## CASTLE CARY
Somerset

**CASTLE CARY AND DISTRICT MUSEUM**
Market Place
Museum based on themes from the County of Somerset, including the internationally renowned *Diaries of a Country Parson* by Parson Woodford. Also military and agricultural developments within Somerset.

✆ 0963 50277.
Open: Apr–Oct Mon–Fri 10.30–12.30 & 2.30–4.30. Donations. Guided tours available by appointment only.

## CAWTHORNE
South Yorkshire

**CANNON HALL MUSEUM & COUNTRY PARK**
(6m W of Barnsley on A635)
Cannon Hall is a late 17th-century house remodelled in the 1760s by John Carr of York, an influential architect of the period. It was opened as a country house museum in 1957, and has a large collection of furniture, paintings, glassware and pottery, some of which is displayed in period rooms. The Regimental Museum of the 13th/18th Royal Hussars (Queen Mary's Own) is also housed here. Cannon →

*Cannon Hall*

lake walk of 10 miles for which a completion certificate is available. Nature trails have many unusual plants and animals. Access to bird hide, best viewing Oct–Dec. The Centre includes a bi-lingual exhibition on geology, archaeology, history and natural history.

𝜙 049082 463.
Open: Exhibition and fishing, daily 8–one hour after sunset. Charge for fishing and watersports. Parties by arrangement.
🍴 (10–5) 🅿 ♿ (most). Fishing platforms for the disabled and free fishing open days. Souvenir & fishing tackle shop.

Hall stands in 70 acres of parkland, landscaped in the 1760s by Richard Woods, that contain several lakes stocked with numerous ornamental and indigenous species of waterfowl.

𝜙 Barnsley 0226 790270.
Open: Tue–Sat 10.30–5 & Sun 2.30–5. (Closed Mon, Good Fri & 23 Dec–2 Jan.) Parking charge. Coach parties must pre-arrange parking: 𝜙 0226 733272 (Countryside Section). ♿ (ground floor only) parking for disabled by arrangement. 🐕

## CENARTH
Dyfed

**THE NATIONAL CORACLE CENTRE**
Set in the grounds of a 17th-century flour mill by the falls and salmon leap at Cenarth. There is a unique display of coracles from all over the world and coracles may be seen on the river throughout the summer.

𝜙 Newcastle Emlyn 0239 710209.
Open: Whitsun–Oct daily 10.30–5. Donations. Guided tours charged for. ♿ (ground floor). Shop.

## CERNE ABBAS
Dorset

**CERNE GIANT**
(On footpath 0.25m NE of village)
This colossal hill figure is cut into the turf exposing the natural chalk

rock below. He is 180ft long from head to foot, and appears to be striding towards the left. In his right hand he brandishes a club 120 ft long. His body is outlined and detailed by narrow trenches up to 2ft wide and his condition has been maintained by periodic scouring by the local people, an activity which traditionally occurred every seven years. Today he is maintained by the National Trust. The Cerne Ciant is thought to be a Romano-British figure, dating perhaps from the second-century AD and is still the subject of a great deal of folklore. Above the Giant is a small near-rectangular earthwork known as the 'Trendle' or the 'Frying Pan' which may well have been associated with the Giant. The best view of the Giant is from the A352 Sherbourne to Dorchester Road. A footpath from the village leads up through the Churchyard. The Giant and the Trendle are fenced off to protect them from erosion and visitors are asked to remain outside the fence.

Open: accessible at all reasonable times.
(NT)

## CERRIGYDRUDION
Clwyd

**LLYN BRENIG VISITOR CENTRE & WELSH WATER AUTHORITY ESTATE**
A 1,600 acre estate with a unique archaeological trail and round the

* **GUERNSEY** *

## CATEL
Guernsey

**GUERNSEY TELEPHONE MUSEUM**
Hermes, Cobo Road
The museum is run on a voluntary basis by a small group of Guernsey Telecom staff, and offers working demonstrations of exchanges, telephones, telex and fax. Popular with children.

𝜙 0481 711221.
Open: Apr–Sep Tue & Wed 7pm–9pm. Free guided tours available. Donations requested. Coach parties welcome by prior arrangement.

## ST PETERS
Guernsey

**COACH HOUSE GALLERY**
Les Islets (on main road from airport to L'Eree)
A sympathetically restored complex of old farm buildings, housing an art gallery, etching studio and pottery workshops. The work of many accomplished artists can always be seen, including prints and paintings of Guernsey subjects by

the gallery artists. Also pottery, glass and porcelain.

℘ 0481 65339.
Open: Feb–Dec daily 11–5 (times may be restricted in winter.) Small parties welcome, but no coaches. ♿ (ground floor only).

## ST SAMPSON
Guernsey

**OATLANDS CRAFT CENTRE**
Route du Braye
The workshops are set in seven acres, with ancient brick kilns, thatched barns and a farmhouse. Crafts which can be seen include glassblowing, pottery, patchwork, stonecasting, silversmithing and glass engraving. There is also a bee centre and shire horse centre (both charged for), plus croquet, bowls and mini-golf, and horse driving for the disabled.

℘ 0481 44282.
Open: daily 10–5.30 (5 Nov–Etr). Closed Sun Nov–Etr). Coach Parties welcome.
🖵 🛆 ♿ toilets & parking for the disabled. Shop. Garden centre.

## ✦ JERSEY ✦

## GOREY VILLAGE
Jersey

**JERSEY POTTERY**
Visitors are able to watch all processes, including throwing, casting, hand painting etc, through to the finished article. Notices in each department explain in detail the work being carried out. The pottery is set in delightful gardens and has a particularly good restaurant.

℘ 0534 51119.
Open: all year Mon–Fri 9–5.30 (Closed BH). Coach parties welcome, must book in advance for parties of children.
🖵 (licensed) ♿ (ramps) toilets for the disabled. Shop.

## ST HELIER
Jersey

**JERSEY PHOTOGRAPHIC MUSEUM**
Lido De France, St Saviours Road
The museum contains one of the largest collections of European cameras that can be seen anywhere in the world. There are also around 150 photographs on show, the display changing approximately every two months.

℘ 0534 73102.
Open: all year Mon–Fri 9–5.30; Sat 9–12. Coach parties welcome. Guided tours available.
🖵 (licensed) ♿ (part) Shop.

## ST OUEN
Jersey

**JERSEY GOLDSMITHS**
Five Mile Road
Visitors can watch craftspeople producing items of gold jewellery in the workshops, then browse through the large display of gold jewellery. Bergerac's car, from the television series, is also on show here.

℘ 0534 82098.
Open: all year Mon–Sat 10–5.30. Coach parties welcome. Guided tours available on request.
🖵 ♿ toilets & parking for the disabled, ramp to restaurant.

**KEMPT TOWER INTERPRETATION CENTRE**
Five Mile Road
This Martello tower has recently been converted into an interpretation centre displaying artifacts mostly relating to Les Mielles, Jersey's 'mini national park'. Ornithological walks are held on most Sun afternoons around the adjacent Le Mielle de Morville area and nature walks on Thu pm (May–Sep); check local press for details.

℘ Jersey 0534 83651.
Open: Apr & Oct, Thu & Sun only 2–5; May–Sep daily 2–5. Parties by arrangement. Guided tours by arrangement. Correspondence:

Planning Office, South Hill, St. Hellier, Jersey.
Shop 🛆

**PLEMONT CANDLECRAFT**
Portinfer
Small, family-run cottage craft industry. Visitors can watch making and hand carving of a wide range of decorative candles.

℘ 0534 82146.
Open: Mar–Oct daily 9.30–5.30; Nov–Feb Mon–Fri only. Coach parties welcome.
♿ (part).

**SUNSET CARNATION NURSERIES**
St Ouen's Bay
Two acres of flower crops and exotic plants, including the beautiful Jersey Lily. Tropical garden, aviary and fish pools.

℘ 0534 82090 (482090 from Apr 1992).
Open: all year daily 10–5; (Mon–Fri only Nov–Mar). Coach parties welcome.
🖵 ♿ (part) parking for disabled. Shop.

## CHATHAM
Kent

**CAPSTONE FARM COUNTRY PARK**
Capstone Road, Capstone (3m E of Chatham)
A countryside environment on the urban fringe astride an attractive North Downs valley. The park provides a range of facilities and activities within its 113-hectare site. There is a visitor centre with ranger assistance, and a series of walks and informative talks. Dry skiing, riding and fishing (charge) are available, plus a programme of special events including wildlife treasure hunts, kiteflying, orienteering and children's picnics.

℘ Medway 0634 812196.
Open: all year, daily, 7am–sunset. Guided tours available by prior arrangement only.
🖵 (Mar–Sep 10–6) ♿ disabled parking close to main facilities; toilets for the disabled. 🛆

## CHEDDLETON
Staffordshire

**FLINT MILL**
(Beside Caldon Canal, Leek
Road, off A520)
Two watermills standing side by
side. The South Mill was a corn mill
from 1253, but was converted to
grind flint for the pottery industry;
the North Mill was purpose-built in
the 18th century. Exhibits include
explanations of the preparation of
materials for pottery, a 100 hp
Robey steam engine and the narrow
boat *Vienna*, moored on the Caldon
Canal.

✆ 078139 2561.
Open: all year most weekdays 10–5
and weekend afternoons 1–5.30
(closed 25 & 26 Dec). Parties by
advance booking (access unsuitable
for heavy vehicles). Donations
welcome.
⌂ ⑁ (part).

## CHELMSFORD
Essex

**CHELMSFORD AND ESSEX MUSEUM**
Oaklands Park, Moulsham
Street
Long-term exhibitions, selected
from the permanent collection, on
social and local history, natural
sciences, costume, glass, paintings
and coins. A new History of
Chelmsford display is due to open
by the time this book is published.
The Essex Regiment Museum is
also in the same building. Tactile
Exhibitions for the blind can be
arranged.

✆ 0245 353066.
Open: all year Mon–Sat 10–5, Sun
2–5. Coach parties welcome, booking
advisable. Guided tours can be
arranged by appointment.
⑁ (ground floor only).

## CHELTENHAM
Gloucestershire

**ART GALLERY & MUSEUM**
Clarence Street
Foremost Arts and Crafts Movement

collection inspired by William
Morris. Notable 17th-century Dutch
and 17th–20th century British
paintings. Also a large collection of
English and Oriental ceramics,
pewter, social history and
archaeological material relating to
the area. Special exhibitions are
held throughout the year.

✆ 0242 237431.
Open: Mon–Sat 10–5.20; also Sun,
May–Sep 2–5.20. (Closed BH.)
⑁ Shop ⌂ ⑁

**GUSTAV HOLST BIRTHPLACE
MUSEUM**
4 Clarence Road
The composer's birthplace
containing rooms with period
furnishings and working Victorian
kitchen. Displays tell the story of
the man and his music.

✆ 0242 524846.
Open: Tue–Fri 12–5.20, Sat 11–5.20.
(Closed Sun, Mon, BH.) Donation.
Parties by prior arrangement. Guided
tours available by prior arrangement
with Keeper of Museums ✆ 0242
237431.
Shop ⑁

## CHEPSTOW
Gwent

**STUART CRYSTAL**
Bridge Street (opp Castle)
Visitors can view craftsmen
applying decoration to hand-made
crystal; included in the self-guided
tour is a museum section displaying
past and present Stuart crystal
produced over 150 years. A video of
the techniques used in present day
manufacture can also be seen.

✆ 02912 70135.
Open: daily 9–8 May–Sep; 9–5 Oct–
Apr. Evening lectures by appointment.
⑁ (ramps) toilets for the disabled.
Shop ⌂

## CHERTSEY
Surrey

**CHERTSEY MUSEUM**
33 Windsor Street
A late Georgian house, The Cedars,

containing Matthews collection of
costumes and accessories, local
history collection, including a 10th-
century Viking sword, silver, glass,
dolls and collection of Meissen
porcelain figures. Also various
exhibitions throughout the year.

✆ 0932 565764.
Open: Tue & Thu 2–5, Wed, Fri & Sat
10–1 & 2–5. (Closed Xmas.) Guided
tours by arrangement. Donation.
Parties by appointment.
⑁ Shop.

## CHESTER
Cheshire

**CHESTER VISITOR CENTRE**
Vicars Lane
Over 2,000 years of Chester's
history are illustrated by a video
and a life-size reconstruction of a
scene in the Rows during Victorian
times. There is a tourist information
desk and guided tours of Chester
depart from here (charge). Craft
fairs take place on Bank holiday
weekends.

✆ 0244 351609.
Open: all year daily 9am–9pm
(closes at 7pm Nov–Mar). Coach
parties welcome
⑁ (part; ramp to entrance). Shop.

**GROSVENOR MUSEUM**
27 Grosvenor Street
One of the finest collections of
Roman remains in Britain, including
special Roman Army gallery. The
Sculptured Stones and Natural
History gallery will be reopened
during 1992, hopefully in March,
after being upgraded. Period house
with Victorian and Georgian rooms.
Temporary exhibitions. No smoking
or eating in the museum. Access for
pushchairs can be difficult.

✆ 0244 321616.
Open: Mon–Sat 10.30–5, Sun 2–5.
Donation box. Parties by
appointment. Guided tours available
for pre-booked groups by
arrangement. Shop ⑁

## CHESTERFIELD
Derbyshire

**PEACOCK INFORMATION AND HERITAGE CENTRE**
Low Pavement
A timber-framed building dating from 1500, thought to have been a guildhall. First floor is now used as an exhibition room. A video on the history of Chesterfield is available for showing on request. Medieval market in July.

✆ 0246 207777.
Open: Information centre Apr–Oct 9–6; Nov–Mar Mon–Sat. 9–5; Heritage centre Mon–Sat 11–4.
🍴 ♿ (ground floor only) Shop.

## CHESTER-LE-STREET
Co Durham

**ANKERS HOUSE MUSEUM**
Parish Centre, Church Chare
The Ankers House, adjoining the Parish Church, is thought to be the most complete example of its kind in England. The small museum on three floors gives insight into the life of an anchorite who would be walled up for life to pass his or her time in prayer and contemplation.

✆ Durham 091 388 3295.
Open: Apr–Oct Mon–Sat 10–4.
Donations welcomed. Guided tours by arrangement.
💻 10–3.

## CHICHESTER
West Sussex

**DISTRICT MUSEUM**
29 Little London
Discover how people have lived and worked in this attractive town and its region. Especially rich in evidence from the Stone Ages and Roman periods, and in local life and work during the last 100 years.

✆ 0243 784683.
Open: all year, Tue–Sat 10–5.30.
(Closed BH & PH.) Donation box.
Parties by appointment. Guided tours available by prior arrangement.
Donation.

♿ (ground floor only) Some tactile displays. By prior arrangement staff can be available to guide or assist. Shop ♿ (ex guide dogs).

**GUILDHALL MUSEUM**
Prior Park
Branch of District Museum in medieval Greyfriars church, later used as City Guildhall, containing archaeological finds from district. The small public park contains mound of Norman Castle.

✆ 0243 784683.
Open: Jun–Sep, Tue–Sat 1–5; other times by appointment. Donation box. Park open daily.
♿ toilets for the disabled in nearby park; some tactile displays. Shop ♿ (ex guide dogs).

## CHIPPENHAM
Wiltshire

**YELDE HALL MUSEUM**
Market Place
15th-century, timber-framed old Town Hall or 'Yeld Hall' renovated and opened as a museum, staffed entirely by volunteers. It houses the town's records and items of local interest.

✆ 0249 652922.
Open: mid Mar–Oct Mon–Sat ex BH 10–12.30 & 2–4.30. Donations. Guided tours by application to Hon Curator. Parties (max 25).

## CHRISTCHURCH
Dorset

**CHRISTCHURCH CASTLE AND NORMAN HOUSE**
Early 12th-century Norman keep, and Constable's House built c1160.

Open: at all reasonable times.
(AM)

**CHRISTCHURCH PRIORY**
Church Street
The longest parish church in England, the priory was begun in 1094 and has examples of Norman, Early English, Perpendicular and

Tudor architecture. It is a complete medieval monastic church. Of particular interest are the ancient misericords, the Norman turret and the Miraculous Beam.

✆ 0202 485804.
Open: all year daily, 9.30–5. (Sun 2.30–5.30, subject to services). Donations. Guided tours by arrangement with Head Verger (donations). Admission to tower & museum charged for.
♿ (entrance ramp) Shop.

**HIGHCLIFFE CASTLE GROUNDS**
(On A337 between Highcliffe & Christchurch)
Highcliffe Castle was built as a house between 1830–34 in the French style of the 15th century. It is surrounded by scaffolding and protective covers, so is not currently open to the public. The grounds offer a unique setting for walking and picnicking, and access to a fine sandy beach below allows superb views across Christchurch Bay to the Isle of Wight.

✆ 0202 486321.
Open: daily until 8pm (summer) or 5pm (winter).
🍴 ♿ toilets for the disabled. Charge for parking.

## CHURCH LENCH
Hereford and Worcester

**ANNARD WOOLLEN MILL**
Handgate Farm
Turn towards 'The Lenches' in Harvington. Turn left after 1.25m and it is the next farm (about 0.25m) signposted. A workshop in a rural setting specialising in mohair yarns and knitwear made to in-house designs. Visitors can see angora goats, ball winding and the mill shop.

✆ Evesham 0386 870270.
Open: all year, Thu–Mon 10–5.
Guided tours for parties (donation to Cancer Research requested) by prior arrangement.
🍴 ♿ toilets for the disabled. Mill shop.

## CHURCHSTANTON

Somerset

**Somerset Spring Water**

The Firs, Biscombe

Natural spring water bottling plant.

✆ 082 360 385.

Open: Mon–Sat 10–4, Sun 10–12.30. Coach parties not accepted.

## CIRENCESTER

Gloucestershire

**Cirencester Park**

Three thousand acres of superb park and woodland easily accessible by foot from the town centre via Cecily Hill. The park was laid out by the first Earl Bathurst in association with Alexander Pope in the early 18th century. Special events (charge) include polo, horse-driving trials and the Cotswold Country Fair in September.

✆ 0285 653135.

Open: all year, daily 8–5. No vehicles permitted in Park.

♿

**Brewery Court**

Brewery Court

Resident craftsmen and women including a blacksmith, baker, ceramic sculptress, jewellers, weaver, willow basket-maker, printer and publisher, leatherworker, textile artists and designers and bookbinder. There is a contemporary craft shop, coffee house and education workshop, and a gallery for temporary exhibitions of contemporary art and craft.

✆ 0285 651566.

Open: all year (ex some BHs) Mon–Sat 10–5. Coach parties by appointment only.

☕

## CLAPHAM

North Yorkshire

**Yorkshire Dales National Park Centre**

Visitor Centre with interpretative display on 'The Limestone Dales'. Audiovisual theatre. Maps, walks, guides and local information available.

✆ 05242 51419.

Open: daily Apr–Oct 9.30–5.

Ħ

## CLAVA CAIRNS

Highland

(6m of E of Inverness)

Situated on the south bank of the River Nairn, this group of burial cairns has three concentric rings of great stones.

Open: at all reasonable times.

(AM)

## CLAWDD-NEWYDD

Clwyd

**Bod Petrual Visitor Centre**

(On B5105 3m W)

On the southern edge of Clocaenog Forest, with way-marked walks. Forest Interpretation Centre is housed in a converted keeper's cottage. An exhibition illustrates the history and ecology of the forest using local information, pictures, etc.

✆ 08245 208.

Open: Visitor Centre, daily Etr–Oct 10–5, forest 10–dusk.

♿ toilets for the disabled. Ħ

## CLEVEDON

Avon

**Clevedon Craft Centre**

Moor Lane

The craft centre comprises 14 studios currently showing silver, porcelain, woodturning, house signs, weaving, machine knitting, leather carving, glass engraving, furniture stripping, garden ornaments, upholstery, flower arranging and picture framing.

✆ 0272 872149.

Open: all year, daily (some studios shut Mon), 11–5. Parties not accepted Mon.

☕ (tearoom closed Mon) ♿ toilets for the disabled.

## CLUN

Shropshire

**Clun Local History Museum**

Situated in lower floor of town hall. Original court house, built in 1780. Fine display of flints, agricultural and domestic relics, smocks, geological finds, remains of Bronze Age burial. Many other exhibits.

✆ 05884 576

Open: Etr–Oct, Tue & Sat 2–5 and BH weekends Sat, Mon & Tue 11–1 & 2–5. Donations. Guided tours available by prior arrangement.

## COATBRIDGE

Strathclyde

**Summerlee Heritage Trust**

West Canal Street

Winner of the Scottish Museum of the Year award in 1990, this museum of social and industrial history has indoor and open-air exhibits. These include a recently extended working electric tramway, belt-driven machinery, 1810 coal mine and an Ironworks Gallery. Regularly changing exhibitions and special events.

✆ 0236 31261.

Open: all year, daily (ex Xmas & New Year BH), 10–5. Donation box.

☕ (10–4.30) Ħ ♿ (ramps; wheelchairs available on loan). Shop.

## COLCHESTER

Essex

**Hollytrees Museum**

High Street

Two centuries of fascinating toys, costume, decorative arts and curios, displayed in an attractive Georgian town house of 1718.

✆ 0206 712931.

Open: Mon–Sat 10–1, 2–5

Shop 🚫

**Natural History Museum**

All Saints Church, High Street

Displays of the natural history of northeast Essex, including impressive dioramas, housed in the former All Saints Church.

✆ 0206 712931.
Open: Mon–Sat 10–1 & 2–5.
♿ Shop ✖

**OLIVERS ORCHARD**
Shrub End (Off Gosbecks Road)
Olivers Orchard is a working fruit
farm in the Roman River Valley
Conservation Zone. Here you can
visit the orchard, pick your own
fruit and vegetables, stock up at the
farm shop and visit the countryside
centre.

✆ 0206 3320208 shop, 331369 office.
Open: Jun–Dec, daily. Jun–Oct & Dec
Mon–Fri 9–dusk, Sat & Sun 9–6; Sat &
Sun only Nov. Guided tours available
for pre-booked groups up to 28
(charge).
⊡ (licensed) barbeque. ⊼ ♿
(ground floor)

**TRINITY MUSEUM**
Holy Trinity Church, Trinity
Square
Town and country life in the
Colchester area over the last 200
years, displayed in the medieval
former church of Holy Trinity,
complete with Saxon tower.

✆ 0206 712931.
Open: Mon–Sat 10–1 & 2–5 (Closed
Sun, Good Fri & afternoons 23–27
Dec).
♿ Shop ✖

**TYMPERLEYS CLOCK MUSEUM**
Trinity Street
A fine collection of clocks made in
Colchester, displayed in a restored
late 15th-century house.

✆ 0206 712931.
Open: Mon–Sat 10–1 & 2–5.
♿ (steps at front) Shop ✖

## COLLIESTON
Grampian

**SLAINS CASTLE**
(1m NE)
Spectacular but fragmentary Keep
on a rocky headland, home of the
Hays of Erroll for three centuries.
Nearby are two cannon salvaged
from the Spanish galleon *Santa
Caterina*, wrecked in 1594. A coastal

path from Collieston leads to the
castle.

Open: accessible at all reasonable
times.
(AM)

## COLONSAY, ISLE OF

### KILORAN
Colonsay

**KILORAN WOODLAND GARDEN**
(2m N of Scalasaig)
Set close to Colonsay House, these
peaceful gardens and woodlands
are a maze of colour during the
Spring, and are noted for their fine
display of rhododendrons and
shrubs, including embothriums and
magnolias. The Gulf Stream
encourages plants not normally
found at this latitude.

Open: daily, dawn to dusk.

## COMPTON
Surrey

**THE POTTERY**
Brickfields
Take road signposted to
Binscombe and Farncombe
from B3000 (2m from
Guildford), 'Brickfields' is 100
yds down Farm Lane.
Mary Wondrausch is a potter with
an overwhelming passion for the
17th-century English tradition of
slipware pottery. Much of the work
is individually commissioned
commemorative plates, but there
are also traditional pots such as owl
jugs, salt kips, egg stands and
pitchers.

✆ 048341 4097.
Open: all year Mon–Fri 9–1 & 2–5, Sat
& Sun 2–5. Telephone before group
visit.

## CORFE CASTLE
Dorset

**CORFE CASTLE MUSEUM**
West Street
The museum occupies the ground
floor of one of the smallest Town

Hall buildings in England. This tiny
rectangular building was partly
rebuilt in brick in 1680 after a fire.
The small museum displays old
village relics, dinosaur footprints
130 million years old and pictorial
wall displays of the old local stone
and clay industries. The Ancient
Order of Marblers and Stone
Cutters meet on Shrove Tuesday in
the Council Chamber on the first
floor (open by appointment only).

✆ 0929 480415.
Open: daily, Apr–Oct 10–6 (Nov–Mar
weather permitting).
♿ (ground floor only)

## CORRIESHALLOCH GORGE
Highland

(On A835 12m SSE of Ullapool)
This spectacular mile-long gorge,
one of the finest examples in Britain
of a box canyon, is 200 ft deep and
varies in width from 50–150 ft. The
river which carved this channel
through hard metamorphic rock,
plunges 150 ft over the Falls of
Measach. The suspension bridge a
little way down-stream from the
Falls gives breathtaking views. It
was built by John Fowler (1817–
98), joint designer of the Forth
Railway Bridge, who bought the
estate of Braemore in 1867. Farther
downstream, a viewing platform
provides an excellent vantage point
looking up towards the Falls. The
gorge is a special habitat for plant
life, with high humidity and poor
light.

Open: accessible at all times.
Voluntary donations welcome.
♿ (view from bridge only)
(NTS)

## CORRIS
Gwynedd

**RAILWAY MUSEUM**
In village, 300 yds from A487
Museum in century-old railway
building with photographs of
operation of Corris narrow gauge
railway from 1890–1948. Items
connected with railway are          →

constantly added, and some old wagons are on show, half mile of track between museum and old engine shed at Maespoeth has now been reinstated. Passengers not carried. Children's playground nearby.

Open: BH periods & Mon–Fri mid Jul–early Sep 10.30–5; Jun–mid Jul and first fortnight in Sep, 12–5, and as advertised locally. Parties by appointment. Guided tours available by arrangement with Corris Railway Society Chairman, Brynderw, Aberllefenni, Machynlleth, Powys SY20 9RR.
& (ground floor only) Shop.

## COVENTRY
West Midlands

**COOMBE ABBEY COUNTRY PARK**
Brinklow Road, Binley
On the Rugby to Coventry road, signposted off the M6 at junction 2.
Over 200 acres of beautifully landscaped parkland including a 90-acre lake and 10 acres of formal gardens. There are good visitor facilities all year round and a programme of special events and guided walks. Fishing available (charge).

℘ 0203 453720.
Open: all year, daily 8–dusk. Parking charge. Guided tours by prior arrangement (charge).
⌂ (public house) & adapted bird hide, all weather paths & toilets for the disabled. ⊼

**HERBERT ART GALLERY AND MUSEUM**
Jordan Well
Collections include social history, archaeology, folk life, industry, natural history, visual arts. Of special interest are the collection of Graham Sutherland's studies for the 'Christ in Glory' tapestry in Coventry Cathedral, and the Frederick Poke collection of fine 18th-century English furniture and silver. There is a Natural History live animal display.

℘ 0203 832381.
Open: Mon–Fri 10–5.30. (Closed Good Fri & part Xmas.)
& (lift) Shop ⊗ (ex guide dogs).

**OLD CATHEDRAL OF ST MICHAEL**
Bayley Lane
Coventry cathedral ruins adjacent to the new Cathedral. Tells the story of the Blitz; at the altar is the Cross of Nails, formed from nails found and now made into a symbol of reconciliation. Admission charge to tower.

Open: accessible any reasonable time.

**ST MARY'S GUILDHALL**
Bayley Lane
Medieval guildhall, with minstrels' gallery and buttery, restored hall with portraits and Flemish tapestries. Caesar's watchtower, housing one of Mary Queen of Scots' resting-places on the road to Fotheringay

℘ 0203 832381.
Open: Etr–Oct, Mon–Sat 10–5, Sun 10–4 (subject to civic requirements – enquiry advised before visiting).
& (ground floor only) ⊗ (ex guide dogs).

## COWES
**See Wight, Isle of**

## COXWELL, GREAT
Oxfordshire

**GREAT BARN**
Stone-built 13th-century barn with fine roof timbers.

Open: at all reasonable times. Donations welcomed.
(NT)

## CRANBROOK
Kent

**CRANBROOK UNION MILL**
Grade I listed, 70 ft high smock mill with eight-sided, three-storey brick base and a four-storey, fixed wooden tower. Built in 1814, it is

wind powered, and now fully restored to working use for milling. Maintained by the Cranbrook Windmill Association.

℘ 0580 712256.
Open: Etr–Sep Sat & BH Mons 2.30–5, also last two Sun in July and all Suns in Aug. Donations towards restoration. Guided tours are available by arrangement out of public viewing times. Parties by arrangement. Shop.

## CRANHAM
Gloucestershire

**PRINKNASH ABBEY AND POTTERY**
(On A46 between Cheltenham and Painswick)
The abbey dates from 1928 when a Benedictine community moved here from Caldey Island. The 'Old Abbey' was built in the 14th century as a grange of the abbots of Gloucester. Rich beds of clay were discovered when the foundation were being dug for the new building and so the pottery was established, producing distinctive ware.

℘ 0452 812239.
Open: all year daily 9–5.30 (closed Good Fri, 25 & 26 Dec). Coach parties welcome. Guided tour of pottery viewing gallery available (charge).
⌂ ⊼ & (part; ramps at entrance) toilets for the disabled. Shop.

## CRASTER
Northumberland

**KIPPER CURING (L ROBSON & SONS LTD.)**
Haven Hill
The small fishing village is the home of the Craster Kipper. Curing kippers has been carried out in this original smokehouse building since 1856, using traditional methods which visitors can see.

℘ Embleton 066 576 223.
Open: Jun–Sep (ex BH), Mon–Fri 9–5. Parties can see round the kipper shed but restaurant room is limited.
⌂ & (two steps) ⊗ Shop.

## CRATHIE
Grampian

**ROYAL LOCHNAGAR DISTILLERY AND RECEPTION CENTRE**
(By Balmoral Castle)
Distillery in country setting near Balmoral Castle where visitors can enjoy a guided tour of the distillery followed by a free dram.

✆ 03397 42273/42375.
Open: daily Mar–Oct, Mon–Sat 10–5, Sun 11 4; Nov–Feb weekdays only 10–5. Guided tours available. Parties accepted by prior appointment.
🖫 ♿ all disabled visitors will receive a tour of the distillery, but routed differently). Shop.

## CRESWELL CRAGS
Nottinghamshire

**CRESWELL CRAGS VISITOR CENTRE**
(Off Crags Road 1m E off B6042. Gorge is adjacent to A616 Sheffield to Ollerton and A60 Mansfield to Worksop.)
Small limestone gorge once the home of early man and prehistoric animals. Caves have revealed numerous Ice Age fossils. The visitor centre explains the archaeological significance of the site with an exhibition and audiovisual programme which shows what life was like for our ancestors. Wide range of events every weekend.

✆ Worksop 0909 720378.
Open: Feb–Oct, daily 10.30–4.30; Nov–Jan Suns only 10.30–4.30.
Guided tours available (Sats as advertised). Group tours by arrangement (fee).
🛋 ♿ free wheelchair loan; audio loop; Shop.

## CRIEFF
Tayside

**STUART STRATHEARN GLASS**
Muthill Road
Handmade lead crystal includes vases, rose bowls, honey pots, decanters and whisky glasses. The range is engraved with a wide variety of flowers and Scottish game

and self-conducted tours enable the visitor to see engraving at close hand. Video on glassmaking and decoration. Children's playground.

✆ 0764 4004.
Open: Factory daily 9–5; Shop daily 9–5 (Jun–Sep 9–7). (Closed Xmas & New Year). Group visits can be arranged on request.
♿ 🛋 ✎

## CROMER
Norfolk

**LIFEBOAT MUSEUM**
Traces history of lifeboats since 1804. The 37 ft lifeboat, *Oakley*, is on display, plus model exhibits of previous lifeboats used on station. The *H F Bailey*, stationed at Cromer from 1935 to 1947, which saved over 500 lives, is being restored to its original condition and will go on display by early 1992. Also

*Glass from the Strathearn Collection, at Stuart Strathearn Glass, Crieff*

operational lifeboat on display at Boathouse on end of Cromer Pier.

✆ 0263 512503.
Open: daily May–Sep 10–5. Pre-booked guided tours available. Donations. Parties by arrangement.
♿ Shop.

## CROWTHERWOOD
South Yorkshire

**SANDALL BEAT NATURE RESERVE**
(2m NE of Doncaster, off the A18).
The trees were planted in the early part of the last century to provide a source of timber for ship building during the Napoleonic wars. Today, as neighbouring older woodlands have been cleared, it has become an important refuge for many forest creatures. Sandall Beat has been a nature reserve since 1966 and a Site of Special Scientific Interest since 1984.

✆ 0302 873401 (Doncaster Metropolitan Borough Council).
Open: please telephone for information.

## CULROSS
Fife

**CULROSS ABBEY**
Cistercian monastery, founded by Malcolm, Earl of Fife in 1217. The choir is still used as the parish church and parts of the nave remain. Fine central tower, still complete.

Open: Apr–Sep Mon–Fri 9.30–6, Sun 2–6.
(AM)

**LITTLE HOUSES**
The Study
This small Royal Burgh on the north shore of the Forth has fine examples of 16th- and 17th-century domestic architecture, restored over a period of 60 years by the National Trust for Scotland. The Ark, Bishop Leighton's House, The Old Jail and other restored houses may be viewed from the outside. There is a Visitor Reception, exhibition and video at the Town House (admission charge).

✆ New Mills 0383 880359.
Open: exterior of buildings can be viewed at any time. Audio-visual programme at Town House has induction loop for the hard-of-hearing.

# CUSWORTH
South Yorkshire

**CUSWORTH COUNTRY PARK**
(1m NW of Doncaster, off A638).
Created as ornamental parkland in the 1740s. The deer may have gone, but today's visitor may see grey squirrels and a variety of bird life by day and a famous bat colony by night. Acres of open space and lakeside walks. Within the park is Cusworth Hall, home of the Museum of South Yorkshire Life – see separate entry below.

✆ 0302 782342.
Open: at all times.
&. toilets for the disabled.

**MUSEUM OF SOUTH YORKSHIRE LIFE**
Cusworth Hall (2m NW Doncaster)
18th-century house with fine chimney pieces and chapel in south-west wing. Museum of South Yorkshire life and sections of interest to children. Temporary exhibitions and many annual events. Also extensive grounds which are open all year, with fishing in ponds, cricket and football pitches. Children's study base, and research facilities.

✆ Doncaster 0302 782342 (786925 for school visits).
Open: Mon–Fri 10–5, Sat 11–5, Sun 1–5 (Closed 4pm Dec & Jan). (Closed 25 & 26 Dec & 1 Jan). Parties by appointment. Guided tours available by pre-arrangement.
&. (lift to ground floor) Shop ⚒ (ex in park)

# CWMCARN
Gwent

**CWMCARN FOREST DRIVE VISITOR CENTRE**
(On A467 7m junction 28 M4)
The Visitor Centre (free) is situated near the entrance of seven-mile scenic drive (charge). There is an interpretive exhibition on the working of the forest and uses of the timber grown. A programme of special events includes guided walks.

✆ 0495 272001.
Open: all year (ex Xmas) daily 9–5. (The Drive is closed Oct–Etr). Coach parties must book in advance.
⛺ (summer weekends only) &.

# DAGENHAM
Essex

**FORD MOTOR COMPANY**
(A13)
The Ford plant in Dagenham is the largest centre of employment in Ford's UK empire. Since October 1931 more than 10 million vehicles have been built there and it has the capacity to produce 1,200 Fiestas a day. Comfortable shoes are recommended as a tour of the plant involves a walk of approximately 2½ miles.

✆ 081 526 2570 for tours.
Open: all year Mon–Fri ex public & plant holidays. Tours 9.30–12 & 1.15–3.45 (book well in advance). Min age 15 yrs for educational groups and min 10 yrs for family groups accompanied by at least one adult.

# DALWHINNIE
Highland

**DALWHINNIE DISTILLERY**
An opportunity to see single malt

whisky in the making and to sample the final product. There is also an exhibition area.

✆ 052 82 264.
Open: all year Mon–Fri 9.30–4.30. Guided tours by prior arrangement – 052 82 208. Coach parties must book in advance.
&. (partial tour) toilets for the disabled. Shop.

# DANBURY
Essex

**DANBURY COUNTRY PARK**
Woodland, lake and ornamental gardens.

✆ 024 541 2350.
Open: all year, daily 8–dusk. Guided tours by arrangement. Parties by arrangement only. Charge for parking Sun & BH Apr–Oct (ex OAP, disabled & motorbikes).
⛽ &. toilets for the disabled.

# DANBY
North Yorkshire

**THE MOORS CENTRE**
Lodge Lane
The former shooting lodge offers full information and countryside interpretation service to visitors to the North York Moors National Park. The grounds include riverside meadow, woodland and terraced gardens, children's play area and brass rubbing centre. Video shown daily, and also an exhibition about the North York Moors. Bookshop information desk.

✆ Guisborough 0287 660654.
Open: daily Apr–Oct 10–5; Nov–Mar Sun 11–4. Donations appreciated. Parties by appointment only.
⛺ ⛽ &. (ground floor) toilets for the disabled. Shop ⚒

# DANEBURY RING
Hampshire

(Off unclass road 2.5m NW of Stockbridge)
A fine Iron Age fort rising to 469 ft, much of it thickly wooded with beech trees. Extensive excavations have been carried out since 1969.

There is a nature trail and leaflets are available at the site.

Open: accessible at all reasonable times.

## DARLINGTON
Co Durham

**ART GALLERY**
Crown Street
Contains a permanent collection of pictures but also has temporary loan exhibitions throughout the year.

✆ 0325 462034.
Open: Mon–Fri 10–8, Sat 10–5.30. (Closed Sun & all weekends BH.) Parties by arrangement. Nearest car park closes 6pm.
✖

**DARLINGTON MUSEUM**
Tubwell Row
Local social and natural history, archaeology and bygones. Observation beehive and beekeeping exhibits, approx May–Sep, each year.

✆ 0325 463795.
Open: all year Mon–Wed & Fri 10–1 & 2–6; Thu 10–1; Sat 10–1 & 2–5.30. (Closed Good Fri, May Day, Xmas & New Year's Day.) Guided tours by prior arrangement only. Groups by appointment only.
♿ (ground floor only) Shop ✖ (ex guide dogs).

## DARTINGTON
Devon

**DARTINGTON CIDER PRESS CENTRE**
Shinners Bridge (On the A384 Buckfastleigh to Totnes road)
An unusual complex of 12 shops and two restaurants set in a 4.5-acre landscaped site, specialising in crafts, Dartington Glass, kitchenware, fashion, herbs, plants and fresh farm foods.

✆ Totnes 0803 864171.
Open: 2 Jan–31 Dec, Mon–Sat, Sun mid Jul–mid Sep, 9.30–5.30.
🍽 (licensed) 🚻♿ (ground floor) parking & toilets for disabled.

## DARTMOUTH
Devon

**BAYARD'S COVE FORT**
Small artillery fort built 1509–10 to cover the entrance to the inner haven.

Open: accessible at all reasonable times.
(AM)

## DEDDINGTON
Oxfordshire

**DEDDINGTON CASTLE**
(E of Deddington, S of B4031)
Extensive earthworks enclosing a large outer and a smaller inner bailey.

Open: at all reasonable times.
(AM)

## DEERHURST
Gloucestershire

**ODDA'S CHAPEL**
(Off B4213 at Abbots Court SW of church)
Rare Saxon chapel, founded by Earl Odda and dedicated in 1056. The nave survives virtually to its full height.

Open: at all reasonable times.
(AM)

## DERBY
Derbyshire

**DERBY MUSEUM & ART GALLERY**
The Strand
Antiquities, social and natural history, militaria, and also temporary exhibitions. There are paintings by Joseph Wright of Derby (1734–1797). Derby porcelain. Many temporary exhibitions are held.

✆ 0332 255586.
Open: daily, Mon 11–5; Tue–Sat 10–5; Sun 2–5. Donations. Guided tours available by prior arrangement.
♿ lift. Shop ✖ (ex guide dogs).

See also **ELVASTON**

## DEWSBURY
West Yorkshire

**DEWSBURY MUSEUM**
Crow Nest Park
Crow Nest Mansion, parts of which date back to the late 16th century, is the home of Dewsbury Museum. The main galleries are now devoted to the theme of childhood: children at work, at play and at school. Temporary exhibitions feature local history, social history and decorative arts.

✆ 0924 468171.
Open: all year, Mar–Oct Mon–Fri 10–5, Sat & Sun 12–5, Nov–Feb all week 12–5.
Shop.

## DINAS MAWDDWY
Gwynedd

**MEIRION MILL**
In the Dyfi Valley, at the southern end of the Snowdonia National Park, is this working woollen weaving mill and retail shop in rural estate. Pack-horse bridge (AM). Garden's and children's playground. Dog exercise area.

✆ 06504 311.
Open: Apr–Oct daily including BH. Enquire for winter opening. Groups (adults only) by appointment.
🍽 (licensed) 🚻♿ Shop.

## DISS
Norfolk

**100TH BOMB GROUP MEMORIAL MUSEUM**
Common Road, Dickleburgh (E of Diss off A140)
A collection of USAAF uniforms, decorations, combat records, equipment, memorabilia and wartime photographs housed in an original World War II control tower.

✆ 0379 740708.
Open: Sat and Sun all year, Wed May–Sep, 10–5, or by appointment. Guided tours if required.
🍽♿ (ground floor; ramps available & help if needed) Shop.

## DONCASTER
South Yorkshire

**MUSEUM & ART GALLERY**
Chequer Road
Prehistoric, Medieval and Romano-British archaeology, British natural history, local history and costumes. British and European Art Collection, paintings, sculpture, ceramics, glass and silver. Historical collection of the Kings Own Yorkshire Light Infantry. Monthly special exhibitions.

✆ 0302 734293.
Open: all year, Mon–Sat 10–5, Sun 2–5. (Closed Good Fri, Xmas Day & New Year's Day.) Talks available by arrangement for organisations. Coaches setting down only. ☐ (pre-booked parties) ♿ toilets for the disabled. Shop ✖ (ex guide dogs).

## DORCHESTER
Dorset

**MAIDEN CASTLE**
(2.5m SW)
Prehistoric earthworks, the name being derived from Celtic 'Mai-Jun' ('the stronghold by the plain'). Huge, oval, triple-ramparted camp, with extensive plateau on summit. Complicated defensive system of ditches and ramparts. Stormed by the Roman army in c43AD.

Open: at all reasonable times. (AM)

**OLD CROWN COURT**
58/60 High West Street
The court is contained in the Old Shire Hall, dating from 1796–97, and was the scene of the trial of the six Tolpuddle Martyrs in 1834 who were sentenced to transportation to Botany Bay in Australia for swearing an oath of loyalty to the Friendly Society of Agricultural Labourers. The building is now a Tolpuddle Memorial. See also Tolpuddle.

✆ 0305 251010, ext 2408, or 267992.
Open: all year Mon–Fri 9–1 & 2–4. Tour of cells by appointment only. (Closed PH & Tues following Spring & Aug BH.) Other times only by

arrangement at adjacent West Dorset District Council. Guided tours and parties by arrangement.
✖

## DORCHESTER-ON-THAMES
Oxfordshire

**DORCHESTER ABBEY AND MUSEUM**
The Abbey Church of SS Peter and Paul is the only remaining part of the Augustinian Abbey founded around 1140 and enlarged in 13th and 14th centuries. St Birinus, the first Bishop of Dorchester, baptised the pagan King Cynegils in 653 on the site of the Abbey, and he features in the medieval glass and stone carvings. The museum contains archaeological finds from the Bronze Age through to Anglo-Saxon times with maps showing layout of village during Roman times and later.

✆ Museum, Oxford 0865 340056; Abbey, Oxford 0865 340007.
Open: Museum Etr–Apr Sat, Sun; May–Sep Tue–Sat & BH, 10.30–12.30 & 2–6, Sun 2–6; Abbey daily 9-dusk (subject to church services). Guided tours available on request. Donations. ☐ Etr weekend & May–Sep only Wed, Thu, Sat & Sun 3–5.30.
🅿 ♿ toilets for the disabled. Shop ✖

## DORNOCH
Highland

**DORNOCH CATHEDRAL**
Founded in the 13th century by Gilbert, Archdeacon of Moray and Bishop of Caithness and largely destroyed by fire in 1570 but restored between the 18th and 20th centuries. Burial place for 16 Earls of Sutherland with at the western end a fine statue by Chantrey of the first Duke of Sutherland.

Open: daily dawn–dusk
♿ ✖

**DORNOCH CRAFT CENTRE**
Town Jail, The Square
Visitors can observe the weaving of tartans on Saurgr power looms. There is also kilt and soft toy

making. The jail cells have a small exhibition.

✆ 0862 810555.
Open: Mon–Fri (Nov–May) Jun–Oct Mon–Sat 9–5; Sun Jul & Aug 12–5. Parties by appointment.
☐ ♿ (ground floor only) Shop.

## DOUGLAS
*See Man, Isle of*

## DOUNBY
*See Orkney*

## DOWLISH WAKE
Somerset

**PERRY'S CIDER MILLS**
A long established family-run firm using traditional methods of cidermaking, a process which can be seen in a 16th-century barn in the autumn. The museum, which is housed in a thatched barn, includes wagons and carts and a fine collection of small farm tools. Also on display are photographs of cidermaking and nostalgic pictures of village life around 1900. Traditional farmhouse cider and other country-style items can be bought.

✆ Ilminster 0460 52681.
Open: all year Mon–Fri 9–1, 1.30–5.30; Sat 9.30–1, 2–4.30 & Sun 10–1. (Closed winter BHs.) Guided tours available by appointment to special interest groups. Coach parties accepted by prior arrangement. ♿ toilets are accessible by wheelchair and of ample size. Garden centre. Shop.

## DRUMCOLTRAN TOWER
Dumfries and Galloway

(7m NE of Dalbeattie)
A 16th-century tower house, three storeys in height and built to an oblong plan, with a projecting tower or wing.

Open: Apr–Sep Mon–Fri 9.30–6, Sun 2–6.
(AM)

*Perry's Cider Mills at Dowlish Wake*

## DRYSLWYN

Dyfed

**DRYSLWYN CASTLE**
Ruined, 13th-century, native Welsh stronghold on a lofty mound, important for its part in the struggles between the Welsh and English in the 13th century.

Open: accessible at any time. (AM)

## DUDLEY

West Midlands

**MUSEUM & ART GALLERY**
St James's Road
Includes the Brooke Robinson collection of fine and decorative art. Geological Gallery and a wide variety of temporary exhibitions throughout out the year.

℘ 0384 453571.
Open: Mon–Sat 10–5. (Closed BHs.) & (ground floor only) ✇ (ex guide dogs).

## DUFFTOWN

Grampian

**DUFFTOWN MUSEUM**
The Tower, The Square
Small local history museum featuring Mortlach Kirk material. Temporary displays.

℘ Forres 0309 73701.
Open: Etr–Oct Mon–Sat, 10–12.30, 1.30–5.30 (Jun & Sep, Mon–Sat, 10–6, Sun 2–5; Jul–Aug, Mon–Sat 9.30–6.30, Sun 2–6)
& Shop ✇ (ex guide dogs).

**GLENFIDDICH DISTILLERY**
(1m N of town, off A941)
The distillery was founded by William Grant and is still family owned. A visitor's reception centre houses a bar and Scotch whisky museum. The theatre offers a programme in six languages covering the history of Scotland and Scotch whisky and information on the owning family.

℘ 0340 20373.
Open: all year Mon–Fri 9.30–4.30 Etr–Oct also Sat 9.30–4.30, Sun 12–4.30. (Closed Xmas & New Year). All tours accompanied; groups of more than 12 should book in advance.
☇ & (ramps) Shop ✇

## DUFFUS

Grampian

**DUFFUS CASTLE**
(off B9012)
Motte and bailey castle, with 8-acre bailey surrounding re-built 15th-

century hall and 14th-century tower, now broken into two halves.

Open: Apr–Sep Mon–Sat 9.30–6, Sun 2–6.
(AM)

## DUMFRIES

Dumfries & Galloway

**BURNS' MAUSOLEUM**
St Michael's Churchyard
Mausoleum in the form of a Grecian temple containing the tombs of the poet and his wife, Jean Armour, and their five sons. A sculptured group depicts the Muse of Poetry throwing her cloak over Burns at the plough.

℘ 0387 53374 (Dumfries Museum).
Open: at all reasonable times, access inside by prior arrangement with attendant at Burns' House, Burns Street, Dumfries ℘ 0387 55297.

**ROBERT BURNS CENTRE**
Mill Road
Interpretation Centre and exhibition on the life of the poet, situated in 18th-century water mill.

℘ 0387 64808.
Open: Apr–Sep Mon–Sat 10–8, Sun 2–5; Oct–Mar Tue–Sat 10–1, 2–5. Donations. Admission to audio-visual programme charged. Parties by prior arrangement.
& (stair chair lift) toilets for the disabled, induction loop system ☊ Shop.

**DUMFRIES MUSEUM**
The Observatory
Situated in and around the 18th-century windmill tower on top of Corbelly Hill. Large collection of local history, archaeology, geology, local birds and animals.

℘ 0387 53374.
Open: all year, Mon–Sat 10–1 & 2–5. Closed Sun & Mon Oct–Mar. Donations. Charge for Camera Obscura. Parties by arrangement.
& (not windmill tower) toilets for the disabled. Shop.

### OLD BRIDGE HOUSE
Mill Road
Built in 1660, into the fabric of the 15th-century sandstone Devorgilla Bridge, Dumfries' oldest house is now a museum of everyday life in the town. Exhibits include kitchens of 1850 and 1900, an early dentist's surgery and an evocation of Victorian childhood.

☏ 0387 56904.
Open: Apr–Sep, 10–1 and 2–5 Mon–Sat, 2–5 Sun. Donations. Parties by prior arrangement.

## DUNBLANE
Central

### DUNBLANE CATHEDRAL
The Cathedral mostly dates from the 13th century but incorporates a 12th-century tower. After the Reformation it became a ruin but was restored 1889–93. Intricately carved pulpit, nave pews and 15th-century misericord stalls. Pictish cross, fine Victorian and modern stained glass.

☏ 0786 823388.
Open: daily Apr–Sep, 9.30–6 (Sun 2–6); Oct–Mar, 9.30–4 (Sun 2–4).
Guided tours available.
&

## DUNDEE
Tayside

### BARRACK STREET MUSEUM
Barrack Street
Museum of Natural History; Scottish Wildlife of Lowlands and Highlands. Skeleton of Great Tay Whale. Some changes in displays may be caused by redevelopment. The Art and Nature Gallery features temporary exhibitions exploring themes of nature and related art shows.

☏ 0382 23141.
Open: Mon–Sat 10–5. Donation box.
Shop ✵ (ex guide dogs).

### BROUGHTY CASTLE MUSEUM
Broughty Ferry (4m E)
15th-century castle rebuilt as estuary fort in 19th century.

Displays of arms and armour, seashore wildlife, Dundee's former whaling industry and history of former Burgh of Broughty Ferry. The observation area at the top of the castle provides fine views.

☏ 0382 76121 or 23141.
Open: Mon–Thu & Sat 10–1 & 2–5, Sun 2–5 (Jul–Sep only). Donation box.
⚏ Shop ✵

### MCMANUS GALLERIES
Albert Square
Major Art Gallery with changing exhibitions of local and national interest. Important Scottish and Victorian collections. Displays cover Archaeology in Tayside and Ancient Egypt, Dundee's Trade and Industry, Social and Civil History. McManus Galleries is one of Dundee's finest Victorian buildings by Sir George Gilbert Scott.

☏ 0382 23141.
Open: Mon–Sat 10–5.
Donation box. Education staff may be available to give an introductory talk by prior arrangement.
& Shop ✵

### MILLS OBSERVATORY
Balgay Park, Glamis Road
Observatory, built in 1935, with fine Victorian 10-inch Cooke refracting telescope and other instruments. Gallery displays on astronomy and space exploration, and small planetarium. Full-time astronomer. Regular slide shows.

☏ 0382 67138 or 23141.
Open: Apr–Sep Mon–Fri 10–5, Sat 2–5; Oct–Mar, Mon–Fri 3–10, Sat 2–5.
Guided tours by arrangement. Parties by appointment.
⚏ Shop ✵

## DUNFERMLINE
Fife

### ANDREW CARNEGIE BIRTHPLACE MUSEUM
Junction of Moodie Street and Priory Lane.
The cottage in which the great philanthropist was born in 1835.

New displays tell the exciting story of the weaver's son who gave away 350 million dollars and how the Carnegie Trusts still spend his money for the good of mankind. Free guided walks to the museum start at the Louise Carnegie Gates, Pittencrief Park.

☏ 0383 724302. 724505 for guided walks.
Open: all year daily. Apr–Oct Mon–Sat 11–5, Sun 2–5; Nov–Mar 2–4.
Guided walks May–Aug 2pm, other times for groups by arrangement. Donation box. Parties by arrangement.
& (ground floor only) toilets for the disabled. Shop ✵ (ex guide dogs).

### DUNFERMLINE ABBEY
Pittencrieff Park
Benedictine house founded by Queen Margaret. The foundations of her church remain beneath the present Norman nave. The site of the choir is now occupied by a modern parish church, at the east end of which are remains of St Margaret's shrine dating from the 13th century. King Robert the Bruce is buried in the choir and his grave is marked by a modern brass. Guest house was a royal palace where Charles I was born.

Open: Apr–Sep 9.30–7, Sun 2–7; Oct–Mar 9.30–4, Sun 2–4 (Closed 25, 26 Dec, 1 Jan, Thu pm & Fri in winter). (AM)

### DUNFERMLINE DISTRICT MUSEUM
Viewfield Terrace
Interesting and varied displays of local history, domestic bygones and damask linen. The Small Gallery has monthly changing art and craft exhibitions.

☏ 0383 721814.
Open: all year, Mon–Sat 11–5. (Closed Sun & PH.)
Shop ✵

### PITTENCRIEFF HOUSE MUSEUM
Pittencrieff Park
Situated in a rugged glen, with lawns, hothouses and gardens,

overlooked by the ruined 11th-century Malcolm Canmore's Tower. Fine 17th-century mansion house, with galleries displaying local history, costumes and temporary exhibitions.

✆ 0383 722935 or 721814.
Open: 5 May–2 Sep, Mon & Wed–Sun 11–5.
& (ground floor & gardens only).
Shop ✖

## DUNGENESS
Kent

**'A' POWER STATION**
The Information Centre informs visitors about energy in all its forms, by the use of advanced interactive programmes, videos and models. Guided tours are available by prior arrangement and schools are particularly welcome.

✆ Lydd 0679 21815.
Open: Guided tours every afternoon but it is advisable to phone 2 days in advance of visit.
& toilets for the disabled. ✖

## DUNKELD
Tayside

**HERMITAGE**
(2m W, off A9)
A tree garden was created here by the Second Duke of Atholl in the 18th century. Today, there are 33 acres of mixed conifer and deciduous woodlands, with a wide variety of trees including a Douglas Fir over 180 ft tall. Among the wildlife is the red squirrel. Two follies, Ossian's Hall and Ossian's Cave above the wooded gorge of the River Braan, can be visited on the nature trail.

✆ Pitlochry 0796 3233 (Ranger/Naturalist, Killiecrankie Visitor Centre).
Open: accessible at all reasonable times. Parking charged for (Honesty Box).
(NTS)

**LITTLE HOUSES & THE ELL SHOP**
The Cross
The National Trust for Scotland owns 20 restored houses in Cathedral and High Streets which may be seen externally, dating from after the Battle of Dunkeld in 1689. The restored Ell House is now the Trust's Ell Shop. Trust display of photographs of the restoration scheme and an audio-visual show are in the adjacent Tourist Information Centre.

✆ 03502 460.
Open: Ell Shop Apr–23 Dec Mon–Sat 10–1 & 2–5. (Closed 28 Oct–4 Nov).
Shop.
(NTS)

**LOCH OF THE LOWES VISITOR CENTRE**
High-powered binoculars in the observation hide look over the wildlife reserve, which is frequented by ospreys as well as waterfowl. The surrounding woodland is also interesting for its birdlife. There is an exhibition and slide programme in the visitor centre.

✆ 03502 337.
Open: Apr–Sep daily 10–5. Coach parties welcome by prior arrangement.
⊼ & (pat, including observation hide). Shop.

## DUNOON
Strathclyde

**SCOTTISH WHITE HEATHER FARM**
Toward (5m SW of Dunoon)
Extensive gardens, including azaleas, white heathers, sprays, coloured heather and conifers for sale.

✆ Toward 036987 237.
Open: Etr–Oct Mon–Sat 9.30–6, Sun 12–6. Visitors advised to phone in advance during winter months. Guided tours available by private arrangement.
& (grounds) disabled visitors may park in private drive.

## DUNWICH
Suffolk

**DUNWICH MUSEUM**
St James's Street
Contains the history and relics of the ancient town of Dunwich. Also flora and fauna of the area.

✆ Westleton 072873 358.
Open: Mar, Apr & Oct, Sat & Sun 2–4.30. Also May–Sep daily 11.30–4.30.
Groups (20 max.) by appointment.
Shop ✖

## DURHAM
Co. Durham

**ST AIDAN'S COLLEGE GROUNDS**
Windmill Hill
The College was designed by Sir Basil Spence, and built in the early sixties. The spacious and well-stocked grounds, landscaped by Professor Brian Hackett, are at their best during July, when the shrub beds are in flower. Features include a laburnum walk and a reflecting pool, well stocked with aquatic plants and fish. From the garden there are fine views of Durham Cathedral.

✆ 091 374 3269.
Open: all year, daily 9–dusk. Donations to NGS. Guided tours by prior arrangement only.
⊟ (by prior aarangement) &
(ground floor and grounds only) toilets for the disabled.
✖ (garden only).

## EAST BERGHOLT
Essex

**BRIDGE COTTAGE**
Flatford
National Trust cottage with a small exhibition of John Constable's connection with the village.

✆ 0206 298 260.
Open: Etr–Oct; Wed–Sun Apr–May & Sep–Oct, every day Jun–Aug, 11–5.30. Donation box. Parking charge (disabled free).
⊟ & Shop.

## EASTBOURNE
East Sussex

**THE PIER**
Grand Parade
One of the finest and most elegant of England's Victorian piers with glorious views to Hastings and Beachy Head. The pier has many amenities and entertainments to offer and the front has recently been rebuilt to coincide with the 121st anniversary of its opening.

✆ 0323 410466.
Open: all year, daily 8am–2am.
☐ (licensed 9–5.30) Catering for coach parties must be pre-booked.
♿ (ground floor; toilets accessible)
Shop.

**TOWNER ART GALLERY & LOCAL HISTORY MUSEUM**
High Street, Old Town
Elegant Georgian manor house (c1777) set in pleasant gardens. Collection of mainly 19th- and 20th-century British art. Lively temporary exhibition programme. Museum traces the history of Eastbourne from pre-history to Edwardian era.

✆ 0323 411688.
Open: all year Tue–Sat 10–5 Sun & BH 2–5. (Closed Mon, Good Fri, 24–25 Dec & 1 Jan). Donation box. Guided tours available on application.
♿ (ground floor & gardens only) Shop ✖

## EAST CARLTON
Northamptonshire

**EAST CARLTON COUNTRYSIDE PARK**
(Between Corby & Market Harborough off the A427)
Steelmaking heritage centre, craft workshops, working blacksmith's forge and campsite set in 100 acres of beautiful countryside with views into Leicestershire across the Welland Valley. Various tours and music events on Sundays in summer.

✆ 0536 770977.
Open: daily, Apr–Oct 10–6, Nov–Mar 10–4. Donations. Guided tours available to pre-booked groups by

prior arrangement and on certain special days.
☐ ♿ (part; ramps to school room, surfaced paths) toilets for the disabled. Shop ⚓

## EAST DEREHAM
Norfolk

**BISHOP BONNERS COTTAGES MUSEUM**
40 Crown Road
Timber-framed, thatched cottages with a rare coloured frieze dated 1502. The cottages, in front of the detached bell-tower of the parish church, house the local folk museum.

✆ 0362 693107.
Open: May–Sep, Tue–Fri 2.30–5, Sat 3–5. Donations. Guided tours are available. Parties by prior arrangement.
♿ (ground floor).

## EAST FORTUNE
Lothian

**MUSEUM OF FLIGHT**
East Fortune Airfield
The former airship base now displays the history of aircraft and rockets and has working exhibits which visitors may operate. Include a Supermarine Spitfire Mk 16, De Havilland Sea Venom, Hawker Sea Hawk and Comet (4c).

✆ 062 088 308.
Open: Etr–1 Oct Mon–Sun 10.30–4.30. Guided tours available by arrangement.
♿ Shop ✖ (ex guide dogs).

## EASTHAM
Merseyside

**EASTHAM WOODS COUNTRY PARK**
Green Lane, off Ferry Road
Country park of about 100 acres with a fine nature trail, unique views across the Mersey estuary and historical features that include a bear pit and the site of an ancient river crossing, 'Job's Ferry', originally operated by a brotherhood of monks. Close to the Manchester Ship Canal, Speke Airport and Queen Elizabeth II dock.

✆ 051 327 1007.
Open: Park, at all reasonable times; Visitor Centre by arrangement. Pre-booked guided tours available.
☐ (daily in summer, 11am to early evening) ⚓ ♿ (ramp into Visitors Centre) toilets for the disabled.

## EAST HOATHLY
East Sussex

**SPECIALLY FOR YOU**
Warnham Cottage
(A22 London-Eastbourne rd)
A workshop and showroom showing a range of clothing for adults and children designed around the traditional English smock. Displays of intricate handsmocking by skilled needle-women in a charming 18th-century cottage.

✆ 0825 840397.
Open: all year Thu–Sat 10–4; other times by appointment. Guided tours max 20 people.
♿

## EASTLEIGH
Hampshire

**EASTLEIGH MUSEUM**
The Citadel, 25A High Street
Museum of town life including railway exhibits with art gallery adjacent. The museum has changing displays about every five weeks.

✆ 0703 643826.
Open: all year Tue–Fri 10–5, Sat 10–4. Parties by prior arrangement.
♿ Shop.

## EAST MERSEA
Essex

**CUDMORE GROVE COUNTRY PARK**
Grassland adjoining the beach with fine views across the Colne and Blackwater Estuaries. There is an information room.

✆ 0206 383868.
Open: all year, daily 8-dusk. Parking charged Sun & BH in summer (ex OAP, disabled, motorbikes). Guided tours & coach parties by prior arrangement.

&. (grounds only) toilets for the disabled. ⛱

## ECTON
Northants

**SYWELL COUNTRY PARK**
Washbrook Ln
Developed on the site of the former Sywell Reservoir, the Park covers an area of 143 acres and consists of pastureland around the water and an arboretum below the dam. A number of events are run at the Park as part of the County Council's Countryside Event Programme.

✆ 0604 810970.
Open: all year, summer 8.30–6, winter 8.30–5. Guided tours at the discretion of the Rangers. Coach parties by prior arrangement only. Donations welcome.
&. toilets for the disabled. Shop ⛱

## EDINBURGH
Lothian

**CLAN TARTAN CENTRE**
James Pringle Woollen Mill, 70–74 Bangor Road, Leith (1m N)
Visitor centre highlighting the history of the Scottish clans and their tartans, with a computer facility to find out if your name is linked to any of the clans. History and development of the tartan. Shop selling a range of Pringle knitwear and full range of Highland dress.

✆ 031 553 5161.
Open: all year May–Oct daily 9–5.30, Nov–Apr Mon–Sat 10–5.
⛯ (licensed) &. toilets for the disabled. ✎

**FRUIT MARKET GALLERY**
29 Market Street
The leading venue for major Scottish and international exhibitions of contemporary and 20th-century art. Programme of painting, design, sculpture, photography and video. Annual all-Scotland Open Exhibition. Free workshops, tours and events accompany performances.

✆ 031 225 2383.
Open: times not decided for 1992 – please phone for information. Donations. Guided tours available.
⛯&. (ground floor only). Shop ✎

**GENERAL REGISTER HOUSE**
(East end of Princes Street)
Designed by Robert Adam, it was founded in 1774. Headquarters of the Scottish Record Office and the repository for National Archives of Scotland. Changing historical exhibitions. Historical and Legal Search Rooms available to visitors engaged in research.

✆ 031 556 6585.
Open: all year Mon–Fri 9–4.30. Exhibitions Mon–Fri 10–4. (Closed certain PH.)
&. (ground floor only) ✎

**GEORGE HERIOT'S SCHOOL**
Lauriston Place
Dates from 1628 and was founded by George Heriot, the 'Jingling Geordie' of Scott's 'Fortunes of Nigel'.

✆ 031 229 7263.
Open: Jul–Aug Mon–Fri 9.30–4.30. Guided tours available. Coach parties not accepted.
&. (ground floor only) ✎

**HUNTLY HOUSE**
142 Canongate
Dating from 1570 and housing Edinburgh's principal museum of local history. Includes period rooms, collections of silver, glass and pottery and reconstructions relating to the city's traditional industries.

✆ 031 225 2424 Ext 6689 (031 225 1131 after 5pm & weekends).
Open: Mon–Sat, Jun–Sep 10–6; Oct–May 10–5. (During Festival period only Sun 2–5). Donations. Guided tours available for special parties by arrangement.
&. (ground floor only) Shop ✎

**LADY STAIR'S HOUSE**
Lady Stair's Close,
Lawnmarket
A restored town house dating from

1622, now a treasure house of portraits, relics and manuscripts relating to three of Scotland's greatest men of letters – Robert Burns, Sir Walter Scott and Robert Louis Stevenson.

✆ 031 225 2424 Ext 6689 (031 225 1131 after 5pm & weekends).
Open: Mon–Sat, Jun–Sep 10–6; Oct–May 10–5. (During Festival also Sun 2–5). Donations. Guided tours available for special groups by arrangement.
Shop ✎

**MUSEUM OF CHILDHOOD**
42 High St (Royal Mile)
A wonderful collection of childhood memories for all ages, this was the first museum in the world to be devoted solely to the history of childhood. Naturally popular with children, it has also been described as 'the noisiest museum in the world'!

✆ 031 225 2424 Ext 6645.
Open: Mon–Sat 10–6 & Sun 2–5 during Festival; Oct–May 10–5. Donations. Guided tours for special parties by arrangement.
&. (ground floor, lifts to first floor, ramp to other floor) toilets for the disabled. Shop ✎

**NATIONAL GALLERY OF SCOTLAND**
The Mound
One of the most distinguished of the smaller galleries in Europe, whose interior has been completely restored to that of the 1860s. It contains collections of Old Masters, Impressionists and Scottish paintings including: Raphael's *Bridgewater Madonna*, Constable's *Dedham Vale*, and masterpieces by Titian, Velasquez, Raeburn, Van Gogh and Gauguin. Drawings, water-colours and original prints by Turner, Goya, Blake etc (shown on request Mon–Fri).

✆ 031 332 4939 (recorded message).
Open: Mon–Sat 10–5, Sun 2–5; in winter, (Oct–Mar) some lunchtime closure. (Mon–Sat 10–6, Sun 11–6 during Festival.)
&. Shop ✎

*An enchanting exhibit at Edinburgh's Museum of Childhood*

and pastimes of Edinburgh's people from the late 18th-century to the present day. Filled with the sights, sounds and smells of the past, it includes reconstructions of a prison cell, cooper's workshop, draper's shop, bookbinders workshop and 1940's kitchen among its fascinating displays.

✆ 031 225 2424 Ext 6638.
Open: all year Mon–Sat, 10–6, 10–5 Oct–May (Sun during Festival 2–5). Donations. Special parties by arrangement.
♿ toilets for the disabled. Shop.

### NATIONAL LIBRARY OF SCOTLAND
George IV Bridge
Founded in 1682, this is one of the four largest libraries in Great Britain with several million books. There is an extensive collection of manuscripts, together with 19th-century music, Caxton bible, a map collection and the Scottish Science Library.

✆ 031 226 4531.
Open: Reading room Mon–Fri 9.30–8.30, Sat 9.30–1 (opens at 10 on Wed); Exhibition room Mon–Sat 9.30–5, Apr–Sep Sun 2–5 (open until 8.30pm every day Aug–early Sep); Science Library Mon–Fri 9.30–5 (closes 8.30pm on Wed).
♿ ✖

### NATIONAL MUSEUM OF SCOTLAND
I Queen Street
Scottish collections and archaeological finds from earliest times to the present, illustrating everyday life and history.

✆ 031 225 7534.
Open: Mon–Sat 10–5, Sun 2–5.
♿ Shop ✖ (ex guide dogs).

### NATIONAL MUSEUM OF SCOTLAND
Chambers Street
The most comprehensive display in

Britain under one roof comprising the decorative arts of the world and ethnography, natural history, geology, technology and science. Lectures, gallery talks and films at advertised times.

✆ 031 225 7534.
Open: Mon–Sat 10–5, Sun 2–5.
🚻 ♿ toilets for the disabled. Shop ✖ (ex guide dogs).

### PARLIAMENT HOUSE
High Street (Royal Mile) on S side of St Giles Cathedral
Dates from 1639, but façade was replaced in 1829. The Hall has a fine hammer-beam roof. The Scottish Parliament met here before the Union of 1707. Now the seat of Supreme Law Courts of Scotland.

✆ 031 225 2595.
Open: all year Mon–Fri 10–4. Parties by arrangement.
🚻 (9–2.30) ♿ (ground floor and 2nd floor east wing only) toilets for the disabled. ✖ (ex guide dogs).

### THE PEOPLE'S STORY
Cannongate Tolbooth, 163 Canongate
A 16th-century building with museum displays of the life, work

### ROYAL BOTANIC GARDEN EDINBURGH
Inverleith Row
Famous garden, noted especially for the rhododendron collection, rock garden, plant houses and exhibition hall. Diverse programme of exhibitions and educational activities all year.

✆ 031 552 7171.
Garden open all year (ex Xmas Day and New Year's Day). Mar–Oct Mon–Sat 9–1 hr before sunset, Sun 11–1 hr before sunset; Oct–Mar Mon–Sat 9–sunset, Sun 11–sunset. Plant houses, exhibitions hall & Inverleith House Visitor Centre open Mon–Sat 10–5, Sun 11–5. Guided tours available. Donation box.
🚻 (Mon–Sat 10–5, Sun 11–5; closes 15 mins before Garden when this is before 5). ♿ toilets for the disabled; a small number of wheelchairs are available at the Garden entrances at no charge. Shop ✖ (ex guide dogs).

### SCOTTISH NATIONAL GALLERY OF MODERN ART
Belford Road
The national collection of 20th-century painting, sculpture and graphic art. The work of the established masters includes Derain, Picasso, Giacometti, Magritte, Henry Moore, Barbara

Hepworth, Lichtenstein and major
Scottish artists, as well as leading
figures of the contemporary
international scene. Some sculpture
is displayed. The gallery print room
is also open to the public by
appointment.

✆ 031 332 4939 (recorded message).
Open: all year. Mon–Sat 10–5 & Sun
2–5; in winter (Oct–Mar) some
lunchtime closure. (During Festival
Mon–Sat 10–6, Sun 11–6.)
🚻 (licensed) ♿ Shop ✿

**SCOTTISH NATIONAL PORTRAIT
GALLERY**
Queen Street
Striking red Victorian building
containing portraits of men and
women who have contributed to
Scottish history. The collection
includes such historical
personalities as Mary Queen of
Scots, James VI and I, Burns, Sir
Walter Scott and Ramsay
MacDonald as well as modern
figures such as The Queen Mother,
Sean Connery and Muriel Spark.
Many other artists, statesmen,
soldiers and scientists are
portrayed in all media, including
sculpture. There is an extensive
reference section of engravings, and
photographs.

✆ 031 332 4939 (recorded message).
Open: all year daily, Mon–Sat 10–5 &
Sun 2–5; in winter (Oct–Mar) some
lunchtime closure. (During Festival
Mon–Sat 10–6, Sun 11–6.)
♿ Shop ✿

**SOUTH QUEENSFERRY MUSEUM**
Council Chambers, High
Street, South Queensferry
This small museum tells the story
of the river crossing, including the
Forth Bridges, and the ancient
Royal Burgh. There are superb
views of the bridges

✆ 031 331 1590.
Open: Thur–Mon 10–1 & 2.15–5 (Sun
12–5). Donations. Volunteer guides
occasionally available for guided
tours.

**TRINITY APSE**
Chalmers Close, High Street
Trinity Apse is the surviving
fragment of Scotland's finest
medieval collegiate. Currently in use
as Edinburgh's brass rubbing
centre. Admission is free although a
charge is made for brass rubbing.

✆ 031 556 4364.
Open: all year Mon–Sat, 10–6 Jun–
Sep, 10–5 Oct–May (Sun during
Edinburgh Festival 2–5). Donations.
Coach parties should pre-book if
brass rubbing required.
Shop.

**WEST REGISTER HOUSE**
Charlotte Square
The former St George's Church,
designed by Robert Reid in the
Greco-Roman style in 1811. Now an
auxiliary repository for the Scottish
Record Office and housing an
exhibition '800 years of Scottish
History'. Search Room available to
researchers.

✆ 031 556 6585.
Open: Mon–Fri 9–4.45. Exhibitions
10–4. (Closed some PHs.)
♿ ✿

**EDWINSTOWE**
Nottinghamshire

**SHERWOOD FOREST & VISITOR
CENTRE**
(0.5m N on B6034)
Probably the most famous forest in
Britain but now consisting of
scattered areas of woodland. The
Visitor Centre has an exhibition on
Robin Hood with information on
forest wildlife found in the forest
and walks, including one to the
Major Oak, which lies about half a
mile west.

✆ Nottingham 0623 823202.
Open: Forest accessible at all
reasonable times; Visitor Centre
permanent exhibition open all year.
Mar–Sep 10.30–5; Oct–Feb 10.30–
4.30. Tourist Information Office, cafe
and shop open 11–5 in summer;
winter opening limited.
🚻♿🚻

**ELCOT**
Berkshire

**ELCOT PARK HOTEL**
(5.5m W of Newbury off A4)
16–acre garden overlooking the
Kennet Valley with extensive views.
Mainly lawns and woodland laid out
by Sir William Paxton in 1848.
Magnificent display of daffodils and
shrubs in Spring.

✆ Kintbury 0488 58100.
Open: all year, daily 10–6.
🚻 (licensed restaurant) ♿

**ELGIN**
Grampian

**PLUSCARDEN ABBEY**
(6m SW on unclass road)
The original monastery was
founded by Alexander II in 1230.
Restoration took place in the 14th
and 19th centuries, and the Abbey
has been re-occupied by the
Benedictines since 1948. Planned
restoration of west wing. New
Women's building, retreats and
Information Centre.

✆ Dallas 034389 257.
Open: daily, 5am–8.30pm. Guided
tours available.
♿ parking for the disabled. Shop.

**ELSTREE**
Hertfordshire

**ALDENHAM COUNTRY PARK**
Dagger Lane (Signposted from
A5 or A41, leave M1 at junction
5)
Home of the Aldenham herd of
Longhorn cattle and a variety of
other rare breed animals. The 175-
acre park offers woodland walks,
picnic areas, children's corner,
adventure playground, fishing and a
ranger service. Special events.

✆ 081 953 9602.
Open: all year, every day (ex Xmas
Day) 9–5 winter, 9–dusk summer.
Parking charge. Guided tours for
specialist groups. Donations. Coach
parties by prior arrangement.
♿ (access to animal winter quarters, →

disabled angling facility, nature trail & lakeside walk) toilets for the disabled. ᚷ

## ELVASTON
Derbyshire

**ELVASTON CASTLE COUNTRY PARK**
Borrowash Road (6m SE Derby off B5010, signs from A6 & A52)
Two hundred-acre country park with 19th-century landscaped parkland, ornamental woodlands, formal gardens and topiary. Other facilities include the Park Centre, Nature Trail Centre, and the Working Estate Museum (admission charged). There is a programme of special events.

✆ 0332 571 342.
Open: all year, daily 9–dusk (most facilities Etr–Oct). There is a charge for parking.
☕ (tearoom Tue–Sun & BH Etr–Oct 11–4). ♿ (ground floor & grounds) parking & toilets for the disabled. Shop ᚷ

## ENFIELD
Gt London

**FORTY HALL MUSEUM**
Forty Hill
Built in 1629 for Sir Nicholas Raynton, Lord Mayor of London, the Mansion was modified in the early 18th century. Contemporary plaster ceilings and screen, 17th- and 18th-century furnishings and paintings, ceramics and glass. Also temporary exhibitions. In park.

✆ 081 363 8196.
Open: all year Tue–Sun 10–5 (Closed Mons ex BHs.) Donations. Guided tours available by arrangement & subject to staff availability. Parties by appointment.
☕ (Oct–Etr 11–4, summer 11–6) ᚷ ♿ (ground floor only) toilets for the disabled. Shop ✺

## ERPINGHAM
Norfolk

**ALBY CRAFTS**
(On A40 between Cromer & Aylsham)

The craft centre comprises a gallery, gift shop, honey-pot shop, six studio workshops and a furniture showroom, in converted Norfolk farm buildings set in four acres of grounds with a bee garden. Also lace museum (small charge) and bottle museum (small charge).

✆ 0263 761590.
Open: early Mar–mid Dec Tue–Sun 10–5. Coach parties by appointment only.
☕ (table licence) ♿ (ground floor; ramps). Shop.

## EWLOE
Clwyd

**EWLOE CASTLE**
(NW of village on A55)
Remains of native Welsh castle in Ewloe woods near where Henry II was defeated in 1157.

Open: at all reasonable times. (CADW)

## EXETER
Devon

**DEVONSHIRE REGIMENTAL MUSEUM**
Wyvern Barracks, Barrack Road
The exhibits cover the history of the Devonshire Regiment from its formation in 1685 to 1958 when the Regiment amalgamated with the Dorset Regiment. Exhibits include uniforms, weapons, medals, historical documents and military souvenirs collected by the Regiment over the years.

✆ 0392 218178.
Open: all year Mon–Fri 9–4.30. (Closed Sat, Sun & BHs.) Donations. ♿ (ground floor only) Shop ✺

**GUILDHALL,**
High Street
Dates from 1330, partially rebuilt 1446; arches and façade, added 1592–5. Fine displays of oil paintings, Guild Crests and civic silver and regalia.

✆ 0392 265500.
Open: all year Mon–Fri 10–1 & 2–4, Sat 10–12 (ex when used for Civic functions).
♿ (ground floor only) ✺ (ex guide dogs).

**QUAY HOUSE INTERPRETATION CENTRE**
46 The Quay
Exhibition of the historical development of the Quay and Port of Exeter and 'A Celebration of Exeter', an audio-visual presentation.

✆ 0392 50115.
Open: all year, daily (ex 25–26 Dec) 10–5 (6pm Jul & Aug). Guided tours by arrangement charged according to circumstances. Parties accepted (max 50).
♿ (ground floor) Shop.

**ROYAL ALBERT MEMORIAL MUSEUM**
Queen Street
A Victorian treasure-house of displays including natural history, local history, archaeology including the Romans, Exeter silver, Devon pottery and glass. Ethnography shows the way of life of Eskimos and Red Indians. Paintings by British artists and lively exhibitions. Holiday activities for children.

✆ 0392 265858.
Open: all year Tue–Sat 10–5.30. ♿ (by arrangement) ✺ (ex guide dogs).

**ST NICHOLAS PRIORY**
The Mint, off Fore Street
Former guest wing of a Benedictine Priory, founded around 1087, later becoming an Elizabethan merchant's home. Today visitors see its Norman crypt and kitchen and the guest hall, where the Prior used to entertain. Brass rubbing available.

✆ 0392 265858.
Open: Tue–Sat 10–1 & 2–5. ♿ (by arrangement). ✺ (ex guide dogs).

## FAIRFORD

Gloucestershire

**ST MARY'S CHURCH**

Late 15th-century 'wool' church
with glorious stained glass: 28
windows installed in the late 15th
century have, despite the ravages of
the Reformation and the Civil War,
been preserved intact. It is the only
parish church in Britain to have
retained its complete set of
medieval glass, which covers an
area of over 2000 sq ft.

✆ Cirencester 0285 712467.
Open: daily 9–6 (summer), 9–5
(winter). Donations.
♿ (2 wheelchairs available for loan)
toilets for the disabled nearby. Shop
❀

## FALKIRK

Central

**FALKIRK MUSEUM**

15 Orchard Street
District history museum which
traces the development of the area
from earliest times to the present.
There are displays of Roman and
Medieval pottery, Dunmore pottery,
locally produced cast-iron objects
as well as photographs and archives
of rural and industrial life in Falkirk.

✆ 0324 24911 Ext 2472.
Open: Mon–Fri 10.30–12.30 & 1.30–5,
Sat 10–5.
♿ (ground floor only) Shop ❀

**ROUGH CASTLE**

One of the most remarkable forts
on the Antonine Wall built by the
Roman army c140 AD. The site
covers one acre with double ditches
and defensive pits.

Open: Apr–Sep Mon–Fri 9.30–6, Sun
2–6.
(AM)

## FARNHAM

Surrey

**ALICE HOLT FOREST VISITOR
CENTRE**

(5m SW on A325, signposted)

Forest visitor centre and forest
shop in an attractive location with
walks and trails, car parks and
picnic places.

✆ 0420 23666 Ext 229.
Open: Mar–Sep Tue–Sun 10–4.30
Guided tours for school parties &
professional groups by arrangement.
🌲 ♿ (part, including Visitor Centre)
toilets for the disabled. Shop.

**FARNHAM MUSEUM**

Willmer House, 38 West Street
Geology, archaeology, local history
and art housed in Willmer House, a
fine example of Georgian brickwork.
Special events. Museum garden.

✆ 0252 715094.
Open: Tue–Sat 10–5. Guided tours
available for small parties and school
groups if requested in advance.
♿ (ground floor & garden only)
entrance and toilets for the disabled.
Shop ❀

**NEW ASHGATE GALLERY**

Wagon Yard, Lower Church
Lane, Downing Street
Monthly changing exhibitions by
leading contemporary artists and
craftspeople and a large stock of
ceramics, prints, jewellery and
wood. Jewellery studio and framing/
restoration workshop on the
premises.

✆ 0252 713208.
Open: all year Tue–Sat (ex BH) 10–
1.30 & 2.30–5. Parking charge.
♿ (ground floor) Shop.

## FAWLEY

Hampshire

**CALSHOT CRAFTS CENTRE**

Badminston Farm, Calshot
Road (Alongside B3053/A326
Fawley to Calshot Road)
Seven acres of grounds with nature
trail and picnic area with views of
the Solent and Isle of Wight. Crafts
shop and gallery.

✆ 0703 898846.
Open: all year, every day (ex 25 & 26

Dec & 1 Jan) 10–5 (6 in summer).
Prior booking for coach parties
requiring cream teas.
🍽 (licensed) ♿ Shop 🌲

## FENCE

Lancashire

**SLATE AGE (FENCE) LTD**

Visitors can see slate from Coniston
and Elterwater being cut with
diamond saws and made up into
fancy goods and gifts.

✆ Nelson 0282 66952.
Open: Workshop and Shop Mon–Sat
9–4. (Closed Xmas.)

## FINCHINGFIELD

Essex

**FINCHINGFIELD GUILDHALL AND
MUSEUM**

(On B1053 between Saffron
Walden & Braintree)
Exhibitions of arts and crafts most
weekends Easter to September.

✆ Great Dunmow 0371 810456.
Open: Museum: Etr–Sep Sun & BHs
2–5.30, Guildhall art exhibitions as
arranged 10–6. School parties by
arrangement. .
Shop.

## FINDON

West Sussex

**CISSBURY RING**

(1 mile E)
Well preserved 60-acre Iron Age fort
– the largest on the South Downs. It
was occupied between the 5th and
the 1st centuries BC and again in
the 4th century AD. Extensive
excavations have revealed flint
mines, ploughing patterns and sites
of huts. There are good views from
the ramparts.

Open: accessible at all reasonable
times.

## FINSTOWN
### See Orkney

## FLAMBOROUGH HEAD & BEMPTON CLIFFS

Humberside

(4m NE of Bridlington off B1259, B1255 & B1229)
Great chalk cliffs rising high above the North Sea between Flamborough Head and Bempton where the largest breeding colony of seabirds in England include gannets and kittiwakes. The cliffs are extremely dangerous and visitors should keep to footpaths and observation points. A good place for wildflowers.

Open: accessible at all times by public footpath.

## FLINT

Clwyd

**FLINT CASTLE**
Ruined late 13th-century castle, erected by Edward I, with circular detached keep originally surrounded by moat.

Open: accessible at all reasonable times.
(CADW)

## FLIXTON

Suffolk

**NORFOLK & SUFFOLK AVIATION MUSEUM**

A collection of aircraft and aviation spanning the early years of flight to present day. There are 16 aircraft, with some housed in a new hangar; other buildings contain smaller items relating to the history of flight.

✆ Thurton 0508 480778.
Open: Apr–Oct, Sun & BH 10–5; Jun–Aug, Sun Wed & Thu 7pm–9pm; also Jul & Aug Thu 11–5. Parties at other times by prior arrangement. Voluntary donations welcome.
⛾ (ramp) Shop ⚮ (in museum).

## FOCHABERS

Grampian

**BAXTERS VISITOR CENTRE**
(1m W of Fochabers on A96 Aberdeen–Inverness road)
The Visitor Centre tells the story of how Baxters first began over 120 years ago up to present day, now supplying customers in over 60 countries. There is a guided tour of the factory, a video show, a Victorian kitchen and the 'old shop' where it all began.

✆ 0343 820393 Ext 241.
Open: Mon–Fri 9.30–4.30, Sat & Sun May–Sep 11–4.30 (Closed 2 weeks over Xmas & all BH; also certain dates in Apr, Jun, Jul & Aug). Telephone before visit if requiring tour. Coach parties must book in advance.
⛁ 🚻 ⛾ (ground floor only) parking & toilets for the disabled. Shop ⚮

## FOLKESTONE

Kent

**MUSEUM & ART GALLERY**
Grace Hill
Local history, archaeology and natural science. Temporary art exhibitions. Located on first floor of building; no lift.

✆ 0303 850123.
Open: all year, Mon, Tue, Thu & Fri 9–5.30, Wed 9–1 & Sat 9–5. (Closed BH). Parties restricted to maximum of thirty.
⚮

**ROWLANDS CONFECTIONERY**
17 Old High Street
Manufacture of confectionery including lettered rock can be viewed by interested visitors.

✆ 0303 54723.
Open: daily 9–5.30. Coach parties not accepted. Shop.

## FORDINGBRIDGE

Hampshire

**ALDER MILL**
Sandleheath Road (Take the B3078 from Fordingbridge to Damerham, turn left in

Sandleheath signposted Alderholt, the mill is half a mile at bottom of hill.)
Picturesque watermill on a tributary of the Hampshire Avon restored to full working order, milling and selling flour. Local crafts are on sale with three-weekly exhibitions by local artists.

✆ 0425 653130.
Open: Etr–Sep, mid Nov–Xmas Tue–Fri & Sun 2–6 (10–6 Sat & BHs). Donations. Guided tours by arrangement (charge). Coach parties by appointment.
⛁ ⛾ (ground floor). Shop.

## FORRES

Grampian

**FALCONER MUSEUM**
Tolbooth Street
Displays of local history, wildlife, geology, and archaeology. Temporary exhibitions.

✆ 0309 73701.
Open: all year Mon–Fri 9.30–6.30; also Sat May–Oct 9.30–12.30 & 1.30–6.30; Sun Jul–Aug 11 & 2–6.
⛾ (ground floor only) Shop ⚮ (ex guide dogs).

**SUENOS' STONE**
A notable 20 ft-high Dark Age monument with a sculptured cross on one side and groups of warriors on the reverse.

Open: Apr–Sep Mon–Fri 9.30–6, Sun 2–6.
(AM)

## FORTROSE

Highland

**FORTROSE CATHEDRAL**
Partly dismantled by Cromwell for a fort at Inverness; the surviving portions of the 14th-century cathedral include the south aisle with vaulting and fine detail.

Open: accessible at all reasonable times.
(AM)

## FORT WILLIAM
Highland

### INVERLOCHY CASTLE
A well-preserved example of a 13th-century and later stronghold. Noted for the famous battle fought nearby in 1645, when Montrose defeated the Campbells.

Open: Apr–Sep Mon–Fri 9.30–6, Sun 2–6.
(AM)

## FOVANT
Wiltshire

### REGIMENTAL BADGES
(0.75m SE on footpath)
The Regimental Badges line the scarp slope of Fovant Down and were cut into the chalk by regiments encamped in the area during the First World War. The badges can be viewed from the A30 east of Fovant or from the footpath which runs between Fovant and Chiselbury Hill Fort.

Open: accessible at all reasonable times.

## FOWEY
Cornwall

### ST CATHERINE'S CASTLE
(0.75m SW off A3082)
Ruined stronghold erected in 16th century by Henry VIII to defend the coast and restored in 1855.

Open: all year, any reasonable time.
(AM)

## FRANKBY
Merseyside

### ROYDEN PARK AND THURMASTON COMMON
(Take the B5139 from Upton via Greasby to Frankby Green. Turn left along Hillbark Road to Royden Park gates.)
Nearly 250 acres of heathland, woodland and open parkland. The main point of access is at Royden Park where there is a visitor centre, toilets, a walled garden, model

railway (runs Sunday afternoons) and picnic sites.

℘ 051 677 7594.
Open: all year, walled garden 10–5 (Closed Xmas & New Year). Guided tours by arrangement with Countryside Rangers.
⋔ ♿ (garden).

## FULBECK
Lincolnshire

### MANOR STABLES CRAFT WORKSHOPS
(On A607 between Lincoln & Grantham)
Craft workshops in converted stone stables with saddlers and other working craftspeople. Quality crafts for sale in showroom. Talks on weaving, spinning, dried flower arranging or ceramic painting by prior arrangement.

℘ 0400 72779.
Open: all year (ex 24 Dec–9 Jan) Tue–Sun & BH Mons 10.30–4.30. Prior booking for coach parties.
⋤ ⋔ ♿ (ground floor) toilets for the disabled. Shop.

## GALASHIELS
Borders

### PETER ANDERSON CASHMERE WOOLLEN MILL & MUSEUM
Nether Mill, Huddersfield St
The museum brings aspects of the town's past to life by the clever use of early photographs and captions. A central unit displays artefacts of the town's involvement with the woollen trade and also every day items in common use in days gone by.

℘ 0896 2091.
Open: all year Mon–Sat 9–5 (Jun–Sep, Sun 12–5). Mill Tours (charge, children under 6 free), Mon–Fri at 10.30, 11.30, 1.30 & 2.30 or by appointment.
♿ (ground floor only) Shop.

### OLD GALA HOUSE
Scott Crescent
Former home of the Lairds of Gala

dating from 1583. Displays tell the story of the house, the Lairds and the early growth of the town. Important features include painted cciling (1635) and painted wall (1988), and temporary exhibition galleries.

℘ 0750 20096.
Open: Mid Mar–Oct Mon–Sat 10–4, Sun 2–4. Donations. Guided tours & coach parties by prior arrangement.
⋤ ♿ (ground floor) toilets for the disabled. Shop.

## GLASGOW
Strathclyde

### BELLAHOUSTON PARK
Sports Centre
171 acres of parkland only 3 miles from the city centre. Site of the Empire Exhibition of 1938. Sunken garden, walled garden and rock garden. Multi-purpose Sports Centre situated at west end of park, with adjacent all-weather Athletic Centre. Glasgow show.

℘ 041 427 4224 (041 427 5454 Sports Centre).
Open: daily end Apr–Aug 8am–10pm, Sep–Apr 8–5 (times approximate).
⋤ (Sports Centre) ♿

### BOTANIC GARDEN
Queen Margaret Drive (off Great Western Rd)
Established in 1817, it contains an outstanding collection of plants. The Kibble Palace is a unique glasshouse with, among others, a famous collection of tree ferns. The main glasshouse contains numerous tropical and exotic plants. The 40 acres of gardens include systematic and herb gardens, and a chronological border.

℘ 041 334 2422.
The Kibble Palace. Open: daily 10–4.45 (4.15 in winter). The main glasshouse, Open: Mon–Sat 1–4.45 (4.15 in winter) Sun 12–4.45 (4.15 in winter). Gardens, Open: daily 7–dusk.
♿ (garden only) toilets for disabled.

## THE BURRELL COLLECTION
Pollok Country Park (2.5m SW)

The Burrell Collection is housed in an award-winning gallery, which makes the most of its superb natural setting. The Collection was formed by Sir William and Lady Burrell and comprises more than 8,000 items. These include Chinese ceramics, bronzes and jades, Near Eastern rugs and carpets, Turkish pottery and artefacts from the ancient civilisations of Iraq, Egypt, Greece and Italy. European medieval art is represented by metalwork, sculpture, illuminated manuscripts, ivories and two of the most important museum collections in the world of stained glass and tapestries. The paintings range from the 15th to the early 20th centuries and include works by Memling, Bellini, Cranach, Rembrandt, Courbet, Millet, Boudin, Degas, Manet and Cezanne. There are also important collections of British silver and needlework.

✆ 041 649 7151.
Open: Mon–Sat 10–5, Sun 12–6. (Closed: 25 Dec & 1 Jan.) Donations. Guided tours available. Parking charged for.
🚻 🅿 ♿ (lifts) toilets for the disabled. Shop ✖ (ex guide dogs).

## CATHEDRAL
Castle Street

The most complete medieval Cathedral surviving on the Scottish mainland, dating mainly from the 13th and 14th centuries.

Open: Apr–Sep Mon–Fri 9.30–6, Sun 2–6.
(AM)

## CITY CHAMBERS
George Square

Opened by Queen Victoria in 1888, this impressive building, designed by William Young, occupies the eastern side of George Square and is the headquarters of Glasgow District Council. The building was built in Italian Renaissance style and is noted for its loggia, marble staircase and banqueting hall.

✆ 041 227 4017/8 (Curator's office).
Open: Guided tours Mon–Fri 10.30 & 2.30. Advisable to telephone before visiting. (Closed PHs & civic receptions.) Parties by prior arrangement.
♿ ✖ (ex guide dogs).

## COLLINS GALLERY
University of Strathclyde, Richmond Street

A modern exhibition hall with a varied programme of temporary exhibitions throughout the year, ranging from contemporary painting and sculpture, craft and photography to local history and architecture. Most exhibitions include demonstrations, talks, film or workshops, with special events for children.

✆ 041 553 4145.
Open: all year, Mon–Fri 10–5 & Sat

12–4. (Closed BH.) Guided tours available. ⚿ toilets for the disabled. Shop ⌖

## GLASGOW ART GALLERY & MUSEUM
Kelvingrove (0.25m NW)
The finest civic art collection in Great Britain. All schools and periods of European painting with emphasis on Dutch 17th century, French 19th century and Scottish art from 17th century to the present day. Collections of pottery, porcelain, silver, sculpture, arms and armour, also archaeology, ethnography and natural history.

℘ 041 357 3929.
Open: Mon–Sat 10–5, Sun 12–6. (Closed Xmas Day & New Year's Day.) Donations. Guided tours available.
⌷ ⚿ (lifts) toilets for the disabled. Shop ⌖ (ex guide dogs).

## HAGGS CASTLE
100 St Andrews Drive, (2m SW)
Built in 1585, the castle houses a museum for children. The emphasis is on the exploration of history through activities and a 'hands on' approach to the displays. These include a 16th-century kitchen, 17th-century bedroom and a Victorian nursery. There are also regular temporary exhibitions and children's activities.

℘ 041 427 2725.
Open: Mon–Sat 10–5, Sun 12–6. (Closed Xmas Day & New Year's Day.) Donations. Guided tours only if booked in advance. Maximum of 30 accepted for tours or parties.
⋔ ⚿ (ground floor & workshops only) toilets can accommodate disabled and wheelchair-bound visitors. Shop ⌖ (ex guide dogs).

## HUNTERIAN MUSEUM
The University of Glasgow (0.25m NW)
The museum takes its name from William Hunter (1718–83), a student at Glasgow University in the 1730s, who later acquired fame and fortune as a physician and medical

teacher in London. Hunter bequeathed to the University his substantial collections which included coins, paintings and prints, books and manuscripts, South Seas curiosities, zoological specimens, fossils and minerals, together with anatomical and pathological specimens relating to his medical work. Opened in 1807, it was Scotland's first public museum. There have been many additions since Hunter's time, with an emphasis now on geology, archaeology, coins and art.

℘ 041 330 4221.
Open: Mon–Sat 9.30–5. (Closed PHs.) Guided tours available if pre-booked. Parties by prior arrangement.
⌷ ⚿ (ground floor. Lift by prior arrangement) Shop ⌖

## HUTCHESONS' HALL
158 Ingram St
This elegant listed building was built in 1802–5 to a design by David Hamilton. It incorporates on its frontage the statues of founders of Hutchesons' Hospital, George and Thomas Hutcheson, from an earlier building of 1649. A major reconstruction in 1876 by John Baird heightened the Hall to its present proportions and provided an impressive staircase.

℘ 041 552 8391.
Visitor centre and Function Hall open all year Mon–Fri 9–5, Sat 10–4. (Closed PH & 1–5 Jan) Shop open Mon–Sat 10–4. Hall open subject to functions in progress. Coach parties not accepted.
⚿ (ground floor only) toilets for disabled.
(NTS)

## MITCHELL LIBRARY
North Street
The largest public reference library in Western Europe with more than a million volumes, founded in 1874 and named after Stephen Mitchell, a Glasgow tobacco manufacturer. There is a special collection on Robert Burns and Scottish Poetry. Various small exhibitions.

Glasgow: Museum of Transport

℘ 041 221 7030.
Open: all year, Mon–Fri 9.30–9 & Sat 9.30–5. (Closed PHs.) Guided tours available by prior arrangement.
⌷ (10–4.30) ⚿ toilets for the disabled. Shop ⌖ (ex guide dogs).

## MUSEUM OF TRANSPORT
Kelvin Hall, 1 Bunhouse Road
This museum tells the history of transport with displays of Glasgow trams and buses, Scottish-built cars and other vehicles, railway locomotives and horse drawn vehicles. There is also a large display of ship models and a reconstruction of a typical Glasgow side street of 1938.

℘ 041 357 3929.
Open: Mon–Sat 10–5 & Sun 12–6. (Closed Xmas Day & New Year's Day.) Guided tours available.
⌷ (Mon–Sat 10.15–4.30, Sun 2–4.30) ⚿ (ramps/lifts to all areas) toilets for the disabled. Shop.

## PEOPLE'S PALACE MUSEUM
Glasgow Green, off London
Road (0.25m SE)
Contains a fascinating visual record
of the history and life of the City.
Exhibits include Medieval Glasgow,
interesting relics of Mary, Queen of
Scots, the Battle of Langside, the
Tobacco Lords of the 18th century,
and the history of the music hall.
Fine examples of Glasgow
craftsmanship, particularly pottery
and special displays illustrating
social and domestic life, including
women's suffrage, temperance and
the two world wars. A wide range of
pictures of noteworthy people and
places. Winter gardens with
adjoining tropical house.

℘ 041 554 0223.
Open: Mon–Sat 10 5, Sun 12–6;
(Closed Xmas Day & New Year's
Day.) Donations. Guided tours
available by advance request.
⬚ ♿ Shop ⚥ (ex guide dogs).

## POLLOK COUNTRY PARK
Formerly a private estate, there are
361 acres of land containing an
extensive collection of flowering
shrubs and trees in a natural
setting. There is a herd of Highland
cattle, a display rose garden, nature
trails and jogging track. A 2-acre
Demonstration Garden has been
designed with the interests of the
amateur and professional gardener
in mind. Demonstrations held
fortnightly on Sat mornings. Ranger
service. Countryside Rangers
Interpretation Centre.

℘ 041 632 9299.
Park always open. Demonstration and
display garden open: daily Mon–Thu
8–4, Fri 8–3.30; weekends 8–6.30
(Winter 8–4).
🅿 ♿

Also POLLOK HOUSE
Situated within the grounds, a neo-
Palladian building first constructed
in 1752, with Edwardian additions
containing the famous Stirling
Maxwell Collection of Spanish
paintings, furniture, etc.

℘ 041 632 0274.
Open: Mon–Sat 10–5, Sun 12–6.
(Closed Xmas Day & New Year's
Day.) Donations. Guided tours
available.
⬚ ♿ (all parts accessible if
wheelchair suitable for lift)
Shop 🅿 ⚥ (ex guide dogs).

## PROVAND'S LORDSHIP
3 Castle Street
Built in 1471 as a manse serving the
Cathedral, this is the oldest house
in Glasgow. Period displays from
1500 onwards and a fine collection
of 17th-century furniture. Latterly a
confectioner's shop, the machines
which made the sweets can also be
seen.

℘ 041 552 8819.
Open: Mon–Sat 10–5 & Sun 12–6
(Closed Xmas Day & New Year's
Day.) Donations. Parties by prior
arrangement.
♿ (ground floor only with assistance)
Shop ⚥ (ex guide dogs).

## PROVAN HALL
Auchinlea Park (6.5m E off
B806)
Well restored 15th-century house
considered most perfect example of
a simple pre-Reformation house
remaining in Scotland. In the
adjacent grounds are formal and
informal gardens including garden
for the blind.

℘ 041 771 6372.
For information on opening hours
please telephone.
♿

## REGIMENTAL MUSEUM OF THE ROYAL HIGHLAND FUSILIERS
518 Sauchiehall Street
The history of the Highland Light
Infantry, The Royal Highland
Fusiliers and the Royal Scots
Fusiliers from 1678 to the present
day. Exhibits include medals, silver,
pictures, uniforms, weapons,
memementoes and records.

℘ 041 332 0961.
Open: all year, Mon–Fri 9–4. Guided
tours are available. Coach parties

must book visits 2 weeks in advance.
(Closed BHs.)
♿ ⚥

## ROSS HALL PARK
Crookston (5m W on A736)
Beautifully kept gardens with
artificial ponds, featuring a variety
of aquatic plants and stocked with
fish. Extensive heather and rock
gardens and woodland nature trails

℘ 041 882 3554.
Open: Apr–Sep daily 1–8, Oct–Mar
daily 1–4.
♿

## RUTHERGLEN MUSEUM
King Street, Rutherglen
Museum of the former Royal Burgh
with a new gallery celebrating
Rutherglen's identity and a rich
collection of old photographs.
Regularly changing displays and
temporary exhibitions.

℘ 041 647 0837.
Open: all year ex 25 Dec & 1 Jan,
Mon–Sat 10–5, Sun 12–6. Guided
tours available for school groups by
arrangement. Coach parties by prior
appointment.
♿ Shop.

## VICTORIA PARK
Whiteinch (2.5m W on A814)
This park has the best-known
fossilized prehistoric tree stumps,
discovered in 1887 and housed in
the Fossil Grove building. The park
has extensive carpet bedding
depicting centennial events.

℘ 041 959 1146.
Fossil Grove building open: Mon–Fri
8–4, Sat, Sun pm only. Park open:
daily 7–dusk.
🅿 ♿

# GLASTONBURY
Somerset

## GLASTONBURY TOR
(0.75m E of town centre on the
N side of A361)
Rising to 521 ft, legend-rich
Glastonbury Tor is also an excellent
viewpoint, overlooking the
Somerset levels. Crowning it is a

15th-century tower, the remains of St. Michael's Church, destroyed in a landslip in 1271; near the foot is the Chalice Spring. Footpaths climb to the summit.

Open: accessible at all reasonable times.
(NT)

## GLENDRONACH
Grampian

**GLENDRONACH DISTILLERY**
(On B9001, 19m N of Inverurie)
Visitors can see the complete process of whisky making including the malting barley rooms and distilling of spirits. Whisky has been made on the premises for over 160 years.

℘ Forgue 046682 202.
Open: Guided tours Mon–Fri 10 & 2. Parties by prior arrangement.
✿ Shop.

## GLENLIVET
Grampian

**THE GLENLIVET DISTILLERY VISITORS CENTRE**
(Off B9008 10m N of Tomintoul)
The visitor centre contains an exhibition of ancient artefacts used in malting, peat cutting and distilling, and an audio-visual presentation. Distillery tour. Whisky and souvenir shop.

℘ 05422 7471.
Open: Etr–Oct, Mon–Sat 10–4. Guided tours. Coach parties must pre-book.
▱ ὁ (Visitors Centre only) toilets for the disabled ㅈ Shop ✿ (ex guide dogs).

## GLOUCESTER
Gloucestershire

**CITY MUSEUM & ART GALLERY**
Brunswick Road
The Marling bequest of 18th-century walnut furniture barometers and domestic silver. Paintings by Richard Wilson, Gainsborough, Turner, etc,

supplemented by art exhibitions throughout the year. Local archaeology including Roman mosaics and sculptures, natural history and a freshwater aquarium.

℘ 0452 524131.
Open: Mon–Sat 10–5. Donations.
ὁ Shop ✿

**FOLK MUSEUM**
99–103 Westgate Street
A group of half-timbered houses, (Tudor and Jacobean), furnished to illustrate local history, domestic life and rural crafts. Civil War armour, toys from 18th century onwards, Severn fishing tackle, farming equipment. New extensions with 'Double Gloucester Dairy', ironmonger's shop, wheelwright and carpenter's workshops. Pin factory with 18th-century forge. Victorian school room.

℘ 0452 526467.
Open: Mon–Sat 10–5. Donation box. Guided tours available for school groups by prior appointment. Parties accepted (max 40), advance notification essential.
ὁ (ground floor only; assistance necessary for access) Shop ✿

**GLOUCESTER ANTIQUE CENTRE**
1 Severn Road
In a carefully restored 19th-century warehouse, the Antique Centre comprises 67 shops on four floors. Follow the signs to the Historical

Docks, the centre is situated on the north-east corner of the main basin.

℘ 0452 529716.
Open: all year, Mon–Fri 9.30–5, Sat 9.30–4.30, Sun 1–4.30, or by appointment. Guided tours by prior arrangement, free if cream tea is taken.
▱ (licensed) ὁ (ground floor; lift from loading bay area).

**GLOUCESTER DOCKS**
An inland Victorian port still preserved virtually intact in the heart of Gloucester, developed as a major tourist, cultural and commercial centre. Famous as the location for filming the *Onedin Line*, the area has many listed buildings. Principal attractions are the National Waterways Museum; Robert Opie Museum, Glorious 'Glosters' Regimental Museum and the Gloucester Antique Centre.

℘ Information Centre 0452 421188 (Leisure Services Dept) or 525524 (Regional British Waterways Board). Open: Vantage points at all times, contact Docks Trading Company, 0452 311190. Guided tours available by arrangement with information centre.

*Gloucester Docks*

## GODALMING
Surrey

**GODALMING MUSEUM**
109A High Street
Local history displays. Wool and
knitting related artefacts. Garden in
Jeykll and Lutyens style. Local
studies reference library.

✆ 0483 426510.
Open: Tue–Sat 10–5. Donation box.
Guided tours by arrangement –
advance booking essential. Parties by
prior appointment.
Shop ✖

## GOLDEN GROVE
Dyfed

**GELLI AUR COUNTRY PARK**
(between A476–B4300
signposted from Cross Hands,
Ffaifach & A40)
Overlooking the beautiful Towy
Valley, the Country Park includes a
deer park, nature trails, picnic
areas, children's play area, gardens
and arboretum. There is a visitor
centre and restaurant. Special
events include craft demonstrations
and guided walks.

✆ 0558 668885.
Open: all year, daily (ex 25–26 Dec).
Guided tours available.
🍴 (restaurant May–Sep) ♿ (ground
floor & part of grounds) toilets for the
disabled. 🅿

## GRANGEMOUTH
Central

**GRANGEMOUTH MUSEUM**
Victoria Public Library, B'ness
Road
Displays showing the town's
development from its origins as the
terminus of the Forth and Clyde
Canal to its present status as a
major international chemical and
petrochemical centre.

✆ 0324 24911 Ext 2472.
Open: all year Mon–Sat 2–5. (Closed
local public holidays).
Shop.

## GRASSINGTON
North Yorkshire

**YORKSHIRE DALES NATIONAL PARK
CENTRE**
Colvend, Hebden Road
Visitor Centre featuring display on
Wharfedale. Audio-visual
programme, maps, guides and local
information. Charge for parking.

✆ 0756 752774.
Open: Apr–Oct daily 9.30–5, plus
some winter weekends.
🅿 ♿ toilets for the disabled.

## GRAYS
Essex

**THURROCK MUSEUM**
Orsett Road
Local history, agriculture, trade and
industrial collections. Also
Palaeolithic to Saxon archaeology
and maritime and riverside history.

✆ Grays Thurrock 0375 390000 Ext
24145.
Open: all year, Mon–Fri 10–8 & Sat
10–5. (Closed BHs.) Coach parties
not accepted. Guided tours available
for school groups by arrangement.
♿ toilets for the disabled ✖ (ex
guide dogs).

---

### GREAT
### ✦ CUMBRAE ✦
### ISLAND

---

## MILLPORT
Strathclyde

**MUSEUM OF THE CUMBRAES**
Garrison House
Small local history museum housed
in the former barracks for the crews
of the ship *The Royal George*. It
tells the story of life on and around
the Cumbraes and features many
old photographs, including some of
steamers which achieved fame on
the Millport run.

✆ 0475 530742.
Open: Jun–Sep Tue–Sat 10–4.30.
Donations.
♿ (prior notice of visit required).

## GREENOCK
Strathclyde

**MCLEAN MUSEUM & ART GALLERY**
15 Kelly Street
The museum displays exhibits
relating to local history,
ethnography, natural history,
geology and shipping, including
river paddle steamers and cargo
vessels. Also relics of James Watt.
The Inverclyde Biennial is held
here.

✆ 0475 23741.
Open: Mon–Sat 10–12 & 1–5. (Closed
Sun & PHs.) Guided tours available
by appointment. Donation box.
♿ (ground floor only) Shop ✖

## GREENSTED
Essex

**ST ANDREWS CHURCH**
(1m W of Chipping Ongar on
unclass road)
The only surviving wooden Saxon
church in Britain with walls of solid
oak which are believed to date from
the 9th century. In 1013 the body of
King Edmund rested here on its way
to Bury St Edmunds.

✆ Ongar 0277 364694.
Open: daily, 9–dusk. Guided tours
available.
♿ Shop ✖

## GRIZEDALE
Cumbria

**GRIZEDALE FOREST PARK**
(Between Esthwaite Water &
Coniston Water 1m S
Hawkshead)
Visitor Centre showing the history
of the forest from wildwood to
woodland managed for timber,
wildlife and recreation. There are
way-marked walks, orienteering
courses, cycle trails and woodland
sculpture. Also theatre and gallery
in the forest. There is a charge of
£1 for parking.

✆ Satterthwaite 022984 373
Open: Visitor Centre & Shop Apr–Oct
daily 10–5. Guided tours available

(charge ex Aug).
& (circular way-marked trail of approximately 0.5m) toilets for the disabled. Shop ⊼

## GROSMONT

Gwent

**GROSMONT CASTLE**
(on B4347)
Ruined Marcher stronghold, rebuilt in 13th century by Hubert de Burgh, on hill above Monnow Valley. One of three 'tri-lateral' castles of Gwent.

Open: at all reasonable times.
(CADW)

## GUILDFORD

Surrey

**GALLERY 90**
Ward Street
Exhibition gallery in a restored 19th century Unitarian church. Wide range of monthly exhibitions including major historical and contemporary art, schools artwork, sculpture and crafts.

℘ 0483 444740.
Open: all year Mon–Fri 10–4.30 Sat 10–12.30 & 1.30–4.30. Coach parties by prior arrangement.
& (part) Shop.

**GUILDFORD MUSEUM**
Castle Arch, Quarry Street
Local history, new archaeology gallery and needlework.

℘ 0483 444750.
Open: Mon–Sat 11–5. Donations. Coach parties (maximum 60 persons) accepted by appointment only.
& (ground floor only) toilets for the disabled. Shop ⊗

**THE GUILDHALL**
High Street
With the famous clock hanging from its front, this is the focal point of the High Street. The building itself is part medieval, part Tudor and part Jacobean; it was formerly the law court and council chamber and still houses the Borough Civic Plate.

℘ 0483 444035.
Open: all year Tue & Thu afternoons (tours at 2, 3 & 4) or by appointment. Coach parties by appointment (25 max).
& (ground floor, ramps from street level).

**WOMEN'S ROYAL ARMY CORPS MUSEUM**
Queen Elizabeth Park
Exhibits include The Queen's and Princess Mary's uniforms, a model gunfight, anti-aircraft guns and medals. Video displays.

℘ 0252 340565 or 314598.
Open: Mon–Fri 9–4. Donation box. Military security applies, cars and bags may be searched.

## HADLEIGH

Essex

**HADLEIGH CASTLE**
Founded in 1231 by Hubert de Burgh and rebuilt by Edward III in the 14th century. The walls are of Kentish rag and the castle retains two of its original towers.

Open: accessible at any reasonable time.
(AM)

**HADLEIGH CASTLE COUNTRY PARK**
Fields and woodlands overlooking the Thames Estuary near the castle remains. Accessible by footpath with access via Chapel Lane.

℘ 0702 551072.
Open: all year daily 8–dusk. Parking charged Sun & BH only in summer (ex OAP, disabled & motorbikes). Guided tours & coach parties by arrangement.
& (part) toilets for the disabled.

## HADLEIGH

Suffolk

**WOLVES WOOD**
(1.5m E on A1071 Ipswich road)
An RSPB reserve located in an ancient woodland coppice. Many wild flowers, including orchids and heliborenes with other type site species. Several nightingale

territories with many woodland birds. The best time to visit is late April to early June. Footpath around the reserve can be muddy at times, but visitors are asked to keep to the route marked with blue arrows and not to disturb the protected areas.

℘ 0767 680551.
Open: daily until dusk. Information Centre open weekends Apr–Sep. Guided tours available (summer only) by pre-arrangement. Charge for breakfast on dawn chorus events. Groups should contact reserve in advance. No parking facilities for coaches.
& (Information Centre only)
⊗ (ex guide dogs).

## HADRIAN'S WALL

Cumbria/Northumberland

Stretching 73 miles between Bowness on Solway and Newcastle-upon-Tyne, Hadrian's Wall was begun in 122 AD to separate the Romans from the Barbarians. Originally about 15 ft high and 10 ft wide it had milecastles at every Roman mile (1620 yds) and two equidistant turrets between them. Seventeen forts for up to 1000 soldiers each were built along the wall, and running parallel to the south of Hadrian's Wall is the Vallum, a ditch with mounds on either side. The best places to see the wall are between Banks in Cumbria and Chollerford in Northumberland.

The following places are accessible at all reasonable times:
BIRDOSWALD, off B6318, 1.25m W of Gilsland. Roman fort of *Camboglanna* visible and section of wall.
GILSLAND, W. of village, Milecastle 48 and Willowford Roman bridge.
CARVORAN, 0.75m E of Greenhead. Fine section of wall running along crest of ridge.
CAWFIELDS, 2m N of Haltwistle on unclass road. Remains of Milecastle 42 and sections of wall.
BROCOLITIA, 4m W of Chollerford on B6318. Remains of Roman Fort and traces of the ditch Vallum.

## HALESWORTH
Suffolk

**THE HALESWORTH GALLERY**
Steeple End
Gallery with regularly changing
exhibitions.

✆ 098 687 3064.
Open: mid May–mid Sep daily 11–5
(Sun 2–5). Donations.
🐾 (ex guide dogs).

## HALEWOOD
Merseyside

**HALEWOOD 'TRIANGLE' COUNTRY PARK**
Former railway junction now a
country park of woodlands,
meadows and ponds. Facilities for
walking, cycling, horse-riding,
angling and picnicking. Events and
walks organised by Knowsley
Countryside Ranger Service.
Beginning of Aintree-Halewood
Cycle Way. Access from Lydiate
Lane, Arncliffe Road, Higher Road
and Okell Drive.

✆ 051 443 3682 (Hayton Office).
Open: all year. Guided tour available.
🚶 (part) 🚻

## HALIFAX
West Yorkshire

**BANKFIELD MUSEUM & ART GALLERY**
Boothtown Road, Akroyd Park
Built by Edward Akroyd in the
1860s, this Renaissance-style
building, set in the centre of
parkland on a hill overlooking the
town, contains one of the finest and
most representative collections of
costume and textiles from all
periods and all parts of the world.
There are new galleries of costume
and toys. There is also the museum
of the Duke of Wellington's
Regiment. The Museum mounts
regular temporary exhibitions, both
from its collection, and also
travelling art exhibitions.

✆ 0422 354823 & 352334.
Open: Tue–Sat 10–5, Sun 2–5.
(Closed 25 & 26 Dec & New Year's

*Cloth was sold in the 315
rooms of Halifax Piece Hall*

Day but open other BHs.)
🚶 (ground floor & park only) Shop
🐾 (ex guide dogs).

**PIECE HALL**
Unique 18th-century building,
consisting of colonnaded galleries
which completely enclose a massive
open-air courtyard. It was originally
a market-place for cloth produced
by local weavers before the days of
mills and the Industrial Revolution.
The lengths of cloth were known as
'pieces', hence the name. The
galleries now house a multitude of
art and craft shops, Art Gallery,
Pre-industrial Museum, Industrial
Museum and Calderdale Museum
(charge) and Tourist Information
Centre. Fleamarket Thu, open
market Fri–Sat.

✆ 0422 368725/358087.
Open: Mon–Sat 9–6, Sun 10–6.
Individual attractions may vary.
(Closed many shops shut Mon; Xmas
& New Year's Day.) May be a charge
for special events. Guided tours
available – contact Mr. G. Washington
✆ 0422 362369.
🚻 (10–5) 🚶 (lift) toilets for the
disabled. Shop.

## HALNAKER
West Sussex

**HALNAKER MILL**
(1.5m NE off A285)
Standing on Halnaker Hill (416 ft)
the windmill is a local landmark and
has been partially restored. Built in
1740, it is the oldest tower mill in
Sussex. Interior not open.

Open: accessible at any reasonable
time.

## HAMILTON
Strathclyde

**HAMILTON DISTRICT MUSEUM**
129 Muir Street
Local history museum in a 17-
century coaching inn with original
stable and 18th-century Assembly
Room with musicians gallery.
Displays include prehistory, art,
costume, natural history,
agriculture and local industries of
the past. Transport museum and
reconstructed Victorian kitchen.
Temporary exhibitions throughout
the year.

✆ 0698 283981.
Open: Mon–Sat 10–5. (Closed 12–1
on Wed & Sat). Donation box.

Guided tours are available. Parties by appointment only. ♿ (ground floor only; some object labelling is at wheelchair level). Shop ⚜

## HAMPTON COURT
Gt London

**BUSHEY PARK**
(Off A308)
Less formal than its neighbour Hampton Court Park, with herds of deer roaming free. The Diana Fountain marks the junction with an avenue of limes, a formal highway through an otherwise wild part of the park. North of the limes is the Longford River.

Open: all year 6.30 am–midnt.
🚻

## HAMSTALL RIDWARE
Staffordshire

**RIDWARE ARTS CENTRE**
Hamstall Hall, (8m N of Lichfield between B5014 & A515)
The Arts Centre comprises galleries, craft shops, studios, bookshop, picture framing, restaurant, gardens, animals and historic buildings all within the walls of the ancient manorial complex. There are demonstrations by craftspeople at weekends April to December.

✆ 088 922 351.
Open: 3rd Tue in Mar–24 Dec Tue–Sun 10.30–5.30 (weekends only end Dec–mid Mar). Guided tours available (charge). Coach parties by arrangement (not Sun).
🚻 (licensed restaurant) ♿ (ground floor & grounds) Shop.

## HARDKNOTT CASTLE ROMAN FORT
Cumbria

W end of Hardknott Pass
375 ft square fort with three double gateways enclosing walled and ramparted area of almost three acres. Fort was occupied in mid-2nd

century. Visible remains include granaries, headquarter's building, commandant's house, bath house and parade ground.

Open: accessible at all reasonable times. Access may be hazardous in winter.
(AM)

## HARLOW
Essex

**HARLOW MUSEUM**
Passmores House, Third Avenue
The exhibits cover various aspects of local history from Roman to modern and also natural history and geology. Finds displayed include those from the Roman temple and the post-medieval metropolitan ware pottery industry centred on Harlow. Housed in an early Georgian building, set in gardens; part of the medieval moat from the earlier house can be seen. Temporary exhibitions. Displays in the courtyard illustrate farming and country life in the area.

✆ 0279 446422.
Open: Tue & Thu 10–9, Wed, Fri, Mon 10–5, Sat & Sun 10–12.30 & 1.30–5. Guided tours available by arrangement. Parties by appointment.
♿ (ground floor & gardens only) Shop ⚜

**MARK HALL CYCLE MUSEUM & GARDENS**
Muskham Road, off First Avenue
History of the bicycle 1819–1980s, with 60 machines on display from an 1819 hobby horse to a 1982 plastic machine. Behind the museum are three walled period gardens: a 17th-century herb garden, and an ornamental fruit garden and a large garden divided into sections, including vegetable gardens and a typical cottage garden.

✆ 0279 39680.
Open: daily 10–1 & 2–5 (gardens close at dusk in winter). (Closed

Xmas.) Guided tours available by prior arrangement only. Parties by appointment only.
♿ (ramps) toilets for the disabled. Shop ⚜

**THE PLAYHOUSE GALLERY**
The High
One of the largest exhibition spaces in Essex, the Gallery shows monthly exhibitions of art and craft work with an emphasis on solo and small group shows. On the top floor of the theatre complex.

✆ 0279 424391.
Open: all year Mon–Sat 11–5.30. (Closed Xmas Day). Donations. Parking: hourly charge, but free if you leave after 9.30–10pm.
🚻 (licensed, 10–2.30) ♿ toilets for the disabled.

## HARTLEPOOL
Cleveland

**GRAY ART GALLERY & MUSEUM**
Clarence Road
Permanent collection of pictures. Museum collections feature local history, archaeology, engineering, Indian idols, porcelain, British birds, working blacksmith's shop in museum grounds. New Japanese gallery. Monthly temporary exhibitions.

✆ 0429 266522 Ext 259.
Open: Mon–Sat 10–5.30, Sun 2–5. (Closed Good Fri, 25–26 Dec & New Year's Day.)
♿ (ground floor only; attendants will assist) toilets for the disabled. Shop ⚜

**HARTLEPOOL MARITIME MUSEUM**
Northgate
Collections feature the maritime history of the town and its shipbuilding industry. Also reconstructed fisherman's cottage, a ship's bridge and an early lighthouse lantern.

✆ 0429 272814.
Open: Mon–Sat 10–5. Donation box. Shop ⚜

## HARWICH
Essex

**THE GUILDHALL**
Church Street
Of particular interest are the records, council chamber and carvings in the old jail room which are available for viewing on application.

✆ 0255 507211.
Open: all year (ex BH) Mon–Fri 10–12. Please phone before visiting. Guided tours by prior arrangement. ✖ (ex guide dogs).

## HASTINGS
East Sussex

**FISHERMEN'S MUSEUM**
Rock-a-Nore Road
Former fishermen's church,˙now museum of local interest, including the last of Hastings luggers built for sail.

✆ 0424 424787.
Open: May–Sep Mon–Fri 10.30–12 & 2.30–5, Sun 2.30–5. Donations. ♿ (ground floor only) ✖

**HASTINGS COUNTRY PARK**
E of Hastings off Fairlight Road
Extending over an area of 600 acres, the country park has approximately five kilometres of the most attractive stretch of the Sussex coast, with several fine walks and nature trails. Much of the area is well wooded. Visitor Centre near Fairlight contains interesting displays about the history, geology and wildlife of the country park.

✆ 0424 813225 (Ranger Service).
Open: Country Park accessible at all reasonable times. Visitor Centre: Etr–Sep, Sat, Sun, BH 2–5. Guided tours available.
♿ (contact Ranger Service for advice) toilets for the disabled. ⊼ Shop ✖ (in Visitor Centre).

## HATTON
Warwickshire

**HATTON CRAFT CENTRE**
George's Farm
The largest complex of its kind in the country with a number of awards to its credit. The craft centre comprises 40 workshops with a variety of skills represented. There is also a garden centre, one stop animal shop, fruit park (pick-your-own Jun–Sep), farm shop and café, farm trail, adventure play area and agricultural machinery museum, rare breed farm park and a butcher. Programme of special events.

✆ 092 684 2436.
Open: all year, daily, 10–5. Coach parties should pre-book restaurant ✆ 092 684 3350.
⌕ ♿ (ground floor) toilets for the disabled. Shop & Garden centre ⊼

## HAVANT
Hampshire

**HAVANT MUSEUM**
East Street
The museum shares this late 19th-century building with a flourishing Arts Centre. New local history galleries. A display of firearms and their history, formed by C.G. Vokes, is on the first floor of the museum.

✆ 0705 451155.
Open: Tue–Sat 10–5. Donation box. Guided tours can be arranged for booked parties by prior arrangement. ♿ (ground floor only) Shop.

## HAWES
North Yorkshire

**YORKSHIRE DALES NATIONAL PARK CENTRE AND DALES COUNTRYSIDE MUSEUM**
Station Yard
Visitor Centre featuring interpetative display. Maps, guides and local information available. Also part of the complex is the Dales Countryside Museum, which has an extensive collection of bygones and farm implements, displayed to explain the changing landscapes and communities of the area.

✆ 0969 667450.
Open: daily Apr–Oct, 9.30–5, plus some winter weekends.
♿

**W R OUTHWAITE & SON, ROPEMAKERS**
Town Foot
Visitors are welcome to come in and watch work in progress. See many thin strands of yarn being rapidly twisted into strong rope for all sorts of purposes from macrame to tow ropes.

✆ 0969 667487.
Open: all year (ex Xmas) Mon–Fri 9–5.30 (10–4 Sat most school hols & BH Mons). Parties please contact before visit. Parking charge.
♿ (some widths of wheelchair may be restricted. Please contact before visit.)

**THE WENSLEYDALE POTTERY**
Market Place
Located behind the south side of

*The Swaledale sheep – emblem of the Dales National Park*

the market place, signposted. See the potter at work and a wide range of handmade pottery in the shop.

✆ 0969 667594.
Open: Apr–Oct, Mon–Sat (Sun at BH weekends) 10–5.30. School parties by prior arrangement only.
♿ (ground floor; will assist) Shop.

## HAWICK
Borders

**WRIGHTS OF TROWMILL**
(2.5m NE on A698)
There has been a mill here since the 1750s. Trowmill ground meal until about 1880 when it changed to woollen manufacture. The mill was powered by water until 1965 and by electricity until 1977. Visitors can see the various processes and stages of tweed being made at the new automated factory.

✆ 0450 72555.
Open: Mill Mon–Thu 9–5, Shop Mon–Fri 9–5, Sat 9.30–5 & Sun 10–5. Guided tours available by prior arrangement.
♿ Shop ⊼

## HAYFIELD
Derbyshire

**SETT VALLEY TRAIL**
A two-and-a-half mile trail for walkers, cyclists and horseriders on the site of the former railway line from New Mills to Hayfield. At the old Hayfield Station are a car park, picnic area and toilets, also cycle hire (Apr–Oct).

✆ New Mills 0663 746222.
Open: all year, daily. Information Centre Sun & School Hols 9–6.
♿ (grounds) toilets for the disabled. Shop ⊼

## HEACHAM
Norfolk

**NORFOLK LAVENDER**
Caley Mill (On A149 King's Lynn-Hunstanton road
England's only working lavender farm with plants varying in size, fragrance and colour from white to deep purple. Gardens of lavender, including a 'Living dictionary' of lavender varieties, and herb garden with over 50 varieties of culinary aromatic and decorative plants. Farm harvest begins early July/mid August. A twice-weekly coach trip takes visitors to the lavender field.

✆ 0485 70384.
Open: all year daily 10–5 (Closed 2 weeks at Xmas). Guided tours available during summer (charge, except for children in family group). Parties by prior appointment for tours and catering.
♿ ♿ toilets for the disabled. Shop.

## HEANOR
Derbyshire

**SHIPLEY COUNTRY PARK**
(Signposted from junction 26 of M1 & at Heanor off A608 & A6007)
Six hundred acres of country and 1,000 years of change. Woodland, lakes, open parkland, historic buildings, 18 miles of footpaths and bridleways. Visitor Centre has information about walking, cycling (cycle hire centre within park), horseriding, fishing and a variety of countryside activities and events.

✆ 0773 719961.
Open: Park all year; Visitor Centre Etr–Sep Mon–Fri 11–4.30 (Sat & Sun 10–6.30), Oct–Etr Mon–Fri 12–4.30 (Sat–Sun 10–4.30). Guided tours by prior arrangement.
♿ ⊼ ♿ toilets for the disabled. Shop.

## HECKINGTON
Lincolnshire

**THE PEAROOM CRAFT CENTRE**
Station Yard
The Pearoom was built in 1890 and enlarged in 1891. The building, which remained in use until the 1960s, was used to sort peas, often brought to Heckington by special trains. In the late 1970s, the building was given new life. On the ground and first floors are a range of craft workshops including pottery, silver works, spinning and weaving, fabric painting, wood and leather work. On the third floor, there are also Heritage displays and a varied programme of changing exhibitions. Tourist Information Centre.

✆ 0529 60765.
Open: May–Oct Mon–Sat 10–5, Sun 12–5; Nov–Apr Tue–Sat 10–5, Sun 12–5; BHs 10–5. (Closed Xmas Day.) Donations box. For information about craft displays and exhibitions contact the on-site Tourist Information Office
✆ 0529 60088. Guided tours available for The Pearoom.
♿ ♿ (ground floor only) toilets for the disabled. Shop ⊗

## HELSTON
Cornwall

**HELSTON FOLK MUSEUM**
Old Butter Market, Market Place
Folk museum covering local history and articles from The Lizard Peninsula. Various summer exhibitions are regularly held.

✆ 0326 564027.
Open: Mon, Tue, Thu–Sat 10:30–1 & 2–4.30, Wed 10.30–12. Touring schools and visiting groups welcome. Maximum 50 persons. Guided tours available by arrangement. Donation box.
♿ Shop ⊗ (ex guide dogs).

## HEREFORD
Hereford and Worcester

**HEREFORD CITY MUSEUM**
Broad Street
Roman tessellated pavements, natural history, bee keeping display with observation hive, English watercolours, local geology and county's archaeology; also folk life and folklore material. The exhibitions at City Art Gallery are changed every month.

✆ 0432 268121 Ext 207.
Open: Tue, Wed & Fri 10–6, Thu 10–5, Sat 10–5, Oct–Mar Sat 10–4. (Closed Mon ex BHs.)
♿ Shop ⊗

## HERTFORD
Hertfordshire

**HERTFORD CASTLE**
The original castle was built by William the Conqueror; the remaining walls and motte preserve the plan of his structure. The Edward IV gatehouse still remains, with wings added in the 18th and 20th centuries. The grounds are open to the public daily and band concerts are held on open days during the summer.

✆ 0992 552885 or 584322 (Tourist Information Centre).
Open: 1st Sun every month May–Sep 2.30–4.30. Guided tours available. Coach parties accepted on written application to Town Clerk's Office, The Castle, Hertford SG14 1HR.
& (ground floor & gardens only).

## HEYSHAM
Lancashire

**HEYSHAM NUCLEAR POWER STATION VISITOR INFORMATION CENTRE**
(Nr Heysham Harbour off A589)
Information centre with displays and videos on the production of electricity by nuclear fission and other forms of energy. Tours of power station bookable from the centre. Classroom for children to learn how electricity is made. There is also a nature reserve and field study centre.

✆ 0524 55624.
Open: all year, every day, 10–5.30 Mon–Fri, 1.30–5.30 Sat–Sun (Closes at 4pm on winter weekdays). Guided tours available. Parties must pre-book; last tour 1½ hrs before closing.
& (ground floor; ramps) toilets for the disabled. 🍴

## HIGHDOWN
West Sussex

**HIGHDOWN GARDENS**
(N off A259 between Worthing & Littlehampton)
Well known in the world of horticulture, these gardens show a national collection of plants established here by Sir Frederick Stern. They are laid out in chalk pit on Highdown Hill, with rock plants, flowering shrubs and daffodils, as well as excellent views.

✆ Worthing 0903 501054.
Open: all year Mon–Fri 10–4.30; weekends & BHs Apr–Sep 10–8. Guided tours occasionally available out of working hours by appointment.
& toilets for the disabled.
🐕 (ex guide dogs).

## HIGH WYCOMBE
Buckinghamshire

**WYCOMBE LOCAL HISTORY AND CHAIR MUSEUM**
Castle Hill House, Priory Avenue
Set in Victorian grounds, on a medieval site, the museum is housed in a 17th-century house with later additions. The museum explores the history, crafts and industries of the Wycombe district and has an impressive collection of rural furniture.

✆ 0494 421895.
Open: Mon–Fri 10–5; Sat 10–1 & 2–5. (Closed Sun & BHs, but open some Sun in season. Donations. Guided tours occasionally available by prior arrangement.
& (ground floor only) Shop 🐕

## HIMLEY
Staffordshire

**HIMLEY COUNTRY PARK**
(On B4176 off A449, 4m W of Dudley)
184-acre country park. Ancestral home for the Earls of Dudley (hall not open to the public). Activities available at extra charge.

✆ 0902 324093.
Open: daily Jun–Sep 6–½ hr before dusk, Oct–May 7.30–½ hr before dusk. Guided tours available every 3rd Sunday at 11 or at any time for groups by prior arrangement. No charge except when combined with Victorian Cream Tea in the Hall.
🍽 (9–5) 🍴 & (grounds & ground floor areas).

## HITCHIN
Hertfordshire

**HITCHIN MUSEUM & ART GALLERY**
Paynes Park
Displays on local domestic and working life. The costume gallery covers two centuries of fashion, and the regimental collection of the Herts Yeomanry is housed here. There is a fascinating reconstruction of a Victorian chemist's shop, complemented by a physic garden outside. Temporary art exhibitions change monthly.

✆ 0462 434476.
Open: Mon–Sat 10–5, Sun 2–4.30. (Closed BHs.) Donation box. Guided tours available.
& (ground floor only; entrance ramp) Shop 🐕 (ex guide dogs).

## HOLT
Norfolk

**PICTURECRAFT OF HOLT**
23 Lees Courtyard, Off Bull Street, Signposted from Shire Hall Plain, near the town centre.
The gallery operates an unusual 'no commission' system so the customer buys direct from the artist. Artists can be seen working in an exhibition room featuring a different one man show each week. There is also one of the largest art materials shops in the country.

✆ 0263 713259.
Open: all year Mon–Wed & Fri–Sat 9–1 & 2–5. Guided tours by prior arrangement (1 weeks notice min.).
& (ramps & wide entrances).

## HOLYHEAD
Gwynedd

**SOUTH STACK RSPB RESERVE ELLINS TOWER SEABIRD CENTRE**
(2m W on unclass road)
Spectacular 350 ft sea cliffs with the Seabird Centre overlooking the colonies of breeding sea birds including gillemots, razorbills and puffins and South Stack Lighthouse. Closed circuit TV camera relays live sound and pictures of the birds back to Ellin's Tower, which is

staffed by experienced wardens and equipped with binoculars, telescopes (first floor) and displays about the area. In clear weather, Ireland can be seen from the summit of Holyhead Mountain (722ft).

Open: Reserve accessible at all reasonable times; Information Centre Etr–mid Sep 11–5. Donations. Guided tours available (charge, but free to RSPB members). Parties by appointment.
Ġ (ground floor only).

## HOLY ISLAND (Lindisfarne)
Northumberland

**LINDISFARNE LIMITED**
St Aidan's Winery
Visitors, although not allowed into the working area because of Customs and Excise restrictions are welcomed into the winery showrooms where manufacturing of Lindisfarne Mead is explained (the recipe is a closely guarded secret). Products are on sale. Visitors over 18 years may sample the mead in the showroom. Craft shop sells handmade pottery, jewellery, etc and sea shells from all over the world.

℘ 0289 89230.
Open: Etr–Sep daily; Oct–Mar Mon–Fri. Opening hours depend on tide. Holy Island is accessible at low tide across a causeway with tide tables posted at each end. School parties by appointment only. Shop.

## HOLYWELL
Clwyd

**GREENFIELD VALLEY HERITAGE PARK**
Sixty acres of lakeside and wooded walks including 5 reservoirs, a farm and farm museum, monuments and Basingwerk Abbey remains. A nature and industrial heritage trail goes past the remains of cotton and wire mills. Animals. Video show.

℘ 0352 714172.
Open: all year dawn to dusk.

(Admission charge to farm museum.) Guided tours available for pre-booked parties of 10 or more.
🖵 (summer weekends & summer school holidays) Ġ (ground floor and grounds) toilets for the disabled.
🅰

## HONITON
Devon

**HONITON POTTERY**
30–34 High Street
Visitors can tour the pottery at leisure and see all the processes, especially handpainting.

℘ 0404 42106.
Open: Pottery Mon–Fri, Shop Mon–Sat 9–5.
Shop.

## HORSHAM
West Sussex

**HORSHAM MUSEUM**
Causeway House, 9 The Causeway
16th-century timbered house with walled garden planted with herbs and English cottage garden flowers. Displays include: fine arts, early cycles, domestic life, Sussex rural crafts, local history, archaeology and geology. Regular temporary exhibitions throughout the year.

℘ 0403 54959.
Open: Tue–Sat 10–5. Sussex barn open all year (weather permitting). Guided tours available for school parties by arrangement.
Ġ (ground floor & garden) Shop ⊗

## HOVE
East Sussex

**HOVE MUSEUM AND ART GALLERY**
19 New Church Road
The museum is housed in a fine, late Victorian villa surrounded by lawns. The upstairs galleries display English painting and decorative arts from the 17th century to the present day, including fine furniture and textiles. There is also a toy room and a local history display. Downstairs, there is a comprehensive display of ceramics.

Also on the ground floor are temporary exhibition galleries which feature fine art, crafts and photography. On the lawn in front of the museum stands the Jaipur Gate, which formed part of the Indo-Colonial Exhibition held in London in 1886 and was re-erected at the museum in 1926.

℘ Brighton 0273 779410.
Open: Tue–Fri 10–5, Sat 10–4.30, Sun 2–5. (Closed Mon, Xmas & New Year.)
Ġ (ground floor only) Shop ⊗

## HOY
See Orkney

## HUDDERSFIELD
West Yorkshire

**ART GALLERY**
Princess Alexandra Walk
A major regional collection of 20th-century fine art and sculpture, as well as collections of both fine and decorative arts from the mid 19th century. A busy programme of temporary exhibitions and activities.

℘ 0484 513808 Ext 216.
Open: Mon–Fri 10–6, Sat 10–4. (Closed Sun, Good Fri, 25–26 Dec & BHs.)
Ġ toilets for the disabled. ⊗

**CASTLE HILL**
(5m S off A629)
An Iron Age fort with spectacular views of Huddersfield and the Pennines. The 100ft tower was built to celebrate Queen Victoria's Jubilee.

℘ 0484 530591.
Open: all year, daily dawn–dusk (Jubilee Tower (charge) Etr, May BH & Spring BH–Sep 1–4).
Ġ

**TOLSON MEMORIAL MUSEUM**
Ravensknowle Park (1.5m E of centre on A629 Wakefield Road)
An Italianate mansion built 1859–62, where many of the decorative →

features still survive. Three new galleries – Agriculture, Local History, Industry and Transport. New archaeology gallery due to open during 1992. Wide range of events and temporary exhibitions.

✆ 0484 530591.
Open: Mar–Oct Mon–Fri 10–5, Sat & Sun 12–5; Nov–Feb daily 12–5 (subject to revision). (Closed Good Fri & 25–26 Dec.) Parties by arrangement.
♿ (ramp; access bell; stair-lift to first floor not suitable for those confined completely to wheelchairs) toilets for the disabled, reserved parking. Shop ⌀

# HULL

Humberside

### FERENS ART GALLERY
Queen Victoria Square
Contains collection of works by European Old Masters; 19th-century marine paintings from Humberside; 20th-century English art with 'Live Art' space and busy exhibition programme.

✆ 0482 593912.
Open: Mon–Sat 10–5, Sun 1.30–4.30. (Closed Good Fri, 25–26 Dec & 1 Jan.) Guided tours available by appointment. Parties by prior arrangement.
🍴 (10.30–4 ex Sun) Shop ♿ (ground floor only) ⌀

### HULL & EAST RIDING MUSEUM
36 High Street
Development of road transport through the ages. Archaeology of Humberside and Roman mosaics, including the Horkstow Pavement. There is a new permanent exhibition – Celtic World – and the iron-age Hasholme boat is on display.

✆ 0482 593902.
Open: Mon–Sat 10–5, Sun 1.30–4.30. (Closed Good Fri, 25–26 Dec & 1 Jan.) Guided tours available by prior arrangement. Parties by appointment only.
♿ (ground floor only) Shop ⌀ (ex guide dogs).

### TOWN DOCKS MUSEUM
Queen Victoria Square
Displays include 'Whales and Whaling', 'Fishing and Trawling', 'Hull and the Humber', 'Ships and Shipping', plus Victorian Court Room.

✆ 0482 593902.
Open: Mon–Sat 10–5, Sun 1.30–4.30. (Closed Good Fri, 25–26 Dec & 1 Jan.) Guided tours available by appointment. Parties by prior arrangement.
🍴 (10.30–4 ex Sun) ♿ (ground floor only) Shop ⌀

### WILBERFORCE & GEORGIAN HOUSES
23–25 High Street
Early 17th-century mansion, where William Wilberforce was born, with Jacobean and Georgian rooms and slavery displays. Secluded garden.

✆ 0482 593902.
Open: Mon–Sat 10–5, Sun 1.30–4.30. (Closed Good Fri, 25–26 Dec & 1 Jan.) Guided tours available by prior arrangement. Parties by appointment.
🅿 ♿ (ground floor only) Shop ⌀

# HUNTERSTON

Strathclyde

### HUNTERSTON POWER STATION
Nuclear power station of advanced gas-cooled reactor (AGR) type. Guided parties of about 32 taken on tours of main operational areas and also see video presentation on the plant. Nuclear Whizz Kid Fun Club for children with free novelties.

✆ West Kilbride 0294 823668 or Link Line Freephone 0800 838 557.
Open May–Sep Mon–Sat 10–4, Sun pm only. Tours at 10, 11.30, 2, Sun 2 (by telephone appointment only). (Children accepted if accompanied by an adult.)
⌀

# HUNTINGDON

Cambridgeshire

### CROMWELL MUSEUM
Grammar School Walk
Restored Norman building once a school where Oliver Cromwell and Samuel Pepys were pupils, now Museum of Cromwellian relics. The museum collection includes portraits of Oliver Cromwell and his family as well as leading figures of the period. There are also contemporary coins and medals, and objects which are known to have belonged to Cromwell.

✆ 0480 425830.
Open: Apr–Oct, Tue–Fri 11–1 & 2–5, Sat & Sun 11–1 & 2–4; Nov–Mar, Tue–Fri 1–4, Sat 11–1 & 2–4, Sun 2–4. (Closed BHS ex Good Fri.) Donations. Guided tours available for organised groups out of normal hours by prior arrangement.
Shop ⌀

### HINCHINGBROOKE COUNTRY PARK
One hundred acres of mature woodland, lakes and wildflower meadows. There are many woodland and lakeside trails. Fishing is available on a day ticket basis and Hinchingbrooke House (the former home of the Cromwell family) is open to the public on

*Hunterston 'B'*

Sunday afternoons. There is a programme of special events.

✆ 0480 451560.
Open: all year. Guided tours of Country Park available. Groups by prior arrangement only.
👤 (part) toilets for the disabled. 🚻

## HUNTLY
Grampian

**HUNTLY MUSEUM**
The Square
Local history and changing special exhibitions every year. Governed by North East of Scotland Library Committee.

✆ Peterhead 0779 77778.
Open: all year, Tue–Sat 10–12 & 2–4.
Donation box.
Shop 🐾 (ex guide dogs).

## ILKESTON
Derbyshire

**EREWASH MUSEUM**
High Street
A three-storey 18th-century house set in a lovely walled garden, the museum displays items of social history from the 1850s, including a reconstructed wash-house. Victorian kitchen and stable. There are also toys and exhibits from the local civic and industrial past.

✆ 0602 440440 Ext 331.
Open: all year Thu & Fri 10–4; also Sat Etr–Sep 10–4. Other times by arrangement. Donations. Parties by prior appointment only.
👤 (ground floor & garden; access ramp available, please advise of visit)
Shop 🐾 (ex guide dogs).

## ILKLEY
West Yorkshire

**MANOR HOUSE MUSEUM & GALLERY**
Castle Yard, Church Street
Elizabethan manor house, built on site of Roman fort, showing exposed Roman wall, collections of Roman material, archaeology and 17th- and 18th-century farmhouse parlour/kitchen furniture.

Exhibitions by regional artists and craftsmen.

✆ 0943 600066.
Open: Apr–Sep, Tue–Sun 10–6; Oct–Mar 10–5. Also open BH Mon.
(Closed Good Fri & Xmas.)
👤 (ground floor only) Shop 🐾

## INGLISTON
Lothian

**SCOTTISH AGRICULTURAL MUSEUM**
Royal Highland Showground
Displays of original farming tools, equipment and models showing how the land was worked and the living conditions of agricultural workers and their families in rural Scotland. Paintings depict rural life and a slide show 'The Sword and the Plough' tells the story of agriculture from World War I to the present day.

✆ 031 333 2674.
Open: May–Sep, Mon–Fri 10–5, also Sat in Aug. Donations.
🚻 (Mon–Fri 10–4, Sat 12–4)
👤 (ramps; lift) toilets for the disabled. Shop 🐾 (ex guide dogs).

## INVERFARIGAIG
Highland

**FARIGAIG FOREST CENTRE**
(Signposted 100 metres off B852, 2.5m NE of Foyers)
Nestling deep in a wooded gorge at the mouth of the Pass of Inverfarigaig, this Forestry Commission interpretative centre and picnic area forms the hub of a forest trail network catering for a variety of abilities.

✆ Inverness 0463 791575.
Open: daily Apr–Oct 9–6. Guided tours can be provided for educational groups by prior arrangment. Coach parties not accepted.
🚻 👤

## INVERKEITHING
Fife

**INVERKEITHING MUSEUM**
Queen Street
The Old Friary hospice (founded in 1384) is home of the town museum.

Exhibits show the history of this Royal Burgh along with displays on local industries and Admiral Grieg, father of the Russian navy under Catherine the Great.

✆ 0383 413344 or 721814.
Open: all year Wed–Sun, 11–5.
Donation box. Guided tours available by prior arrangement
🐾

## INVERNESS
Highland

**JAMES PRINGLE WEAVERS**
Holm Mills, Dores Road
Two hundred year old mill showing modern-day weaving in operation, with self-guided tours in six languages. Clan tartan centre has computer research facility and mill shop has a wide selection of Scottish Woollens.

✆ 0463 223311.
Open: all year daily, Mon–Fri 9–5.30, Sat 9.30–5, Sun 10–5 (Closed 25 & 26 Dec and 1 Jan). Coach parties welcome.
🚻 👤 (part) toilets for the disabled. Shop.

**MUSEUM AND ART GALLERY**
Castle Wynd
Museum of the Highlands' social and natural history, archaeology and culture with a very good collection of Jacobite relics, bagpipes and Highland silver. Art gallery has interesting pictures of old Inverness and frequently changing exhibitions.

✆ 0463 237114.
Open: all year, Mon–Sat 9–5.
👤 (ground floor only) Shop 🚻 (10–4) 🐾 (ex guide dogs).

## INVERURIE
Grampian

**INVERURIE MUSEUM**
Town House, The Square
Changing thematic displays plus permanent local history and archaeology exhibition.

✆ Peterhead 0779 77778.          →

Open: all year Mon, Tue, Thu & Fri 2–5, Sat 10–1 & 2–4. Donation box. Shop ⌀ (ex guide dogs).

## ✦ IONA, ISLE OF ✦

Strathclyde

**IONA ABBEY**
This tiny island became an important Christian centre when St Columba brought Christianity from Ireland in 563AD, and it is still a place of pilgrimage. On the site of St Columba's monastery is a 13th-century abbey restored during the early part of the 20th century with more rebuilding and excavations since then.

✆ 06817 404.
Open: accessible at all reasonable times. Donations.
Shop ⌑ (Mar–Oct 10–4.30) ⍭
No cars allowed.

## IPSWICH

Suffolk

**CHRISTCHURCH MANSION**
Christchurch Park
16th-century town house with period rooms, furnished up to 19th century. New Suffolk Artists' Gallery, with temporary exhibition programme.

✆ 0473 253246.
Open: all year (ex 24–26 Dec & Good Fri), Tue–Sat 10–5, Sun 2.30–4.30. Guided tours by written request to Curator, Ipswich Museums, High Street, Ipswich IP1 3QH. Donations. ♿ (ground floor & gardens only) tape/guide for visually handicapped. Shop ⌀

**IPSWICH MUSEUMS**
High Street
Geology, new Victorian Natural History gallery, Ogilvie bird collection, Ethnography and Roman Suffolk display. Temporary exhibition programme.

✆ 0473 213761.
Open: Tue–Sat 10–5.
Closed Sun, Xmas, Good Fri & BH.) Donations box.

♿ (ground floor only; ramps) Shop ⌀

## IRCHESTER

Northamptonshire

**IRCHESTER COUNTRY PARK**
Gypsy Lane
At Irchester Country Park there are 200 acres of woodland and meadow to explore, and a newly renovated Visitor Centre. The Park has been developed on the site of a former ironstone quarry which has left the land lying in 'hills and dales'. Adventure play area, nature trails and woodland walk. A number of events are run at the Park as part of the County Council's Countryside Event Programme.

✆ Wellingborough 0933 76866.
Open: daily, winter 8.30–5, summer 8.30–6. Donations welcome.
♿ (part) nature trail & toilets for the disabled. Shop ⍭

## IRVINE

Strathclyde

**EGLINTON PARK**
Irvine Road, Kilwinning
Castle ruin of late 18th-century, built for 13th Earl of Eglinton, set in a 12-acre garden which is itself part of Eglinton Country Park. Site of the famous Eglinton Tournament of 1839.

✆ 0294 51776 (Ranger).
Open: all year during daylight hours; Visitor Centre Etr–Sep daily 10–4.30. Guided tours available.
⌑ ⍭ ♿ Shop.

**GLASGOW VENNEL MUSEUM AND HECKLING SHOP**
Exhibitions gallery with changing display. Restored heckling shop and lodgings where Robert Burns came to work and live in 1781 at the age of 22 as an apprentice in the trade of flax dressing or heckling.

✆ 0294 75059.
Open: Jun–Sep daily (ex Wed) 10–1 & 2–5, Sun 2–5; Oct–May Tue & Thu–Sat 10–1 & 2–5. Donations. Guided

tours are available.
♿ (ground floor only).

## ISLE OF LEWIS
See Lewis, Isle of

## ISLE OF MAN
See Man, Isle of

## ISLE OF WIGHT
See Wight, Isle of

## KEIGHLEY

West Yorkshire

**CLIFFE CASTLE MUSEUM & GALLERY**
Spring Gardens Lane (NW of town on A629)
Mansion of c1878 given by Sir Bracewell Smith. Contains collections of natural and local history, dolls, ceramics, geological gallery, craft workshops, and interesting exhibitions programme. Play area and aviary in adjacent park. French furniture from Victoria and Albert Museum. A re-creation of the surviving main reception rooms is planned, with their original fittings.

✆ 0274 758230.
Open: Apr–Sep, Tue–Sun 10–6; Oct–Mar, Tue–Sun 10–5. Also open BH Mons.
⌑ Shop ⌀ (ex guide dogs) ⍭ ♿ (ground floor only) toilets for disabled.

## KEITH

Grampian

**STRATHISLA DISTILLERY**
Seafield Avenue
Claimed to be the oldest established distillery in Scotland, dating from 1786. Visitors are given a tour through the production area and shown a film. Whisky sampling is available.

✆ 05422 7471.
Open: early May–mid Sep Mon–Fri 9–4. Guided tours available. Coach parties by prior appointment only. ♿ (ground floor) toilets for the disabled. Shop.

## KELSO
Borders

### KELSO ABBEY
Little but the abbey church remains, and that only in imposing fragments which seem to consist almost wholly of Norman and Transitional work.

Open: Apr–Sep Mon–Fri 9.30–6, Sun 2–6.
&
(AM)

## KESWICK
Cumbria

### CASTLERIGG STONE CIRCLE
(1½m E on unclass road)
Dating from neolithic and post neolithic periods these 38 standing stones are thought to have been constructed for religious or otherwise ceremonial meetings. A further 10 stones nearby form a rectangle.

Open: accessible at all reasonable times.
(AM)

## KETTERING
Northamptonshire

### ALFRED EAST ART GALLERY
Sheep Street
Programme of temporary exhibitions, including collections of paintings by Sir Alfred East and T C Gotch.

℘ 0536 410333 Ext 381.
Open: Mon–Sat 9.30–5. (Closed BHs.) Parties by appointment only.
& (via adjacent public library) ✄

### MANOR HOUSE MUSEUM
Sheep Street
The first phase of Manor House Museum shows glimpses of Kettering's past through collections of social and industrial history, including shoe making, agriculture and town life, archaeology and geology.

℘ 0536 410333 Ext 381.
Open: all year Mon–Sat (ex BH)

9.30–5. Parties by appointment.
& Shop.

## KILMAHOG
Central

### TROSSACHS WOOLLEN MILL
Fascinating demonstration of the art of weaving, with power looms in operation. Mill shop offers traditional woollens and crafts.

℘ 0877 30178.
Open: all year daily, May–Sep, Mon–Sat 9–5.30, Sun 10–5.30; winter Mon–Sat 10–4.30, Sun 11–4. Coach parties welcome.
& (part). Shop.

## KILMARNOCK
Strathclyde

### DICK INSTITUTE
Elmbank Avenue
Exhibits of geology (including fossils), small arms, shells, ethnography, numismatics, and archaeological specimens. Also art gallery, (paintings and etchings) and library.

℘ 0563 26401.
Open: Mon, Tue, Thu & Fri 10–8, Wed & Sat 10–5.
& (ramp, lifts) toilets for the disabled. Shop ✄

### JOHNNIE WALKER PLANT TOURS
Hill Street
Home of the world's largest-selling Scotch whisky. Tour begins with visit to blending, where whiskies from all over Scotland are blended, followed by filtration, and then through the bottling halls at Kilmarnock.

℘ 0563 23401.
Open: Apr–Oct tours Mon–Thu 9.45 & 1.45 Fri 9.45 only. Large parties must book in advance. No unaccompanied children.
Shop. ✄

## KILMARTIN
Strathclyde

### DUNADD FORT
(3m S, off A816)
A prehistoric hillfort incorporating

walled enclosures. It was once the capital of the ancient Scots kingdom of Dalriada.

Open: Apr–Sep Mon–Fri 9.30–6, Sun 2–6.
(AM)

## KILMUN
Strathclyde

### KILMUN ABORETUM
(On A880, 1m from junc with A815)
A large collection of conifer and broadleaved tree species planted in plots and specimen groups. Established by the Forestry Commission in 1930 and now extending to 200 acres on a hillside overlooking the Holy Loch. Guidebooks available at the nearby Forestry Commission Office.

℘ 036984 666.
Open: all year

## KILSYTH
Strathclyde

### COLZIUM HOUSE & ESTATE
Partly a museum, illustrating the Battle of Kilsyth and history of Colzium, with attractive walled garden. Ice house and old castle associated with Montrose's victory over the Covenanters in 1645.

℘ 0236 823281.
House open: Etr weekend–Sep, Mon–Fri 9–5, Sun 10–6. (Closed when booked for private functions). Grounds open at all times. Museum open Wed 2–8.
▣ ⊼ & (ground floor & gardens only) ✄ (in house).

## KINGSTON ST MARY
Somerset

### FYNE COURT
(3m N)
Headquarters of the Somerset Trust for Nature Conservation. 24-acre nature reserve for associated species of plants, with nature trails and walks, aboretum and countryside information centre. Events through the summer, mostly free.                →

✆ 082345 1587.
Open: daily 9–6 or dusk if earlier.
Parties by appointment.
🍴 (afternoon teas summer Sun &
BHs) ♿ (ground floor & part
grounds) nature trail for disabled.
Shop 🅿 ✻ (ex guide dogs). Charge
for parking.

## KINGSWINFORD
West Midlands

**BROADFIELD HOUSE GLASS
MUSEUM**
Barnett Lane
Displays of glass from the Roman
period to the present day, but
concentrating on the coloured, cut
and engraved glass produced in
nearby Stourbridge during the last
century. Slide and video displays.
Glass-making studios.

✆ 0384 273011.
Open: Tue–Fri & Sun 2–5, Sat 10–1 &
2–5, BHs 2–5. Donation box.
♿ (ground floor only) Shop.
✻ (ex guide dogs).

## KINGUSSIE
Highland

**RUTHVEN BARRACKS**
(0.5m SE of Kingussie)
The best preserved of the four
infantry barracks built by the
Hanoverian Government in the
Highlands following the Jacobite
uprising of 1715.

Open: Apr–Sep Mon–Fri 9.30–6, Sun
2–6.
(AM)

## KINROSS
Tayside

**LOCH LEVEN CASTLE**
Castle Island
Built in the 14th century, this castle
is most notable for the escape of
Mary, Queen of Scots after a year's
imprisonment in 1568. The castle is
five storeys in height, with round
towers guarding the outer wall.

Open: Apr–Sep Mon–Fri 9.30–6 & Sun
2–6. Ferry charge.
(AM)

## KINTAIL
Highland

**KINTAIL AND MORVICH
COUNTRYSIDE CENTRE**
(At Morvich Farm, off A87)
National Trust for Scotland
Countryside Centre in 12,800 acres
of magnificent West Highland
scenery including the Five Sisters of
Kintail (four of them over 3,000 ft).
There is a Ranger Naturalist
service.

✆ Glenshiel 059981 218.
Open: Jun–Sep, Mon–Sat 10–6, Sun
2–6. Donations.

## KIRKCALDY
Fife

**KIRKCALDY MUSEUM & ART
GALLERY**
War Memorial Gardens (next to
Kircaldy Station)
A unique collection of fine Scottish
paintings, historical displays and a
full programme of changing art,
craft and local history exhibitions.
Temporary exhibitions and
programme of activities throughout
the year.

✆ 0592 260732.
Open: Mon–Sat 11–5, Sun 2–5.
🍴 🅿 ♿ (ground floor only but
assistance given to first floor) toilets
for the disabled. Shop ✻

**JOHN MCDOUALL STUART MUSEUM**
Rectory Lane, Dysart
Set in the National Trust restored
18th-century house which was the
birthplace of John McDouall Stuart
(1815–1866), the first explorer to
cross Australia. The award-winning
display describes his journeys and
the Australian wilderness.

✆ 0592 260732.
Open: Jun–Aug daily 2–5.
Shop ✻

## KIRKHILL
Highland

**HIGHLAND WINERIES**
Moniack Castle (7m from
Inverness on A862 Beauly road)

Once a fortress of the Lovat chiefs
and their kin, it is today the centre
of an enterprise producing and
bottling country wines and liqueurs.
A selection of preserves are also
made and sold here.

✆ Drumchardine 046383 283.
Open: Mon–Sat 10–5. Guided tours
available. Tastings. Coach parties by
prior appointment.
🍴 (licensed) 🅿 Shop.

## KIRKWALL
*See Orkney*

## KNOCKANDO
Grampian

**CARDHU DISTILLERY**

✆ 03406 204/439.
Open: all year, Oct–Apr Mon–Fri (Sat
& Sun by appointment), May–Sep
Mon–Sat 9.30–4.30. (Sun & evenings
by appointment). Guided tours
available. Coach parties by
appointment.
🍴 (cafe, and licensed restaurant by
appointment) 🅿 ♿ (ground floor)
toilets for the disabled. Shop.

**TAMDHU DISTILLERY VISITORS
CENTRE**
Visitors are able to see the
complete process of whisky being
made.

✆ Carron 03406 221.
Open: Apr–May, Mon–Fri 10–4. Jun–
Sep, Mon–Sat 10–4. Guided tours
available. Parties by appointment
only.
♿ (ground floor only) Shop 🅿

## KNOWLTON
Dorset

**KNOWLTON CIRCLES**
(3.25m SW of Cranborne on
B3078)
Three large henges lying in a row,
the eastern one is bisected by the
B3078 and measures 800 ft across.
The ruined Norman Knowlton
Church stands in the middle of the
centre circle. There are several
round barrows nearby.

Open: accessible at all reasonable times. (AM)

## LAKE VYRNWY
Powys

(SE of Bala on B4393) Large artificial lake with an interesting dam. Focal point for a Royal Society for the Protection of Birds reserve covering 16,000 acres, with three RSPB nature trails and four hides. Wildlife display, video and slide shows at Visitor Centre at the southern end of the lake, plus information on the area before and after the lake was formed.

℘ Llanwddyn 069173 278. Visitor Centre open: May–Sep Mon–Fri 12–6, Sat & Sun 11–6; Oct–Apr weekends only. Donations. Guided walks (charge) Sat & Sun 2.30 or other times by arrangement. ⊼ ♿ (Visitor Centre and spinal-disabled bird watching look-out) toilets for the disabled. Shop.

## LAMB HOLM
*See Orkney*

## LANCASTER
Lancashire

ASHTON MEMORIAL & WILLIAMSON PARK
A 40-acre park created by James Williamson. The Ashton Memorial is an Edwardian folly with an exhibition of the life and times of Lord Ashton. Also British and Tropical Butterfly Houses and Wildlife and Conservation Garden to which admission is charged.

℘ 0524 33318. Open: all year, daily Etr–Sep 10–5, Oct–Etr 11–4. Parties by appointment. ⌂ ♿ parking (Quernmore Rd entrance) & toilets for the disabled. Shop.

CITY MUSEUM
Market Square
Housed in the Georgian former Town Hall building of 1783. Collections include local archaeology and social history and

the Museum of the King's Own Royal Regiment (Lancaster) with uniforms, medals and a splendid archive. There is a changing programme of exhibitions.

℘ 0524 64637. Open: daily Mon–Sat 10–5. (Closed Xmas & New Year.) Donation. Guided tours available for parties by prior arrangement. Vehicle access limited. ♿ (ramp; ground floor only) Shop ♞ (ex guide dogs).

## LANGOLD
Nottinghamshire

LANGOLD COUNTRY PARK
(On A60 5m N of Worksop)
Country park with woodland and lakeside walks (one suitable for prams and wheelchairs). A wealth of flora and fauna, particularly wildfowl. There is an open air swimming pool and children's play facilities.

℘ Worksop 0909 475531. Open: all year, daily dawn–dusk. ♿ (part)

## LAUNCESTON
Cornwall & Isles of Scilly

LAWRENCE HOUSE MUSEUM
9 Castle Street
National Trust-owned Georgian house leased to the Town Council to house the town's museum and Mayor's parlour. Many fascinating exhibits and relics of times past. Monthly exhibitions.

Open: Apr–Oct Mon–Fri 10.30–12.30 & 2.30–4.30. Donations. Guided tours available. Coach parties by prior arrangement with the curators.

## LAXFIELD
Suffolk

LAXFIELD AND DISTRICT MUSEUM
The Guildhall (On B1117 in village centre opposite Church)
Local farming and domestic life through the ages, from the Stone Age, but mostly Edwardian, including a costume display, a 'kitchen' and 'village shop', housed in the early 16th-century Guildhall.

℘ 0986 798368/798218. Open: Spring BH–Sep Sat–Sun 2–5. Donations. Coach parties by prior arrangement. Shop.

## LEAMINGTON SPA
Warwickshire

WARWICK DISTRICT COUNCIL ART GALLERY & MUSEUM
Avenue Road
The art gallery specialises in British, Dutch and Flemish paintings and watercolours of the 16th to 20th century. The museum contains ceramics, Delft, Wedgwood, Whieldon, Worcester, Derby Ware etc, and a collection of 18th-century glass. Temporary exhibitions change monthly. New Local History Gallery due to open early 1992.

℘ 0926 426559. Open: Mon–Sat 10–1 & 2–5; also Thu evenings 6–8. (Closed: Good Fri, Xmas & New Year's Day.) ♿ ♞ (ex guide dogs).

## LEATHERHEAD
Surrey

FIRE AND IRON GALLERY
Rowhurst Forge, Oxshott Road
Gallery and resource centre showing and selling the work of leading designer-blacksmiths.

℘ 0372 375148. Open: all year Mon–Fri 9–1 2–5, Sat 9–1. Guided tours available. Coach parties not accepted. Shop.

## LEEDS
Kent

KENT GARDEN COSTUME DOLLS AND COUNTRY WINES
Yew Tree House, Upper Street
See the processes of making reproduction porcelain dolls in the studio and finished dolls in authentic period costume in the showroom. Visitors are welcome to look around Kent Garden vineyard, vinehouse and winery. Country wines and English wines are produced on the premises and wine tastings are free. Dolls, doll kits and wines for sale.  →

⌀ Maidstone 0622 861638.
Open: all year Thu–Sun & BH 10–5.
Guided tours. Coach parties by prior
appointment only for special
functions – details on request.
ᕒ (ground floor) toilets for the
disabled. ⅜ (ex guide dogs).

## LEEDS
West Yorkshire

### KIRKSTALL ABBEY
Abbey Road
Extensive and impressive ruins of
abbey founded in 12th century by
Cistercian monks from Fountains
Abbey. The chapter house, cloisters
and abbot's lodgings are of interest.

⌀ Leeds 0532 755821.
Open: daily, dawn–dusk.
ᕒ

### LEEDS CITY ART GALLERY
The Headrow (next to Town
Hall)
One of the finest collections of 20th-
century British art outside London,
as well as a splendid Victorian
gallery and an outstanding
collection of early English
watercolours. Housed on the same
premises, The Henry Moore Centre
for the Study of Sculpture
comprises an archive, library and
gallery. There is a regular
programme of changing exhibitions
supported by educational events,
ranging from workshops to talks
and residencies by artists.

⌀ 0532 478248.
Open: Mon, Tue, Thu, Fri 10–6, Wed
10–9, Sat 10–4, Sun 2–5. (Closed 25–
26 Dec & 1 Jan.)
🖵 Mon–Sat 10–3.30 (licensed) ᕒ
toilets for the disabled. Shop.

### LEEDS CITY MUSEUM
Calverley Street
One of Britain's oldest museums
with fine worldwide collections
including geology, natural history,
archaeology, ethnography,
numismatics and changing
exhibitions.

⌀ 0532 478275.
Open: all year Tue–Fri 9.30–5.30, Sat

9.30–4. (Closed BH). Guided tours
available for special interest groups
only by prior appointment.
ᕒ (by prior arrangement). Shop.

### TROPICAL WORLD, CANAL GARDENS
Roundhay Park
Eighty-foot fountain, fantastic
butterfly house, Coronation House
and tropical plant house, including
insects, reptiles, aquaria and birds.
Plus Canal Gardens, Northern Rose
Society trial gardens and a scented
garden for the blind. Band concerts
Sun pm Jun–Jul.

⌀ 0532 661850.
Open: daily, 10–dusk. Donations.
Guided tours available at certain
times of the year – telephone for
details.
🖵 ᕒ Shop 🎋

## LEICESTER
Leicestershire

### JOHN DORAN MUSEUM
British Gas, Aylestone Road
(0.5m S on A426)
Housed in the gatehouse of the
original Aylestone Road Gasworks,
begun in 1878, the collection shows
all aspects of the history of the
manufacture, distribution and use
of gas, with documentary material
as well as old appliances and
equipment.

⌀ 0533 535506.
Open: Tue–Fri 12.30–4.30. (Closed
BHs & Tue following BHs and Good
Fri.) Guided tours available. Parties
accepted by appointment – 20
persons max if a guided tour
required.
ᕒ (ground floor only).

### UNIVERSITY OF LEICESTER BOTANIC GARDENS
Beaumont Hall, Stoughton
Drive South, Oadby (3.5m SE,
A6)
The gardens occupy an area of
about 16 acres and include
botanical greenhouses, rose, rock,
water and sunken gardens, trees,
herbaceous borders and a heather
garden. They comprise the grounds
of four houses; Beaumont,

Southmeade, Hastings and The
Knoll, which are used as student
residences.

⌀ 0533 717725.
Open: Mon–Fri 10–4.30 (3.30 Fri)
(Closed BHs.)
ᕒ ⅜

## LEISTON
Suffolk

### LEISTON ABBEY
(1m N off B1069)
Remains of this 14th-century abbey
for Premonstratensian canons
include choir and transepts of
church, and ranges of cloisters.
Georgian house built into the fabric
of the abbey.

Open: accessible at any reasonable
time.
ᕒ
(AM)

## LEOMINSTER
Hereford & Worcester

### QUEEN'S WOOD COUNTRY PARK AND ARBORETUM
(On A49 Hereford to
Leominster Rd, 8m from
Hereford)
One hundred and seventy acres of
woodland with an arboretum of
nearly 500 varieties of exotic trees.
There is a Visitor Centre and ranger
service.

⌀ 056884 7052.
Open: all year 8–dusk. Donations.
Guided tours available. Coach parties
by prior arrangement.
🖵 (9–6 summer, 9–5 winter) 🎋
ᕒ (grounds) Shop.

## LERWICK
*See Shetland*

## LETCHWORTH
Hertfordshire

### FIRST GARDEN CITY HERITAGE MUSEUM
296 Norton Way South
Part-thatched house with extension
containing the original offices of the
principal architects of the Garden

City, Barry Parker and Raymond Unwin. Displays explain the concept and cover the social, industrial and architectural development of Letchworth as the First Garden City from its beginnings in 1903 up to the present.

✆ 0462 683149.
Open: Mon–Fri 2–4.30, Sat 10–1 & 2–4. (Closed 25–26 Dec.) Donations. Guided tours available (donation). Parties by appointment only.
🚼 ♿ (ground floor only) Shop ✖

**LETCHWORTH MUSEUM & ART GALLERY**
Broadway
Museum contains displays on the archaeology and natural history of North Hertfordshire including important Iron Age and Roman finds from Baldock. Temporary exhibition programme.

✆ 0462 685647.
Open: Mon–Sat 10–5. (Closed BHs.) Guided tours available by appointment.
♿ (ground floor only) Shop ✖

## LEVEN
Fife

**LETHAM GLEN**
Letham Glen has a variety of recreational and educational facilities set in picturesque surroundings. There is a nature centre with informative displays, art exhibitions and in July and August resident artists. There is a putting green (charge), pets' corner, sunken garden, dovecote and nature trail of about a mile (booklet from Nature Centre).

✆ 0333 29231.
Open: garden, walk areas and pets' corner all year, every day. Nature Centre Mon–Fri 12–3, Sat 2–4, Sun 2–4.30. Car park closed in winter. No coach parking. Guided tour available.
🚼 ♿

**SILVERBURN ESTATE**
(E side of Leven on A915)
The Estate offers mature woods, beautiful gardens and a flourishing

population of wild birds. Several paddocks are occupied by Silverburn Shetland ponies, and other animals include Angora goats, Saddleback pigs, geese and ducks. There is also a 'Mini Farm' being developed intended as a resource for schools and other interested groups.

✆ 0333 27568 (Warden).
Open: all year, gardens at all times. Mini Farm Mon–Fri 8.30–4.30, Sat & Sun 2–4. Guided tours available.
🚼 ♿

## ✦ LEWIS, ISLE OF ✦

### CALLANISH
Isle of Lewis

**CALLANISH STANDING STONES**

Unique collection of megaliths comprising an avenue 27 ft in width, with 19 standing stones, terminating in a 37 ft-wide circle containing 13 additional stones. Other stones, burial cairns and circles may be seen in the near vicinity.

Open: accessible at all times. Shop.
(AM)

*Callanish Standing Stones on the Isle of Lewis*

### CARLOWAY
Isle of Lewis

**DUN CARLOWAY BROCH**
Well-preserved broch of late prehistoric date, about 30 ft in height, and one of the finest in the Western Isles.

Open: all year weekdays 9.30–7, Sun 2–7 (closes 4 Oct–Mar).
(AM)

## LICHFIELD
Staffordshire

**THE STAFFORDSHIRE REGIMENT (PRINCE OF WALES) REGIMENTAL MUSEUM**
Whittington Barracks (3m SE)
Uniforms, badges and weapons, relics from the Sikh Wars, Crimea, Egypt, Sudan, South Africa, both World Wars and the Gulf War. A medal display, dating back to 1705 includes 8 of the 13 Victoria Crosses awarded to men of the Regiment.

✆ Whittington 0543 433333 Ext 3240, 3229 or 3263.
Open: Mon–Fri 9–4 (Closed PHs.) Donations. Guided tours available. Parties of 25 or more can request special opening at weekends subject to staff availability.
♿ Shop.

## LINCOLN
Lincolnshire

**HATSHOLME COUNTRY PARK**
Skellingthorpe Road (SW of city centre signposted from A46 bypass)
A 96-acre park with mature woodland, open grassland and a lake. The old stable block houses the Visitor Centre, cafe and Rangers' Office.

✆ 0522 686264.
Open: Park always open, Visitor Centre mid Mar–Oct Thu–Mon 11–5. Guided tours available for groups by prior arrangement with a Park Ranger. Public guided walks in summer.
🚽 (Apr–Oct 11–5) 🚼 ♿ (grounds) toilets for the disabled.

### Lincoln Cathedral

One of the finest medieval buildings in Europe and one of the largest of the English Cathedrals dating from the Middle Ages, The Cathedral Church of the Blessed Virgin Mary was begun in 1072 and completed in 1280. The west front is Norman, the transept, nave, St Hugh's Choir and Angel Choir date mostly from the 13th century. Large-scale restoration took place in the 18th and 19th centuries. Its three towers dominate the skyline for many miles.

✆ 0522 544544.
Open: daily May–Sep 7.15am–8pm; Oct–Apr 7.15–6. Donations. Guided tours are available – 3 tours per day & by arrangement. Donation. Visit to Tower chargeable (accessible during academic vacation period only).
☕ (10–4.30) ♿ (ground floor only) display for the blind, toilets for the disabled. Shop.

## LINDSEY

Suffolk

### St James's Chapel

(On unclass rd 0.5m E of Rose Green)

Small thatched flint and stone chapel with lancet windows and piscina, built in the 13th century but incorporating earlier work.

Open: all year.
♿ (single step)
(AM)

## LITTLEHAMPTON

West Sussex

### Littlehampton Museum

Manor House, Church Street

This museum offers local history with a maritime flavour. Photographs, bygones, historic maps, documents, archaeology, social history and maritime paintings are all displayed here, and there are special exhibitions.

✆ 0903 715149.
Open: Tue–Sat 10.30–4.30. Donation box.
♿ Shop.

## LITTLE NESS

Shropshire

### Adcote

(7m NW Shrewsbury off A5)

Now a school, *Country Life* magazine has described Adcote as 'the most controlled, coherent and masterly of the big country houses designed by Norman Shaw'. Includes William Morris stained glass windows and de Morgan tiled fireplaces. Landscaped gardens.

✆ Baschurch 0939 260202.
Open: Apr–Jun & Sep when school in session 2–5. Guided tours are available. Coach parties by prior appointment only. Donations.
♿ (ground floor & gardens only)
🐕 (ex guide dogs).

## LIVERPOOL

Merseyside

### The Bluecoat

Bluecoat Chambers, School Lane

A fine Queen Anne building in Liverpool's city centre with cobbled quadrangle and garden courtyard. Built as a charity school in 1717, it now houses Merseyside's Arts Centre including Gallery and lively performance programme, plus crafts centre, cinema and artists' studios.

✆ 051 709 5297.
Open: Mon–Sat 10–5. Voluntary donations welcome.
♿ (check accessibility before visit)
☕ (10–5 licensed) Shop.

### Liverpool City Libraries

William Brown Street

One of the oldest and largest public libraries in the country, with over two million books. Temporary Exhibitions.

✆ 051 225 5429.
Open: Mon–Thu 9–7.30, Fri & Sat 9–5. Guided tours by prior arrangement.
♿ 🐕

### Liverpool Museum

William Brown St

Collections include antiquities, botany, decorative arts, geology, zoology (with aquarium and vivarium), physical sciences, social and industrial history and transport. Varied exhibition programme. Museum also houses a Planetarium (charge).

✆ 051 207 0001.
Open: Mon–Sat 10–5 & Sun 12–5. Donations welcome.
☕ ♿ (lift to entrance & upper floors) toilets for the disabled. Shop.

### Museum of Labour History

William Brown Street

✆ 051 207 0001.
Open: all year (ex 24–26 Dec, 1 Jan & Good Fri) Mon–Sat 10–5, Sun 12–5. Donation welcomed.
♿ toilets for the disabled. Shop.

### Sudley Art Gallery

Mossley Hill

Contains the Emma Holt Bequest of fine 19th-century British paintings and sculpture. Permanent display of several hundred shells from all over the world.

✆ 051 724 3245.
Open: Mon–Sat 10–5, Sun 12–5. (Closed: Good Fri, 25–26 Dec & 1 Jan.) Donations. Parties by prior appointment.
♿ (ground floor and grounds only; please give advance notice of visit)
⛩

### University of Liverpool Art Gallery

3 Abercromby Square

Displays from the University's collections of sculpture, paintings, drawings, prints, furniture, ceramics, silver and glass. Works by Epstein, Turner, Frink and Riley and a fine collection of early English watercolours and porcelain. Located in a Georgian terraced house on the University precinct.

✆ 051 794 2347/8.
Open: Sep–Jul (ex BH) Mon, Tue & Thu 12–2; Wed & Fri 12–4. (Other times by appointment.) Donations. Guided tours & coach parties by prior arrangement.
☕ (in University precinct).

## WALKER ART GALLERY
William Brown Street
Outstanding general collection of
European paintings, sculpture and
drawings dating from 1300 to the
present day, especially notable for
Italian and pre-Raphaelite paintings
and contemporary art. A new
sculpture gallery includes 18th and
19th-century works by masters
such as Frampton and Gibson.
Temporary exhibitions throughout
year.

✆ 051 207 0001.
Open: Mon–Sat 10–5, Sun 12–5.
(Closed: Good Fri, 24–26 Dec & 1
Jan.) Donations. Parties by
appointment.
⌨ (10–4.30, 12–4.30 Sun) ♿
(transport lift available; prior notice
appreciated) Shop ⌐ (ex guide
dogs).

## LIVINGSTON
Lothian

### ALMONDELL & CALDERWOOD COUNTRY PARK
(North car park signposted off
A89; South car park at east end
of East Calder Village; Mid
Calder car park (for
Calderwood) on B8046
Pumpherston/Uphall rd)
Consisting of two adjoining estates
formerly owned by the Earl of
Buchan and Lord Torphichen, with
a variety of wildlife, wild flowers and
birds. Calderwood has been left a
natural area, to encourage wildlife.
Almondell has well made paths
along the riverside and through
woodland and a barbecue site
(booking essential) in addition to
its picnic areas. The Visitors' Centre
at Stables Cottage has local and
natural history displays, a slide
show and a small aquarium.

✆ Mid Calder 0506 882254.
Open: Country Park accessible at all
reasonable times; Visitor Centre Apr–
Sep Mon–Wed 9–5, Thu 9–4, Fri
10.30–6. Oct–Mar Mon–Thu 9–5, Sun
10.30–4.30. Guided walks & activities
run by Ranger Service Wed & Sun pm
in summer (advance booking
required).

⌨ 冊 ♿. North car park entrance 2m
S of Broxburn is nearest Visitor Centre
& parking for disabled; please phone
in advance to make sure north
entrance gate will be opened. toilets
for the disabled. ⌐ in Visitor Centre
(ex guide dogs).

## LLANALLGO
Gwynedd

### DIN LLIGWY ANCIENT VILLAGE
(1m NW off A5205)
Remains of 4th-century village, with
two circular and seven rectangular
buildings encircled by pentagonal
stone wall.

Open: accessible at all reasonable
times.
(AM CADW)

## LLANBERIS
Gwynedd

### DOLBADARN CASTLE
Native Welsh stronghold with a
three-storey, 13th-century round
tower.

Open: accessible at all reasonable
times. Charge peak season.
(AM CADW)

## LLANDRINDOD WELLS
Powys

### LLANDRINDOD WELLS MUSEUM
Temple Street (In the
memorial gardens)
Displays on Radnorshire and its
people include reconstructions of a
blacksmith's shop, a Victorian
kitchen and a chemist's shop, finds
from the Roman fort at Castell
Callen, a fine collection of samplers
and an early dug-out canoe. A
permanent exhibition tells 'The
Story of the Spa' in its Victorian and
Edwardian heyday.

✆ 0597 824513.
Open: Mon–Sat 10–12.30 & 2–5
(closed Sat afternoons Oct–Apr &
BH).
Shop.

## ROCK PARK SPA
Norton Terrace
Situated in an 18-acre wooded park
with winding footpaths and
interesting trees, the Pump Room
has been restored to its former
glory and refurbished in Edwardian
style, complete with pumps
providing three spa waters for
anyone to sample. In the Bath
House there is an exhibition of the
history of the spa and others in
Wales. Special events BH Mon.

✆ 0597 824729.
Open: daily Apr–Oct 10–6. Pre-
booked talks available on spa waters.
Parties by prior arrangement.
⌨ 冊 ♿ (ramp) toilets for the
disabled.

## LLANDUDNO
Gwynedd

### GREAT ORME COUNTRY PARK AND NATURE RESERVE
A massive limestone headland with
spectacular cliffs and magnificent
coastal views. An abundance of
wildlife, particularly flowers. Access
by Marine Drive (toll road), cable
car or tramway.

✆ 0492 874151.
Open: Park all year; Visitor centre end
Apr–1st week Oct 10–5.30. Access
unsuitable for coaches. Two hour
guided walks at 2pm every Tues, Thu
and Sun May–1st week in Sep
(charge).
⌨ (summer) 冊 ♿ (part; ramp to
Centre) Shop.

## LLANELLI
Dyfed

### PARC HOWARD ART GALLERY & MUSEUM
Situated in a pleasant park, and
containing paintings, Llanelli
pottery and museum exhibits. From
Mar–Oct a programme of
exhibitions of paintings, porcelain,
sculpture etc is in operation.

✆ 0554 773538.
Open: Mon–Sat 10–4.30. Guided tours
available.
⌨ Shop ⌐

## LLANFIHANGEL-Y-PENNANT

Gwynedd

**CASTELL Y BERE**
(NW of Abergynolwyn on unclass road)
Built by Llywelyn the Great in 1221, Castell y Bere is a keep and bailey castle with two D-shape towers, a typical feature of Welsh castles. Although many of the walls are low there is some fine carved stonework still to be seen.

Open: accessible at all reasonable times.
(AM CADW)

## LLANGYBI

Gwynedd

**ST CYBI'S WELL**
Rectangular structure, known also as Ffynnon Gybi, with dry-stone structure encircling adjacent pool. Interior has wall niches.

Open: accessible at all reasonable times.
(AM CADW)

## LLANIDLOES

Powys

**MUSEUM OF LOCAL HISTORY AND INDUSTRY**
Old Market Hall, Town Centre
The only surviving black and white market hall in Wales, where displays tell the history of this pretty town, once a major centre of the Welsh Woollen industry.

✆ 0597 824513.
Open: Etr week, then Spring BH–Sep 11–1 & 2–5. Donations. Talks and handling sessions by prior arrangement with the Curator. Parties should be prepared to split into smaller groups.
✖

## LLANSTEFFAN

Dyfed

**LLANSTEFFAN CASTLE**
Remains of 12th- to 15th-century stronghold on west side of Towy estuary.

Open: accessible at all reasonable times.
(AM CADW)

## LLANTHONY

Gwent

**LLANTHONY PRIORY**
Augustinian foundation c1108 most of the present structure being 12th or 13th century and including west towers, north nave arcade and south transept. Former Priest's House is now a hotel. The Honddhu valley scenery in the Black Mountains is very picturesque but roads are narrow especially northwards towards lofty Gospel Pass leading to Hay-on-Wye.

Open: at all reasonable times.
(AM CADW)

## LLANTILIO CROSSENNY

Gwent

**HEN GWRT**
(Off B4233)
Rectangular enclosure of medieval house which is still surrounded by moat.

Open: at any reasonable time.
(AM CADW)

## LLANTWIT MAJOR

South Glamorgan

**TOWN HALL**
Originally 12th- and largely 17th-century medieval courthouse and market, known once as the 'Church Loft'. Retains original plan and comprises two storeys; curfew bell now in church.

✆ 04465 3707.
Open: all year Mon–Fri 9–1 & 2–4. (Closed PHs.) Parties not accepted.
✖

## LLANWRTYD WELLS

Powys

**THE CAMBRIAN FACTORY**
Established in 1918 to give employment to ex-service men and women disabled in the First World War. Now a sheltered workshop employing both ex-Service and other disabled persons. Visitors can see an outstanding example of a working mill and all the manufacturing processes including wool sorting, dyeing, carding, spinning, warping, winding and weaving and inspect the finished products.

✆ 05913 211.
Open: Factory, all year Mon–Fri, 8.15–4.30. (Closed BH & Xmas.) Shop Mon–Fri, 8.15–5.15; Sat May–Sep 9–4.30, Oct–Apr 9–noon (Closed Xmas.) Guided tours available.
⌑ (as shop, Mon–Fri only) ♿ (with difficulty; lift to tea room)

## LOCHCARRON

Highland

**STROME CASTLE**
(3m SE)
A fragmentary ruin of a stronghold of the Macdonalds of Glengarry blown up by Kenneth Mackenzie of Kintail in 1602. There are wide views across the Inner Sound to Scalpay, Raasay and the Cuillins of Skye.

Open: accessible at all times.
(NTS)

## LOCHGILPHEAD

Strathclyde

**KILMORY CASTLE GARDENS**
Thirty acres of grounds surrounding the castle. Many rare trees and shrubs have survived years of neglect, but the 18th-century gardens are being restored by the present owners. Woodland walks and nature trails.

✆ 0546 2127 Ext 140.
Open: all year, dawn to dusk.
⧆ ♿ (gardens only) ✖

## LOGGERHEADS

Clwyd

**LOGGERHEADS COUNTRY PARK**
(On A494 3m SW of Mold towards Ruthin; look for the clock tower)
One of the finest country parks in

Wales, set in the beautiful valley of the River Alun. Nature trail from the restored Pentre Water mill takes in panoramic view from the Loggerheads Rocks. Industrial trail shows the former workings of the Gyn Alyn Mine. There is also a countryside centre.

✆ Llanferres 035 285 586.
Open: Country Park, accessible at all reasonable times; Information Centre summer 10–5, winter 10–4 daily (ex Xmas Day). Water mill by prior

arrangement (tour payable). Guided tours of the Park available to pre-booked groups by prior appointment. ⌷ (cafe summer 10–6, winter 10–4 & licensed restaurant) ⊼ ♿ (part of nature trail is suitable for wheelchair users) toilets for the disabled. Shop.

# SHORT WALKS ~TO~ COUNTRY PUBS

One hundred of England's best pubs are included, each at the half-way stage of a pleasant country walk. The round trip will average around five miles and the guide gives full directions for walkers, together with things to see on the way, places of interest nearby and, most important of all, a fine country pub to break the journey and enjoy a good bar meal and a pint of real ale.

*Available at good bookshops and AA Centres*

**Another great guide from the AA**

*Available at good bookshops and AA Centres*

Places to visit of all kinds, for fine weather and rainy days, for young and old - this guide has something for everyone. From Britain's top tourist attractions to some fascinating out-of-the-way places; from Royal castles to country manor houses, theme parks to country parks. If it's worth visiting, you will find it in 2,000 Days Out in Britain.

**Another great guide from the AA**

# ONDON

It is possible to have a really good day out in London for just the price of your fares and food, and the directory which follows has details of all kinds of places with free admission – from the huge national museums and art galleries to fascinating and unexpected delights such as the East Ham Nature Reserve.

By far the best free thing in the capital is the pageantry and there is something to see every day of the year. The Changing of the Guard at Buckingham Palace is the most popular daily event (alternate days from September to April), so arrive early if you want a good view. The ceremony takes place inside the palace railings at approximately 11.25am. Mounting the Guard at Whitehall is another colourful spectacle which takes place at 11am every weekday and 10am on Sundays. You will need a special pass to witness the Ceremony of the Keys at the Tower of London (write to the Resident Governor), which takes place a few minutes before 10pm nightly and lasts for about 20 minutes. It's not all that exciting, but it has been carried out every day for the last 700 years.

Annual events in the capital are well worth a special journey, and the main events are listed below. Full details are available from Tourist Information Offices (addresses below).

## DIARY OF EVENTS

| | | | |
|---|---|---|---|
| **January** | Lord Mayor of Westminster's New Year's Day Parade, 1pm Piccadilly | **June** | Beating Retreat at Horse Guards Parade SW1 |
| **February** | Chinese New Year (sometimes January) around 11.40am, Soho | | Trooping the Colour, Horse Guards Parade with procession along the Mall before and after. |
| | Clowns' Service (first Sunday) 4pm at Holy Trinity Church, Beechwood Road, Dalston E8, with free clown show afterwards | **July** | Swan Upping (third week) on the Thames |
| | | | Doggetts Coat and Badge Race, London Bridge to Cadogan Pier, Chelsea |
| | Gun Salute on Accession Day (6th) | | |
| **March** | Head of the River Race, Mortlake to Putney | **August** | Riding Horse Parade 1pm Rotton Row, Hyde Park |
| | Oxford and Cambridge Boat Race, Mortlake to Putney | | Notting Hill Carnival (bank holiday weekend) |
| **April** | Easter Parade (sometimes in March) 3pm Battersea Park, SW11 (floats congregate from 12.30 onwards) | **September** | Thamesday on the South Bank |
| | | **October** | Judges Service 11am Westminster Abbey, then to Houses of Parliament by 11.45am |
| | London Marathon 8.45am Greenwich, finishing at Westminster Bridge | | |
| | | | Trafalgar Day Parade, 11am Trafalgar Square |
| | Gun Salute on Queen's Birthday (21st) | | |
| | Harness Horse Parade, Regents Park 12 noon | **November** | Remembrance Day Parade (nearest Sun to 11th) |

### TOURIST INFORMATION OFFICES

**Victoria Station Forecourt, W1**
Open Apr–Oct 8am–6pm; bookshop and Britain desk Mon–Sat 8am–7.30pm, Sun 8am–5.30pm

**Selfridges Store, Oxford Street, W1**
Open store hours

**Harrods, Knightsbridge, SW1**
Open store hours

**Liverpool Street Station**
Open Mon–Sat 9.30am–6.30pm, Sun 8.30am–3.30pm

**Tower of London (West Gate) EC3**
Open Apr–Oct daily 10am–6pm.
Telephone enquiries Mon–Fri 9am–5.30pm on 071–730–3488

Places within the London postal area are listed in postal district order under East, North, South and West. Other places within Greater London or the surrounding area are listed under their respective place names.

## ✦ EAST ✦

### E2

**BETHNAL GREEN MUSEUM OF CHILDHOOD**
Cambridge Heath Road
A branch of the Victoria and Albert Museum. Its chief exhibits are toys, dolls and dolls' houses, model soldiers, puppets, games, model theatres and children's costume. Children's art workshops on Sat 11 & 2. School holiday activities.

✆ 081 980 2415 & 081 980 3204.
Open: Mon–Thu & Sat 10–5.30, Sun 2.30–6. (Closed Fri, May Day, 24–26 Dec & New Year's Day.)
♿ (prior arrangement: transport lift can be used to reach upper floor with staff assistance). Shop ✸ (ex guide dogs).

**GEFFRYE MUSEUM**
Kingsland Road
The Museum is named after Sir Robert Geffrye, Lord Mayor of London in 1685 and Master of the Ironmongers' Company. He left in his will provision for 14 almshouses and a chapel for the poor. The buildings were opened in 1714 and in 1914 were converted to a Museum of Furniture Making, the local industry. Set in the East End of London, the Geffrye Museum tells the fascinating story of the British front room. Eleven room displays from 1600 to the 1950s show the changes in design and technology in homes of the middle classes. Exhibits include a reconstruction of John Evelyn's 'closet of curiosities'.

✆ 071 739 8368.
Open: Tue–Sat 10–5 Sun 2–5, BH Mons 10–5. (Closed Mon, Good Fri, 24–26 Dec & New Year's Day.)
🚼 (Tue–Sat 10.30–4.30, Sun 2–5)

♿ (ground floor only) toilets for the disabled. Shop 🚹 ✸ (ex guide dogs).

### E6

**EAST HAM NATURE RESERVE**
Norman Road
Ten acres of 'derelict' churchyard in the heart of urban east London provides a haven for nearly 50 kinds of wild birds, over 20 species of butterfly and much more. Several nature trails explore the areas of grassland, woodland, hedges and the artificial pond; there is a special trail for wheelchair users and a Braille version of the trail guide.

✆ 081 470 4525.
Open: Reserve Mon–Fri 9–5; Sat & Sun 2–5 (closes at dusk in winter); Visitor Centre Sat & Sun only 2–5. Coach parties must book in advance.
♿ (special trail) toilets for the disabled. Shop.

### E15

**PASSMORE EDWARDS MUSEUM**
Romford Road, Stratford
Recently refurbished Victorian museum housing displays on the landscape, archaeology, natural history and history of Newham and neighbouring areas. Special exhibition gallery.

✆ 081 534 0276.
Open: Wed–Fri 11–5, Sat 1–5, Sun & BH 2–5. Prior booking essential for parties.
♿ (ground floor & limited other areas only). Shop.

### E16

**NORTH WOOLWICH OLD STATION MUSEUM**
Pier Road
Imposing restored station building with three galleries of photographs, models and an original turntable pit. From Apr–Oct, on the first Sunday in the month, a locomotive is in steam.

✆ 071 474 7244.
Open: Mon–Wed & Sat, 10–5; Sun & BH 2–5. (Closed 25–26 Dec.) Guided

tours available for advance group bookings by special arrangement. Parties by prior appointment.
♿ toilets for the disabled. Shop ✸ (ex guide dogs).

### E17

**VESTRY HOUSE MUSEUM**
Vestry Road, Walthamstow
Housed in an 18th-century workhouse standing in the Walthamstow Village Conservation Area. The house retains many original features including a mid 19th-century police cell. Historical items of local interest include a reconstructed Victorian parlour, a permanent display, 'Hearth and Home' – the story of domestic life in Waltham Forest one hundred years ago – and the Bremer Car, probably the first British internal combustion engine car seen, which was built locally c1894. Local archives are available for consultation by appointment.

✆ 081 509 1917.
Open: Mon–Fri 10–1 & 2–5.30, Sat 10–1 & 2–5. Guided tours available for special parties by prior arrangment. Parties by appointment.
♿ (ground floor only) Shop ✸

**WILLIAM MORRIS GALLERY**
Lloyd Park, Forest road, Walthamstow
William Morris lived in this house, known as 'Water House' from 1848–56. There are exhibits of his fabrics, wallpapers and furniture. Also ceramics by William de Morgan, furniture by Gimson and Barnsley and work by Mackmurdo and the Century Guild. Pre-Raphaelite pictures, sculpture by Rodin. Events throughout the year.

✆ 081 527 3782, or 081 527 5544 Ext 4390.
Open: Tue–Sat 10–1 & 2–5, and 1st Sun in each month 10–12 & 2–5. (Closed: Mon & PHs.) Donations box. Guided tours available (charge) by prior arrangement, min 10 persons. Parties accepted by appointment only, max 50 persons.
♿ (ground floor & gardens) Shop ✸

## EC1

### MOUNT PLEASANT LETTER DISTRICT OFFICE

Farringdon Road
The largest letter sorting office in Europe. Experience 'the journey of a letter', from the moment it enters the sorting office until it reaches its final destination. See the underground Mail Rail, which conveys a yearly average of ten million sacks of mail across London on automatically-controlled trains. The system was installed in 1927 and several of the original trains have been preserved.

✆ 071 239 2191/2188.
Open: mid Jan–mid Nov Mon–Fri 10 or 10.30, 2 or 2.30 & 7 for organised visits (1½–3 hrs) only. (Closed BH). Prior arrangement required. All bookings must be confirmed in writing at least 10 days before visit date.

### MUSEUM OF THE ORDER OF ST JOHN

St John's Gate, St John's Lane
16th-century gatehouse, former entrance to the medieval Priory of the Order of St John of Jerusalem. Now headquarters of the modern Order, whose charitable foundations include St John Ambulance and the Opthalmic Hospital in Jerusalem. Norman crypt and 15th-century Grand Priory Church. The museum collections include paintings, silver, furniture, medals and insignia. The St John Ambulance museum has medical instruments, photographs, uniforms and personal memorabilia of St John personalities and pioneers with special features on the St John Ambulance role in the Boer War and World Wars.

✆ 071 253 6644.
Open: Mon–Fri 10–5, Sat 10–4. (Closed Etr, Xmas wk and BHs.) Donations. Guided tours 11 and 2.30 on Tue, Fri & Sat (donation requested, about £1 per head). Parties by prior arrangement only. ♿ (ground floor only) toilets for the disabled. Shop.

### NATIONAL POSTAL MUSEUM

King Edward Building, King Edward St
Contains probably the finest and most comprehensive collection of British postage stamps and related material in the world. Included are: the R. M. Phillips collection of 19th-century Great Britain (with special emphasis on the One Penny Black and its creation); the Post Office Collection: a world-wide collection including practically every stamp issued since 1878, and, on microfilm, the philatelic correspondence archives of Thomas de la Rue and Co who furnished stamps to over 150 countries between 1855 and 1965. Within these collections are thousands of original drawings and unique proof sheets of every British stamp since 1840. Special exhibitions.

✆ 071 239 5420.
Open: Mon–Thu (ex BH) 9.30–4.30, Fri 9.30–4. Guided tours available by prior arrangement, Tue–Thu 10–12 & 2–4. Parties by prior appointment (50 max; 25+ split into 2 groups). ♿ (by prior arrangement & in small numbers; ground floor & top galleries only, the latter via Post Office lift.) Shop ✖

## EC2

### BANK OF ENGLAND MUSEUM

Threadneedle Street, Entrance is in Bartholomew Lane
The museum both illustrates the history of this famous British financial institution since 1694 and gives an insight into its current functions. Displays include gold bars, bank notes and a modern dealing desk, with interactive videos.

✆ 071 601 5545.
Open: Mon–Fri and PHs 10–5, Etr–Sep, Sun & BH 11–5. ♿ (with assistance from staff, ramps) 'touch sessions' for blind visitors by prior arrangement, toilets for the disabled.

### GUILDHALL

Off Gresham Street
Rebuilt in 1411 but only the walls of the great hall, porch and crypt survive from the medieval building. It was severely damaged in the Great Fire and the Blitz. Restoration work, completed in 1954 was carried out to designs by Sir Giles Scott. The Court of Common Council, which administers the city, meets and entertains here. The **Guildhall Library** contains an unrivalled collection of books, manuscripts, and illustrations on all aspects of London. The **Guildhall Clock Museum** with 700 exhibits illustrates 500 years of time keeping.

✆ 071 606 3030.
Open: daily May–Sep 10–5, Oct–Apr Mon–Sat 10–5. (Closed Xmas, New Year, Good Fri, Etr Mon & infrequently for civic occasions.) Guided tours available by advance arrangement with Keeper's Office. Parties accepted (40 max). Shop ✖ (ex guide dogs).

### MUSEUM OF LONDON

London Wall
The museum was formed by amalgamating the former London Museum and the Guildhall Museum and is devoted entirely to the story of London and its people during the past 2,000 years. Included are the Lord Mayor's State Coach, a barber's shop from Islington, sculptures from the Temple of Mithras, a 1930 Ford, Selfridge's lift, a medieval hen's egg, a Roman 'bikini' and the Great Fire Experience.

✆ 071 600 3699 Ext 240 or 280.
Open: Tue–Sat 10–6, Sun 2–6. (Closed Mon & Xmas.) Parties by arrangement. ⌷ (licensed) ♿ (ramps & lift) some tactile displays, braille notes & audio facilities, toilets for the disabled. Shop ✖ (ex guide dogs).

## EC3

### LONDON METAL EXCHANGE

Fenchurch Street
Visits (by appointment only) are of

*The 'wedding cake' spire of St Bride's Church, EC4*

interest to people involved in or studying the metal industry or the financial markets of London. The LME is the world's largest futures market for non-ferrous metals.

℘ 071 626 3311.
Open: by appointment only Mon–Fri 12–1. Guided tour consists of video, brief talk & viewing of market in operation.

## EC4
**MIDDLE TEMPLE HALL**
The Temple
A fine example of Tudor architecture built during the reign of Queen Elizabeth I and completed about 1570. Hall features double hammer beam roof. Also stained glass showing shields of past readers. The most treasured possession is the 29 ft long high table, made from a single oak tree of Windsor Forest. Another table was made from timbers of the Golden Hind in which Sir Francis

Drake, a member of the Middle Temple, sailed around the world. Portraits of George I, Elizabeth I, Anne, Charles I, Charles II, James, Duke of York and William III line the walls behind the high table.

℘ 071 353 4355.
Open: Mon–Fri 10–12 & 3–4. (Closed: Aug, Xmas fortnight & week after Etr & Whitsun.) Guided tours available. Coach parties not accepted.

**ST BRIDES CHURCH**
Fleet Street
Internationally known as the 'parish church of the press'. It has been the site of seven previous churches, the existing structure having been meticulously restored to Wren's original design. A wealth of history and relics can be seen on permanent display in the crypt museum. Roman pavement.

℘ 071 353 1301.
Open: daily 9–5 (Closed BHs.)
Guided tours available by appointment.
Shop

**THE STORY OF TELECOMMUNICATIONS**
145 Queen Victoria St
Two display floors featuring the past, present and future of Britain's telecommunications. There are many working exhibits charting 200 years of progress from the earliest telegraphs, to satellites and optical fibres.

℘ 071 248 7444.
Open: Mon–Fri 10–5 (Closed BH.)
Shop (ex guide dogs).

## ✦ NORTH ✦
### N17
**BRUCE CASTLE MUSEUM**
Lordship Lane, Tottenham

An E-shaped part Elizabethan, part Jacobean and Georgian building with an adjacent circular 16th-century tower, which stands in a small park. The museum contains

sections on local history, postal history and the Middlesex Regiment, also known as the 'diehards'.

℘ 081 808 8772.
Open: Tue–Sun 1–5. (Closed Mon, Good Fri, Xmas & New Year's Day.)
Guided tours available only by prior arrangement with the Curator.
(Bruce Castle Park) (ground floor & grounds only)

### N22
**ALEXANDRA PALACE AND PARK**
Wood Green
The Palm Court area and the 196-acre park are free to the public. Alexandra Park facilities include a small animal enclosure, children's playground and paddling pool. The boating lake and pitch and putt are chargeable as are the two major exhibition halls for exhibitions and events.

℘ 081 365 2121.
Open: all year, daily (ex Xmas Day) 10–5.
(10–4.30 & public house) (ground floor & grounds) Health food shop, Garden centre.

### NW1
**CECIL SHARP HOUSE**
2 Regents Park Road
Devoted to the English folk dance, folk music and folk song heritage. Unique Vaughan Williams Memorial Library.

℘ 071 485 2206.
Open: Mon–Fri 9–5.30 (days & times sometimes extended). Guided tours & parties by arrangement only.
Shop.

**REGENT'S PARK**
The elegant charm of this park can be attributed to John Nash who laid it out along with the imposing surrounding terraces. There is a boating lake, open-air theatre and the lovely Queen Mary's Rose Garden. There are a number of Victorian garden ornaments around the park, and a group of fossil tree trunks.

## NW3

### KEATS HOUSE

Keats Grove, Hampstead
Regency house, former home of the
poet Keats. *Ode to the Nightingale*
was written in the garden.
Manuscripts and relics.

℘ 071 435 2062.
Open: Apr–Oct Mon–Fri 10–1 & 2–6;
Sat 10–1 & 2–5, Sun & BHs 2–5; Nov–
Mar Mon–Fri 1–5, Sat 10–1 & 2–5, Sun
2–5. Donations. Guided tours by
appointment only (max 25).
Shop ✻

### KENWOOD, IVEAGH BEQUEST

Hampstead Lane
Mansion re-modelled c1765 by
Robert Adam, with fine grounds,
bequeathed to the nation in 1927 by
Lord Iveagh. Notable library,
furniture and works of art including
paintings by Rembrandt, Hals,
Vermeer, Reynolds and
Gainsborough. Collections of 18th-
century shoebuckles and jewellery.
Summer lakeside concerts.

℘ 081 348 1286.
Open: daily; Apr–Sep 10–6; Oct–Mar
10–4. (Closed 24–25 Dec.)
⌨ ♿ (ground floor & garden only)
toilets for the disabled. Shop
✻ (except in grounds).

## NW4

### CHURCH FARM HOUSE MUSEUM

Greyhound Hill
Old gabled house, dating from
1660s, now museum of local
interest. Period furnished kitchen
and dining room. Changing
exhibitions.

℘ 081 203 0130.
Open: all year, Mon–Sat 10–1 & 2–
5.30 (Tue 10–1 only). Sun 2–5.30.
(Closed Good Fri, 25–26 Dec, 1 Jan.)
Shop ✻

## NW8

### PRIMROSE HILL

St Johns Wood
Once part of the same hunting
forest as Regent's Park, Primrose
Hill retains in its name the rural
character and charm it once had.

The view from the summit is
panoramic, encompassing virtually
the whole of central London.

## NW10

### GRANGE MUSEUM OF COMMUNITY HISTORY

Neasden roundabout
Dating from around 1700, the
building originally formed part of
the outbuildings of a large farm and
was later converted into a Gothic
cottage. Permanent collections tell
the story of the area that is now the
London Borough of Brent. Changing
temporary exhibitions, local history
library, display on the British
Empire Exhibition for which
Wembley Stadium was built. Two
period rooms of late 19th century
and early 20th century, and
reconstructed draper's shop.
Visitors can picnic in the
conservatory.

℘ 081 908 7432.
Open: all year, Tue–Thu, 12–5 Sat
10–12 & 1–5. Parties by advanced
booking only.
⌨ ♿ (ground floor only) Shop
✻ (ex guide dogs).

## ✦ SOUTH ✦

## SE1

### THE MUSEUM OF GARDEN HISTORY

St Mary-at-Lambeth, Lambeth
Palace Road
Historic building and replica 17th-
century knot garden containing
plants of the period. Exhibits
relating to garden history. Replica
17th-century garden in which stand
the tombs of the John Tradescants
(father and son), gardeners to
Charles I & II and famous plant-
hunters, and Captain Bligh of the
*Bounty*. Exhibitions, concerts, plant
fair, craft fair and lectures.
Enquiries to: The Tradescant Trust,
74 Coleherne Court, London SW5
0EF.

℘ 071 261 1891 (11–3).
Open: Mon–Fri, 11–3; Sun 10.30–5.
(Closed Sat & from 2nd Sun in Dec to
1st Sun in Mar.) Donations. Group

visits by prior appointment only.
⌨ ♿ (ramps) Shop.

## SE3

### RANGERS HOUSE

Chesterfield Walk
Suffolk collection of Jacobean and
Stuart portraits housed in 18th-
century villa, former home of Philip
Stanhope, 4th Earl of Chesterfield.
Collection contains a set of
portraits by William Larkin, among
the finest to survive from the
Jacobean period, and a small
collection of Old Masters. Three
first floor rooms house the
Dolmetsch collection of musical
instruments, on loan from the
Horniman Museum. The chintz
bedroom contains walnut furniture
of the early 18th century. Also
chamber concerts and poetry
readings. Educational programmes.

℘ 081 853 0035.
Open: all year, except Mon in Winter.
Summer 10–6, Winter 10–4.
♿ (ground floor only) Shop ✻

## SE5

### SOUTH LONDON ART GALLERY

65 Peckham Road
Presents six exhibitions a year,
mostly of contemporary art, in
media including painting, sculpture,
print, photography, installation and
video; contributors are drawn from
sources throughout the UK. The
purpose-built gallery space, housed
in a Grade II listed building of 1891,
provides one of the finest
environments possible in which to
view modern works of art.

℘ 071 703 6120.
Open: during exhibitions, Tue–Fri 10–
6, Thu 10–8, Sun 3–6 (Closed Mon,
Sat & BH weekends.)
Shop ✻

## SE9

### ELTHAM PALACE

(Off Court Yard)
Royal manor dating from the 13th
century, largely rebuilt from the
15th century onwards. Noted for
great hall with remarkable 15th-

century hammer-beam roof. The bridge over the moat also survives.

✆ 081 854 2242 Ext 4232.
Open: Nov–Mar, Thu & Sun 11–4;
Apr–Oct, Thu & Sun 11–7.
&
(AM)

**WINTER GARDENS**
Avery Hill Park
Approximately 750 species of tropical and temperate plants can be seen here in cold, temperate and tropical houses, a collection second only to the Royal Botanical Gardens at Kew. Tennis and putting available.

✆ 081 850 3217.
Open: all year Mon–Fri 1–4, Sat, Sun & BH 11–4.30 (6pm summer).
(Closed 1st Mon each month & 25 Dec.)
🖃 &

## SE10

**GREENWICH PARK**
On the northern perimeter of this delightful park is the largest children's playground in any Royal Park. It is most famous though, as the home of the Old Royal Observatory (charge) and the Greenwich Meridian which marks Nought Degrees Longitude. There are wonderful views over the Royal Naval College and the Thames. The Wilderness is 13 acres of woodland, inhabited by a herd of fallow deer.

**ROYAL NAVAL COLLEGE PAINTED HALL & CHAPEL**
King William Walk, Greenwich
Group of buildings designed by Webb (late 17th century) and Wren (early 18th century), with additions by Hawksmoor, Vanbrugh and Ripley. Formerly Naval Hospital, becoming College in 1873. Chapel rebuilt in 18th century, and Painted Hall ceiling by Sir James Thornhill.

✆ 081 858 2154.
Open: all year (Painted Hall & Chapel only) daily (ex Thu) 2.30–5 (last admission 4.30). (Closed 24

Dec–1 Jan.) Coach parties not accepted.
✖

## SE15

**LIVESEY MUSEUM**
682 Old Kent Road
Museum has a lively exhibition programme based on popular history and scientific subjects; generally two exhibitions a year, but no permanent displays.

✆ 071 639 5604.
Open: when exhibition is in progress, Mon–Sat 10–5.
✖ (ex guide dogs). & (ground floor only) Shop.

## SE17

**CUMING MUSEUM**
155–157 Walworth Road
Tells the story of Southwark's history from Roman times onwards. Special displays on Shakespeare, Dickens and Michael Faraday. Temporary exhibition programme highlights different parts of the collection.

✆ 071 701 1342.
Open: all year Tue–Sat, 10–5. Parties by arrangement.
Shop.

## SE18

**MUSEUM OF ARTILLERY IN THE ROTUNDA**
Repository Road, Woolwich
Circular structure designed by John Nash, which stood at one time in Carlton House Gardens, near St James's Park. It contains a very interesting collection of artillery.

✆ 081 316 5402.
Open: all year, Apr–Oct, Mon–Fri 12–5, Sat & Sun 1–5; Nov–Mar, Mon–Fri 12–4, Sat & Sun 1–4. (Closed Good Fri, 24–26 Dec & 1 Jan.) Donation box. Guided tours available by prior arrangement.
& (ground floor only) Shop.

**ROYAL ARTILLERY REGIMENTAL MUSEUM**
Old Royal Military Academy, Woolwich

The museum tells the history of the Royal Artillery in pictures, uniforms and militaria. Housed on the upper floor of the central tower block of the old RMA.

✆ 081 854 2242 Ext 5628.
Open: daily Mon–Fri 12.30–4.30, Sat–Sun 2–5 (weekends Nov–Mar 2–4).
(Closed Good Fri, 24–26 Dec & 1 Jan.) Donations. Guided tours occasionally available by prior arrangement only. Parties by prior appointment. Pedestrian access only via the East Gate to the parade ground.

## SE23

**HORNIMAN MUSEUM**
London Road
Ethnographical and large natural history collections including vivaria. Exhibition of musical instruments from all parts of the world. Extensive library and lectures and concerts in spring and autumn. Special exhibitions. Education Centre programmes.

✆ 081 699 2339.
Open: all year Mon–Sat 10.30–6, Sun 2–6. (Closed 24–26 Dec.)
🖃 & Shop ✖ (ex guide dogs).

## SW1

**DESIGN CENTRE**
28 Haymarket
Regular exhibitions, held on the ground floor of the centre, demonstrate the role of design in the British economy. There is a Central Resources Point highlighting all the activities of the Design Council. The most comprehensive design bookshop in Europe and a Young Designers Centre.

✆ 071 839 8000.
Open: Mon–Sat 10–8, Sun 1–6.
Guided tours available for educational groups by prior arrangement. Parties not accepted (ex educational groups).
& (advance notice please).

## GREEN PARK

The smallest of the central London parks, Green Park is situated in the triangle formed by Piccadilly, The Mall and Constitution Hill. Formerly meadowland, its informal character is maintained today. There are no flower borders here, just the springtime crocuses and daffodils which grow among the grass.

## HOUSES OF PARLIAMENT

A mid 19th-century building in Gothic style based on a design by Sir Charles Barry with additional detail by Augustus Pugin, the original building having been destroyed by fire in 1834. Two chambers are set either side of a central hall and corridor, the House of Lords to the south and the House of Commons to the north. The clock tower, 314 ft high, contains Big Ben, the 13½ ton hour bell, while the Victoria tower stands 323 ft high. The House of Commons suffered bomb damage in 1941 and a new chamber designed by Sir Giles Gilbert Scott was opened in 1950.

✆ 071 219 4272.
To gain admission to the Strangers' Galleries join the queue at St Stephen's entrance from approx 4.30 Mon–Thu, approx 9.30 Fri (House of Commons) or from approx 2.30 Tue & Wed, from 3 Thu & occasionally 11 Fri (House of Lords) or by arrangement with MP (House of Commons) or Peer (House of Lords). Tours must be arranged through an MP. Free, although guides require payment if employed.
& (by arrangement) Bookstall ✻ (ex guide dogs)

ALSO **WESTMINSTER HALL**
Built 1097–99 by William Rufus, it is the oldest remaining part of Westminster. The glory of the hall is the cantilever or hammerbeam roof, the earliest and largest roof of its kind in existence, built between 1394 and 1401.

✆ 071 219 4272.
Tours am by arrangement with an MP only. Free, although guides require

payment if employed.
& (by arrangement) ✻ (ex guide dogs).

## ST JAMES'S PARK

Situated between Buckingham Palace and Whitehall, this is the oldest of the Royal Parks, created originally by Henry VIII. Remodelled by Charles II, this latest version was created by Nash for George IV and remains one of the most delightful and popular places to relax. There are band concerts and refreshment facilities.

## TATE GALLERY
Millbank

Opened in 1897 the gallery comprises the national collections of British painting and 20th-century painting and sculpture. Hogarth, Blake, Turner, Constable and the Pre-Raphaelites are particularly well represented in the British Collection and the Modern Collection traces the development of art from Impressionism through postwar European and American art including Abstract Impressionism and Pop, to the present day. Displays from the Collection change annually to explore its wealth and variety, following a chronological sequence from the 16th century to the present day. The Clore Gallery houses the Turner Collection.

✆ 071 821 1313; 071 821 7128 recorded information.
Open: all year (ex Good Fri, May Day, 24–26 Dec & 1 Jan) Mon–Sat 10–5.50, Sun 2–5.50. Free (ex for special loan exhibitions). Guided tours are available. (Groups accepted with prior notice to Education Department.)
♬ (licensed) 12–3 (closed Sun) (coffee shop) 10.30–5.30, Sun 2–5.15.
& (a limited number of wheelchairs can be made available on request) . toilets for the disabled. Shop ✻ (ex guide dogs).

## SW3

### NATIONAL ARMY MUSEUM
Royal Hospital Road
Contains a permanent chronological

display of the history of the British, Indian and Colonial forces from 1485. Life-size reconstructions of the life of a soldier through the ages to the 20th century and audio-visual displays. Uniforms, weapons, prints, photographs, manuscripts, letters, glass, china, silver and relics of British commanders and mementoes of Britain's soldiers. There is a special display of the orders and decorations of the Duke of Windsor and also those of five great field marshals – Lords Roberts, Gough, Kitchener and Wolseley and Sir George White VC. The picture gallery includes portraits by Beechy, Romney and Lawrence, battle scenes and pictures of Indian regiments. Regular special exhibitions and events.

✆ 071 730 0717.
Open: all year daily 10–5.30. (Closed Good Fri, May Day, 24–26 Dec & 1 Jan.) The reading room is open Tue–Sat 10–4.30 to holders of readers' tickets, obtainable by written application to the Director. Guided tours available for parties by prior arrangement. Car & coach parking by prior arrangement.
♬ (Mon–Sat 10–4.15 Sun 12–4.15 & toilets for the disabled. Shop ✻

## ✦ WEST ✦

## W1

### AGNEW'S GALLERIES
43 Old Bond Street

London galleries established in 1860. Annual exhibitions include one devoted to English watercolours and drawings of the 18th and 19th centuries, and an exhibition of Old Master paintings (for sale) from the 14th to 19th centuries. There are also exhibitions of French and English drawings from c1800 to the present day, work by English painters of this century and loan exhibitions in aid of charity. Many works pass through Agnew's on their way to famous art galleries and museums.

✆ 071 629 6176.

Open: all year Mon–Fri, 9.30–5.30 (6.30pm Thu, during major exhibitions). (Closed BH.) Admission charge for some loan exhibitions. ₺ (ground floor only).

**MUSEUM OF MANKIND**
6 Burlington Gardens
Houses the exhibitions and offices of the Ethnography Department of the British Museum. The department has one of the world's greatest collections from the indigenous peoples of Africa, North and South America, Australia and the Pacific Islands and parts of Europe and Asia, with ancient as well as contemporary cultures represented. Some important pieces are on permanent display, but the museum's policy is to mount a number of temporary exhibitions, usually lasting for at least a year.

✆ 071 636 1555 Ext 8043. Open: all year Mon–Sat 10–5, Sun 2.30–6. (Closed Good Fri, May Day, 24–26 Dec & 1 Jan.) Donations welcome. Study sessions available by prior arrangement for educational visits only (✆ 071 323 8065). ₺ (ramps; one room only not accessible). Touch sessions for blind people can be arranged in advance through Education Department. Shop ◈ (ex guide dogs).

**WALLACE COLLECTION**
Manchester Sq
An outstanding collection of works of art bequeathed to the nation by Lady Wallace in 1897, displayed in the house of its founders. Includes pictures by Titian, Rubens, Gainsborough and Delacroix together with an unrivalled representation of 18th-century French art including paintings, especially of Watteau, Boucher and Fragonard, sculpture, furniture, goldsmiths' work and Sèvres porcelain. Also valuable collections of majolica, European and oriental arms and armour.

✆ 071 935 0687.
Open: all year Mon–Sat 10–5, Sun 2–5. (Closed Good Fri, May Day, 24–26 Dec & 1 Jan.) Guided tours available for educational groups (25 max), other groups charged. ₺ Shop ◈

## W2
**HYDE PARK**
Situated to the west of Park Lane between Knightsbridge and Bayswater, this former Royal hunting park now consists of 340 acres of grass and trees. The Serpentine, at its centre, provides a habitat for wild creatures and opportunities for boating. It is probably best known for Speakers' Corner near Marble Arch where, every Sunday, anyone can stand up and say just what they please.

## W3
**GUNNERSBURY PARK MUSEUM**
Gunnersbury Park
Early 19th-century former Rothschild mansion, in fine park, now museum of local interest for the London Borough of Ealing and Hounslow with collections of archaeological discoveries, transport items, costume and topographical and social material Rothschild coaches on display. Rothschild Victorian kitchens open to public on summer weekends. Changing exhibitions.

✆ 081 992 1612.
Open: Mar–Oct (end of British Summer Time) Mon–Fri 1–5, Sat, Sun & BH 1–6; Nov–Feb, Mon–Fri 1–4, Sat, Sun & BH 1–4. (Closed Good Fri, 24–26 Dec & 1 Jan.) Donations. Guided tours & coach parties must be booked at least 2 wks in advance. ₺ (ground floor only) Shop ◈

## W4
**HOGARTH'S HOUSE**
Hogarth Lane, Great West Road
17th-century house where Hogarth lived for 15 years, with engravings, drawings and other relics on display.

✆ 081 994 6757.
Open: all year 11–6, Sun 2–6 (4pm Oct–Mar). (Closed Tue & Good Fri, 1st two weeks Sep, last 3 weeks Dec & 1 Jan.) Guided tours are available. Parties (50 max) must pre-book visit. ₺ (ground floor only) Shop.

## W8
**COMMONWEALTH INSTITUTE**
Kensington High Street
The history, landscapes, wildlife, crafts and economies of the 48 →

countries of the Commonwealth on 3 floors of spectacular galleries. Also lectures and children's holiday workshops.

℘ 071 603 4535.
Open: Mon–Sat 10–5, Sun 2–5. (Closed Good Fri, May Day, 24–26 Dec & 1 Jan.) Special exhibitions admission charge. Guided tours are available: contact Education Division. Parties must be booked in advance. ⌂ (licensed) ♿ (some areas are difficult, but staff are happy to help; prior notice please) toilets for the disabled. Shop ✇ (ex guide dogs).

### KENSINGTON GARDENS

Once part of Hyde Park, then the private garden of Kensington Palace, Kensington Gardens are noted for their tranquility and formality. They include the Round Pond, Queen Anne's Orangery, the Sunken Garden, the Flower Walk and the famous statue of Peter Pan.

## W14

### LEIGHTON HOUSE

12 Holland Park Road
Leighton House is a uniquely opulent and exotic example of High Victorian taste. Built for the President of the Royal Academy, Frederic, Lord Leighton, by George Aitchison, the main body of the house was completed in 1866. The fabulous Arab Hall, with its rare middle-eastern tiles, fountain and gilded decoration, is a 19th-century Arabian Nights' creation finished in 1879. Fine Victorian paintings by Lord Leighton and his contemporaries hang in the rooms, and there are two galleries for exhibitions of modern and historic art. The quiet garden is ornamented with Lord Leighton's sculpture.

℘ 071 602 3316.
Open: all year, Mon–Sat 11–5 (6pm during temporary exhibitions). (Closed Sun & BH.) Garden open Apr–Sep 11–5. Donations.
♿ (ground floor) Shop. ✇

## WC1

### BRITISH MUSEUM

Great Russell Street
Founded in 1753, one of the great museums, showing the works of man from prehistoric to comparatively modern times. The galleries are the responsibility of the following departments: Egyptian; Greek and Roman; Western Asiatic, Prehistoric and Romano-British; Medieval and Later; Coins and Medals; Japanese; Oriental; Prints and drawings. Each year special exhibitions focus more detailed attention on certain aspects of the collections. Programmes on request. Gallery talks (Tue–Sat) Lectures (Tue–Sat) and Films (Tue–Fri). Children's trail at all times.

℘ 071 636 1555.
Open: all year, Mon–Sat 10–5, Sun 2.30–6. (Closed Good Fri, May Day, 24–26 Dec & 1 Jan.) Donations welcome (cash or credit card) Occasional charge for special exhibitions.
⌂ (licensed) ♿ (Bell at main entrance steps; wheelchairs & portable stools available; service lift to basement galleries. Please advise of visit in advance.) Limited parking for the disabled (prior booking essential on 071–636 1555 Ext 8387); some tactile displays & sign language talks (contact Education Dept); lecture theatre induction loop, toilets for the disabled. Shop ✇ (ex guide dogs).

### JEWISH MUSEUM

Woburn House, Tavistock Sq
A collection of ceremonial art, portraits and antiques illustrating Jewish-life, history and religion. There are also two audio-visual programmes explaining Jewish festivals and ceremonies.

℘ 071 388 4525.
Open: Tue–Fri & Sun 10–4 (Opens 12.45 on Fri during winter.) (Closed Public & Jewish Hols.) Donations.
♿ Shop ✇

### PERCIVAL DAVID FOUNDATION OF CHINESE ART

53 Gordon Square

A unique collection of Chinese ceramics, mainly dating between the 10th and 18th centuries: the Song, Yuan, Ming and Quing dynasties. Presented to London University by Percival David in 1951.

℘ 071 387 3909.
Open: Mon–Fri 10.30–5. (Closed weekends & BHs.) Donations welcomed. Guided tours for groups (max 20) arranged in advance, min donation £2 per person. Parties accepted (max 20).
♿ (prior notice required – will provide assistance for entrance steps) lift to all floors, toilets for the disabled. Shop.

## WC2

### AFRICA CENTRE

38 King Street
The Centre is housed in an 18th-century building and is the only one in Britain dedicated to African culture. In the Visual Arts Gallery, there are displays of paintings, photographs and craftware by African artists.

℘ 071 836 1973.
Open: Gallery Mon–Fri 10–6, Sat 11–4. Donations.

### CONTEMPORARY APPLIED ARTS

43 Earlham Street, Covent Garden
Programme of special exhibitions throughout the year and retail display including fine textiles, furniture, studio ceramics, pottery, wood, jewellery etc; books and magazines for craft and design.

℘ 071 836 6993.
Open: all year, Mon–Sat 10–5.30. (Closed Sun & BH.) Parties (max 15) accepted with 1 month's notice.
♿ (ground floor only) Shop ✇

### LONDON SILVER VAULTS

53–64 Chancery Lane
Situated below ground, it comprises approximately 35 vaults owned by different companies and is the largest display of silver in the world. There are also jewellery shops.

✆ 071 242 3844/5.
Open: Mon–Fri 9–5.30, Sat 9–12.30.
(Closed BHs.) Guided tours available
by arrangement. Parties must split into
6 max.
♿ (lift & ramps).

**NATIONAL GALLERY**
Trafalgar Square
Founded by vote of Parliament in
1824, but was first opened in the
present building in 1838. The
gallery houses the national
collection of masterpieces of
Western paintings from the 13th to
early 20th century. Collection
includes van Eyck's *Arnolfini
Marriage*, Velázquez's *The Toilet of
Venus*, Leonardo da Vinci's cartoon
*The Virgin and Child with SS Anne
and John the Baptist*, Rembrandt's
*Belshazzar's Feast*, Titian's *Bacchus
and Ariadne*, and many more.
Lunchtime lectures and guided
tours Mon–Sat only; quizzes and
worksheets available for school
groups pre-booked with Education
Department. Constantly changing
programme of exhibitions, usually
highlighting certain aspects of the
collection.

✆ 071 839 3321 & recorded
information: 071 839 3526.
Open: daily Mon–Sat 10–6, Sun 2–6.
(Closed Good Fri, May Day, 24–26
Dec & 1 Jan.) Guided tours available
Mon–Sat.
🖵 Mon–Sat 10–4.30, Sun 2–4.30,
(licensed) ♿ (lifts; small number of
wheelchairs available on application
to Chief Warder) lectures for the deaf
if booked in advance with Education
Department. Shop 🕮

**NATIONAL PORTRAIT GALLERY**
St Martin's Place
The Gallery was founded in 1856 to
collect the likenesses of famous
British men and women. The
collection includes paintings,
sculpture, miniatures, engravings,
photographs, and cartoons. It starts
from the 15th century and
continues chronologically through
to the present day. Special
exhibitions several times a year.

✆ 071 306 0055.

Open: all year Mon–Fri 10–5, Sat 10–
6, Sun 2–6. (Closed Good Fri, May
Day, 24–26 Dec & 1 Jan.) Donations.
(Charges for special exhibitions).
Guided tours can be booked for
groups through Education
Department.
♿ (part) toilets for the disabled.
Shop.

**THE PHOTOGRAPHER'S GALLERY**
5 & 8 Gt Newport Street
A lively exhibition programme
shows current concerns within the
contemporary independent
photographic sector, both
nationally and internationally.
Reference library, bookshop and
print room.

✆ 071 831 1772.
Open: Tue–Sat 11–7. Donations.
Parties & guided tours by prior
arrangement only.
🖵 (11–5.30) ♿ (ground floor only,
but staff will assist visitors upstairs if
requested). Shop.

**PUBLIC RECORD OFFICE MUSEUM**
Chancery Lane
Contain's permanent display of
records including the Domesday
Book, medieval charters and 19th-
century census returns. Other
items of interest include operations
record book for 73 Squadron, 1940,
poll tax return for Sheffield, 1379,
details of the funeral of the 'Grand
Old' Duke of York and the Police
Strike of 1919.

✆ 081 876 3444.
Open: Mon–Fri 10–5. Guided tours
available for groups by prior
arrangement. Large parties not
accepted.
♿ (ground floor only).

**SIR JOHN SOANE'S MUSEUM**
13 Lincoln's Inn Fields
The house of architect Sir John
Soane (1753–1837), built in 1812
and containing his collections of
antiquities, sculpture, paintings,
drawings, and books. Items of
interest include the Sarcophagus of
Seti I (1292 BC), the Rake's

*National Portrait Gallery*

Progress and the Election series of
paintings by William Hogarth.
Architectural Drawings Collection
open by appointment.

✆ 071 405 2107. Information line:
071 430 0175.
Open: all year Tue–Sat 10.5. Late
evening opening on first Tue of every
month, 6–9pm. Lecture tours Sat 2.30.
Groups must book in advance.
(Closed B.H.)
🕮

# LOTHERTON HALL
West Yorkshire

**LOTHERTON HALL BIRD GARDENS**
The Gardens, close to Leeds, are on
a charming rural estate set in
beautiful landscaped grounds with
waterfalls and ornamental ponds.
Two shire horses make trips
around the estate, which contains
one of the finest collections of
animals in the country – many of
them rare and endangered. Other
animals, such as deer, wallabies
and chinchillas, also live here.

✆ Leeds 0532 813723.
Open: Etr–Oct, Mon–Fri 10–4.15; Sat,
Sun & BH 11–6 (last admission 5.15).
Admission charged at Lotherton Hall.
🖵 📺 ♿

## LOWESTOFT
Suffolk

**ROYAL NAVAL PATROL SERVICE
ASSOCIATION (NAVAL MUSEUM)**
Sparrows Nest Gardens
The museum includes collections of hundreds of photographs from World War II, models of minesweepers and naval ships, war relics, war medals, naval uniforms and the Victoria Cross room.

℘ 0502 586250.

Open: daily Etr BH & May–Oct, 10–12 & 2–4.30. Coach parties by appointment.
☐ (licensed) ♿ (ground floor only) Shop.

## LUDGERSHALL
Wiltshire

**LUDGERSHALL CASTLE**
(7m NW of Andover on A342)
Norman motte and bailey castle with large earthworks and flint walling of later royal castle.

Open: all reasonable times.
♿ (part)
(AM)

## LUTON
Bedforshire

**MUSEUM AND ART GALLERY**
Wardown Park, Old Bedford Road
Collections illustrate natural history, culture, and industries of Luton and Bedfordshire with particular reference to straw hat and pillow lace trade. The Luton Life gallery includes a reconstructed street display.

℘ 0582 36941.
Open: daily, Mon–Sat 10–5, Sun 1–5. (Closed Xmas & New Year's Day.)
Donation box.
♿ (lift) Shop ✖

## LYDFORD
Devon

**LYDFORD CASTLE**
(8m S of Okehampton off A386)
Remains of late 12th-century stone

keep, altered a century later. The lower floor was once a prison and the upper floor became Stannary Court, established to administer local tin mines.

Open: at all reasonable times.
(AM)

## LYNMOUTH
Devon

**WATERSMEET ESTATE**
(1.5m E of Lynmouth on E side of A39 Lynmouth–Barnstaple rd)
Watersmeet is an estate of spectacularly beautiful landscape, fast-flowing rivers, wooded hillsides, high farmland and a small stretch of open moor, near Lynmouth in the Exmoor National Park. The house accommodates an Information Centre, restaurant and shop.

℘ 0598 53348.
Open: Information Centre Apr–Oct daily, refreshments 10.30–5.30, Shop 11–6 (facilities close 1 hr earlier in Oct). Coach parties by arrangement.
☐ 🚻 ♿ (ground floor & grounds; vehicular access by arrangement.)
✖ (in buildings, ex guide dogs).
(NT)

## MACCLESFIELD
Cheshire

**MACCLESFIELD RIVERSIDE PARK**
Beech Lane (Off the A523 Manchester road)
Managed by the Bollin Valley Project, Macclesfield Riverside Park offers country walks, woodland and rare breeds of cattle.

℘ 0625 511086 (Visitor Centre).
Open: Park accessible at all reasonable times; Visitor centre 10–4.
Guided tours are available.
Telephone for details. Parties by prior arrangement.
🚻 ♿ toilets for the disabled.

**WEST PARK MUSEUM**
West Park, Prestbury Road
One of the earliest public parks provides an attractive setting for this small museum, founded in 1898

by the Brocklehust family. Collections comprise a wide range of fine and decorative art, a small but significant collection of Egyptian antiquities and paintings dating from the 19th and early 20th centuries including the early work of Charles Tunnicliffe. There is a varied programme of temporary exhibitions.

℘ 0625 613210.
Open: all year Tue–Sun & BH (ex 25–26 Dec, 1 Jan & Good Fri) 2–5. Guided tours & coach parties by prior arrangement.
♿ (toilets in park). Shop ✖ (ex guide dogs).

## MADRON
Cornwall

**LANYON QUOIT**
(2m NW on unclass road)
A megalithic chambered long barrow dating from between 2000–1600 BC: a huge granite capstone 18 inches thick, almost 9 ft wide and 17 ft long balanced on three upright stones.

Open: accessible at all reasonable times.
(NT)

## MAESGWM
Gwynedd

**MAESGWM VISITOR CENTRE**
(off the A470, eight miles north of Dolgellau)
Depicts the forest environment, the life and work of the forest and the history of the local gold mines. Leaflets are available for the nearby trail and there are many picnic places, 50 miles of waymarked walks and a wildlife observation hide which can be booked by telephone. A slide show is presented in the Visitor Centre, there is an adventure playground and mountain bikes are available for hire.

℘ Dolgellau 0341 40666.
Open: Etr wk, then Whit–Oct daily 10–6. Guided walks Tue & Thu 10.30 (charge).
☐ ♿ toilet for the disabled. Shop.

## MAIDSTONE
Kent

**MUSEUM AND ART GALLERY**
Chillington Manor, St Faith's
Street
Historic Elizabethan manor house,
much extended over the years,
housing outstanding collections of
oil paintings and watercolours,
furniture, ceramics, costume,
natural history and local industry.
Further important collections of
ethnography, archaeology, and
Japanese fine and applied art. Also
on show is the museum of Queen's
Own Royal West Kent Regiment.

℘ 0622 754497.
Open: all year, Mon–Sat 10–5.30, BH
Mon 11–5. Introductory talk by
arrangement with education officer.
Coach parties by prior arrangement.
&. (part ground & 1st floor.) Shop ✇

**TYRWHITT-DRAKE MUSEUM OF
CARRIAGES**
Mill Street
Housed in the 14th-century stables
of the Archbishop's Palace, the
museum contains one of the finest
collections of horse-drawn
carriages in the country. State,
official and private carriages, some
on loan from the Royal collections,
are all represented, together with
livery and associated items.

℘ 0622 754497.

Open: Mon–Sat 10–1 & 2–5, (BH
Mons 11–5). (Closed Good Fri, 25–26
Dec & 1 Jan.) Parties by prior
arrangement only.
&. (ground floor only.) Shop.

## MALDON
Essex

**MALDON MARITIME CENTRE**
The Hythe
Photographs of Thames barges,
plus displays and artefacts of
marine interest. Tourist Information
Centre.

℘ 0621 856503/852290.
Open: all year (ex Feb), Tue–Sun
10–4. Parties by appointment only.
&. Shop.

## MALHAM
North Yorkshire

**YORKSHIRE DALES NATIONAL PARK
CENTRE**
Visitor Centre with interpretative
display and audio-visual theatre for
group use. Maps, walks, guides and
local information available. Picnic
area available.

℘ 0729 830363.
Open: daily Apr–Oct 9.30–5, plus
some winter weekends.
&.

## MALMESBURY
Wiltshire

**ATHELSTAN MUSEUM**
Cross Hayes
This small museum situated within
the Town Hall is named after the
Saxon King whose remains are at
nearby Malmesbury Abbey. The
collection is based on the history
and archaeology of the area, with
special displays of Malmesbury
lace, early costume, coins minted in
the town, early forms of transport
and a Roman burial of a child found
locally.

℘ 0666 822143/823748.
Open: Apr–Sep Tue–Sat 10.30–12.30
& 1–3 (until 4.30 when manned by
volunteers), Oct–Mar Wed, Fri & Sat
1–3. Donations. Parties by
appointment.
&. (ground floor only.)

## ✦ MAN, ISLE OF ✦

## DOUGLAS
Isle of Man

**MANX MUSEUM**
Items illustrate island's
archaeology, history, natural
history, folk life and art. Also
National Reference Library.
Exhibitions.

℘ 0624 75522.
Open: all year, Mon–Sat 10–5.
(Closed 25–26 Dec, 1 Jan, Good Fri &
the morning of 5 Jul.) Donation
requested.

&. (ground floor.) Shop ✇ (ex guide
dogs).

## MANCHESTER
Gt Manchester

**CASTLEFIELD URBAN HERITAGE
PARK**
Castlefield Information Centre,
330 Deansgate
The park includes a reconstructed
Roman Fort, the reclaimed canal
basin and canal, and the gallery of
modern art. The Museum of
Science and Industry and the
Granada Studio tour, also within the
park, have admission charges.

℘ 061 234 3157.
Open: all year Tue–Sat 10–5, Sun
12–5.
Guided tours on occasional basis.
&. Shop.

**CITY ART GALLERIES**
Mosley Street and Princess
Street
A sumptuous display of the city's
treasures in an architectural
masterpiece of the Greek Revival.
Paintings by the Old Masters,
Stubbs, Gainsborough, Turner, and
the Pre-Raphaelites. Outstanding
collections of decorative arts,
furniture, and sculpture. Temporary
exhibitions, workshops, classes and
talks.

℘ 061 236 5244.
Open: all year Mon–Sat 10–5.45, Sun
2–5.45 (ex 25–26 Dec & 1 Jan.)
Donation welcome. Lunchtime talks.
Coach parties by prior arrangement.
▯ Shop ✇

**FLETCHER MOSS MUSEUM AND ART
GALLERY**
Stenner Lane, off Wilmslow
Road, Didsbury (5.5m S of city
off A5145)
Formerly The Old Parsonage, set in
the Botanical Gardens, the Fletcher
Moss Museum and Art Gallery now
displays items made in or
associated with Manchester. There
is an Arts and Crafts Room,
permanent collection of late 19th
and early 20th century paintings
and temporary exhibitions during
the summer. →

℘ 061 236 9422. Ext 223.
Open: Apr–Oct, Wed–Mon 10–5.45
(Sun 2–5.45.) Donation welcome.
Coach parties by prior arrangement.
&. (ground floor) ✆

**FLETCHER MOSS BOTANICAL
GARDENS**
Wilmslow Road, Didsbury, S of
city on A5145)
The park was presented to the city
early this century and has been
transformed into beautiful botanical
gardens. Because of its sheltered
position the rock garden can grow
Alpine, dwarf and other unusual
plants. In addition there are
conifers, rhododendrons, many rare
shrubs and plants, an orchid house
and wild garden.

℘ 061 434 1877.
Open: all year, daily, weekdays 7.45–
dusk, weekends 9–dusk. Guided tours
by prior arrangement.
⌁ (daily 12–5) &. (part grounds)
toilets for the disabled.

**GALLERY OF ENGLISH COSTUME**
Platt Hall, Platt Fields,
Rusholme (2m SE of city)
Famous costume collection
displaying the changing styles of
everyday clothes and accessories of
the last 400 years. The exhibitions
change at regular intervals and no
one period is constantly on display.

℘ 061 224 5217.
Open: daily (ex Tue) 10–5.45, Sun 2–
6. Donation box. Coach parties by
prior arrangement.
&. (ground floor only) ✆ Shop.

**GREATER MANCHESTER POLICE
MUSEUM**
Newton Street
Occupying the old Newton Street
police station, built in 1879, with a
reconstructed 1920s charge room
and cell corridor. The first floor has
police uniforms and equipment, a
forger's den and a photographic
gallery.

℘ 061 855 3290.
Open: to organised groups only by
appointment. All tours escorted.
✆

**JOHN RYLANDS UNIVERSITY
LIBRARY OF MANCHESTER**
Deansgate
World-famous library, built in 1890–
99, an outstanding example of neo-
Gothic architecture retaining most
of its Victorian décor, fittings and
services. Now the special
collections division of a library
which has total resources of more
than 5 million books and
manuscripts. Regular exhibitions
and displays.

℘ 061 834 5343/6765.
Open: daily Mon–Fri 10–5.30, Sat 10–
1. (Other times by prior
arrangement.) (Closed Public and
University hols.) Donations welcome.
Guided tours & parties (25 max) by
prior arrangement only.
&. (prior arrangement necessary)
Shop ✆

**MANCHESTER CRAFT CENTRE**
17 Oak Street
Renovated Victorian market
building now housing around 20
craftshops, including potters,
jewellers, fashion designers and
printers.

℘ 061 832 4274.
Open: Mon–Sat 10–5.30.
⌁ (Tue–Sat 10–4.30) &. (ground
floor & restaurant only) toilets for the
disabled.

**MANCHESTER MUSEUM**
The University, Oxford Road
(1m SE of city)
Contains exhibits of archaeology
and natural history including an
extensive collection from Ancient
Egypt, rocks, minerals, fossils,
coins and native craftsmanship and
huge study collections of over 8
million specimens. Frequent
temporary exhibitions, and
lectures.

℘ 061 275 2634.
Open: daily Mon–Sat 10–5. (Closed
Good Fri, May Day & Xmas–New
Year.) Donation box.
&. Shop ✆

*John Rylands University
Library*

**WHITWORTH ART GALLERY**
University of Manchester,
Oxford Road (1.5m SE of city)
Founded in 1889 by Royal Charter.
The principal collections are British
watercolours including work by
Blake, Turner, the Pre-Raphaelites
and 1939–45 War Artists;
Continental water-colours including
works by Cézanne, Van Gogh and
Picasso; Old Master drawings and
prints, including examples by
leading Renaissance masters such
as Pollaiuolo, Mantegna and Dürer.
An important collection of textiles
including the Whitworth Tapestry,
designed by Paolozzi in 1968;
historic wallpapers; and
contemporary works of art.
Frequent special exhibitions.

℘ 061 273 4865.
Open: daily Mon–Sat 10–5 (Thu until
9). (Closed Good Fri & Xmas to New
Year.) Guided tours & coach parties
by prior arrangement.
⌁ (licensed, Mon–Sat 10.30–4, Thu
10.30–8) &. Shop ✆ (ex guide
dogs).

**WYTHENSHAWE HORTICULTURAL
CENTRE**
Wythenshawe Park,
Northendon (5.5m S of city, off
A5103)
The 5½ acre centre provides a
splendid all year round display of
plants, much of which is used for

the parks and gardens throughout the city. The extensive glasshouses include the Tropical House with pineapples and the Cactus House which contains the Charles Darrah collection.

✆ 061 945 1768.
Open: daily 10–4. Guided tours for parties (charge).
✖ (ex guide dogs) ♿ (ex 2 greenhouses) Shop & plant sales Sat & Sun.

## MANSFIELD
Nottinghamshire

**MUSEUM & ART GALLERY**
Leeming Street
Images of Mansfield, past and present, Buxton Watercolours, Nature of Mansfield and a wide variety of temporary exhibitions.

✆ 0623 663088.
Open: daily Mon–Sat 10–5 (Closed Sun.) Guided tours for school parties by appointment. Coach parties by prior arrangement.
♿ Shop ✖

## MARCH
Cambridgeshire

**MARCH AND DISTRICT MUSEUM**
High Street
Local folk museum, run by volunteers, housing a wide variety of bygones, photographs, documents and historical records.

✆ 0354 55300.
Open: Wed 10–12, Sat 10–12 & 2–4.30. Donations. Guided tours available by arrangement.
♿

## MARSDEN
West Yorkshire

**TUNNEL END CANAL & COUNTRYSIDE CENTRE**
Displays on the history of canals, housed in the former tunnel keeper's cottage at the entrance to the Standedge Tunnel on the Huddersfield Narrow Canal. Also an interpretative centre devoted to this part of the Pennines.

✆ Huddersfield 0484 846062.
Open: Etr–Oct: Tue 2–4, Wed–Fri 10–1 & 2–4, Sat–Sun 10–5. Winter: Tue 2–4, Wed–Thu 11–1 & 2–4, Sat & Sun 10.30–4. (Open BH Mon.)
⌂ ☰ ✖ (ex guide dogs in museum).

## MARYPORT
Cumbria

**MARITIME MUSEUM**
Shipping Brow, I Senhouse Street
Material of local and general maritime interest. Photographic display illustrating Maryport's history. Exhibitions.

✆ 0900 813738.
Open: Etr–Sep, Mon–Sat 10–5, Sun 2–5. (Closed 1–2pm on Sat). Oct–Etr daily ex Wed & Sun 10–12 & 2–4. Donation welcome. Coach parties by prior arrangement.
♿ (ground floor only) Shop.

## MATLOCK
Derbyshire

**JOHN SMEDLEY LTD**
Lea Mills
Set in rural countryside near Matlock, this old established family firm produces high quality knitwear. Spinning, dyeing and knitting can be seen on guided tours. Finished garments and yarns are on sale in the shop.

✆ 0629 534 571.
Open: (Shop) Mon–Sat 10–4. Factory visits by prior arrangement.
⌂ ♿ (shop only).

## MAYBUSH
Hampshire

**ORDNANCE SURVEY**
Romsey Road
Permanent exhibition centre dealing with all aspects of map making and the history of the OS.

✆ 0703 792608/792354.
Open: Mon–Fri 10–4. Guided tours by prior arrangement only (parties 20 max) at 10 & 2. Special tours, lasting up to a day, can be arranged for

professional visits. Significant advance notice required.
⌂ (by prior arrangement) ♿ Map shop.

## MELROSE
Borders

**PRIORWOOD GARDEN**
Special garden with flowers for drying. Visitor centre adjacent to Melrose Abbey and 'Apples through the Ages' orchard walk. Bring and buy plant sale in May.

✆ 089682 2965.
Open: Apr–20 Dec Mon–Sat 10–5.30; also Sun 2–5.30 May–Oct. Guided tours by prior arrangement.
☰ ♿ Shop.
(NTS)

## MENAI BRIDGE
Gwynedd

**TEGFRYN ART GALLERY**
Cadnant Road
A private gallery, standing in its own pleasant grounds near to shores of the Menai Straits. Exhibition of paintings by contemporary and prominent artists including many from North Wales. Pictures may be purchased.

✆ 0248 712437.
Open: Mar–Dec daily 10–1 & 2.5
♿ (ground floor only).

## MERTHYR TYDFIL
Mid Glamorgan

**JOSEPH PARRY'S COTTAGE**
4 Chapel Row
Birthplace of musician and composer Joseph Parry. Exhibition of his life and works and display of mementoes of Welsh male voice choirs. Open-air museum with excavated section of Glamorganshire Canal and exhibits illustrating local industrial and social history.

✆ 0685 73117.
Open: Apr–Aug Mon–Sat 10–1 & 2–5, Sun & BH 2–5; Sep–Mar 2–5 daily. Donation welcome. Guided tours of Chapel Row area charged for. School →

parties by arrangement.
❀ Shop.

## MIDDLESBROUGH
Cleveland

**DORMAN MUSEUM**
Linthorpe Road
Displays of local, social, industrial
and natural history. A permanent
display of regional and Linthorpe
pottery together with a regular
varied programme of temporary
exhibitions.

✆ 0642 813781.
Open: Tue–Sat 10–6. (Closed Xmas
& New Year's Day.) Donation
welcome. Coach parties by prior
arrangement.
♿ (ground floor only) toilet for the
disabled. Shop ❀

**MIDDLESBROUGH ART GALLERY**
320 Linthorpe Road
Attractive late Victorian building,
housing one of the most important
collections of local and national
20th-century art in the north-east.
Active temporary exhibition
programme.

✆ 0642 247445.
Open: Tue–Sat & BH Mon 10–6
(closed between exhibitions). Guided
tours available by prior arrangement.
♿ (ground floor only) toilets for the
disabled. Shop.

**TEES (NEWPORT) BRIDGE**
One of only two similar bridges and
the largest all-steel vertical lift
bridge in the UK. Opened in 1934,
the original timber deck is now
rolled asphalt which carries the
A1085 over the River Tees.

✆ 0642 248155 (County Surveyor's
Office).
Open: all year. School parties by prior
arrangement.

## MILDENHALL
Suffolk

**MILDENHALL & DISTRICT MUSEUM**
6 King Street
Small but lively independent
museum with displays on local

archaeology, Fenland and Breckland
history, bygones and RAF
Mildenhall. Exhibition on High
Lodge – the oldest known Stone
Age site in Britain – founded 5,000
years ago. Occasional special
exhibitions.

✆ 0638 716970.
Open: Wed–Sun 2.30–4.30 (Fri 11–
4.30). Guided tours available for
groups by prior arrangement only.
♿ (ground floor only) toilets for the
disabled. Shop.

## MILNATHORT
Tayside

**BURLEIGH CASTLE**
A 16th-century tower house, with a
courtyard enclosure and roofed
angle tower, dating from 1582.

Open: Apr–Sep Mon–Fri 9.30–6, Sun
2–6.
(AM)

## MILNGAVIE
Strathclyde

**LILLIE ART GALLERY**
Station Road
A permanent collection of 20th-
century Scottish paintings are
included in this modern purpose
built art gallery. There are also
displays of sculpture and ceramics,
and temporary exhibitions of
contemporary art.

✆ Glasgow 041 956 2351.
Open: all year Tue–Fri 11–5 & 7–9,
Sat, Sun 2–5. Guided tours by prior
arrangement. Donations welcome.
♿ (ex toilets). ❀

## MILTON ABBAS
Dorset

**MILTON ABBEY CHURCH**
Blandford
Originally built by King Athelstan as
a monastery but destroyed by fire in
the 13th century. Rebuilt in its
present form during the 15th
century and boasts many
interesting features. The adjacent
Gothic style mansion, with its

ceilings and decorations by James
Wyatt and several Adam fireplaces,
houses an independent boarding
school for boys.

✆ 0258 880484.
Open: daily 9.30–6.30. Donations.
(Admission charge to church & house
during Etr wk & school summer hols.)
Parking charge.
♿ (Jul–Aug daily 10–6).

## MINSTER-IN-THANET
Kent

**MINSTER ABBEY**
The oldest inhabited house in
England, dating back to the 11th
century. Now home of a religious
order.

✆ Thanet 0843 821254.
Open: all year, Mon–Sat 11–noon &
2–4.30, (Closed Sat afternoons &
Sun). (Oct–May Mon–Sat 11–noon).
Donation welcome. Guided tours.
♿ (ex toilets). Shop.

## MINTLAW
Grampian

**ADEN COUNTRY PARK**
(1m W Mintlaw off A950)
Heritage Centre and 230 acres of
beautiful woodland set in open
farmland. The grounds of a former
estate, the Park is the home of
many varieties of plants and animals
which can be explored by a network
of footpaths including a specially
developed nature trail.

✆ 0771 22857.
Open: park all year. Heritage Centre
May–Sep daily 11–5, Apr & Oct wknds
only 12–5. Guided walks by
appointment with Ranger Service.
♿ (May–Sep 11.30–4.30) ♿
(toilets, ground floor & grounds).

## MISTLEY
Essex

**MISTLEY TOWERS**
(On B1352, 9m E of Colchester)
Twin, square porticoed towers,
remaining features of church
designed by Robert Adam and built
in 1776.

Open: towers accessible at all reasonable times. Key keeper. ⅃ (exterior only). (AM)

## MODBURY
Devon

**WOODTURNERS CRAFT CENTRE**
New Road (On the A379 Plymouth-Kingsbridge road)
Small family business specialising in handmade woodcraft. On most days visitors can watch anything from fruit and salad bowls to table and standard lamps, egg cups to coffee tables being made by craftsmen from home-grown hardwoods and Burma teak. There is also a resident carver. Crafts showroom with finished products as well as local pottery, silverware and pressed flower pictures.

℘ 0548 830405.
Open: Feb–Dec, Mon–Sat 10.30–6.
⅃ (ground floor only). Shop.

## MOEL FAMAU
Clwyd

**MOEL FAMAU COUNTRY PARK**
(3.5m NE of Ruthin. N of unclassified road between Loggerheads and Llanbedr-Dyffryn-Clywd)
The country park is situated on the Clwydian Range and includes the highest summit, Moel Famau 1818ft. From here there are excellent views stretching from Snowdonia to Liverpool and beyond. A tower was constructed on the summit to mark George III's golden jubilee, reaching a height of 115ft, but it collapsed during a storm in 1862. The eastern slope of Moel Famau has a forest rich in birdlife. There is a forest trail and a leaflet on the Country Park is available from the Countryside Centre at Loggerheads Country Park – see entry under Loggerheads.

Open: accessible at all reasonable times. Guided tours included in Countryside Service events list.

## MOFFAT
Dumfries and Galloway

**LADYKNOWE MILL**
Small mill where visitors can see garments being made. Showroom for the sale of woollens, tweeds and tartans. Woollen Heritage Centre gives background to the Woollen industry in Scotland with interesting displays.

℘ 0683 20134.
Open: all year daily, 9–5.30 in summer, reduced hours in winter. (Closed 25 & 26 Dec and 1 Jan).
⅃ (licensed) ⅃ (part) 𝍐 Shop ✺

## MONMOUTH
Gwent

**THE KYMIN**
(1.75m E off A4136)
This 800 ft vantage point has views of ten old counties. The hilltop is crowned by a Banqueting House and a Naval Temple. The Banqueting House, built in 1794 by the Kymin Club, is not open to the public. The Naval Temple, built in 1800 by public subscription commemorates famous victories by 16 British admirals whose names are displayed on plaques around the walls.

Open: all year, until dusk. (NT)

## MONTGOMERY
Powys

**MONTGOMERY CASTLE**
Overlooking the small town of Montgomery, the castle was built by Henry III about 1223. For a time it was the home of the powerful Marcher family of Mortimer and the Herberts, and it was here that the poet George Herbert was born in 1593. Assaults by Parliamentarians during the Civil War in 1644 left the castle in ruins.

Open: accessible at all reasonable times. (AM)

## MOORLYNCH
Somerset

**MOORLYNCH VINEYARD**
White wines are produced from the grapes grown here, along with apple wine and cider from local apples. Visitors can see wine-making machinery and follow some of the pleasant walks around the farm and vineyard. Fine views. Rare breeds of fowl and farm animals.

℘ 0458 210393.
Open: May–Sep 10–6. Parties by arrangement only (evening). Coach access difficult.
⅃ (cafeteria 11–6, winebar) ⅃ toilets for the disabled. Shop.

## MOORS VALLEY COUNTRY PARK
Hampshire
(SW of Ringwood on Horton road between Three Legged Cross and Ashley Heath)
Adjacent to the 1000-acre Ringwood Forest, the Country Park is set in 250 acres of river valley and has many leisure facilities as well as river, forest and lakeside walks and a children's adventure playground.

℘ 0425 470721.
Open: Country Park accessible dawn to dusk.
⅃ (footpath routes only) toilets for the disabled. ⅃ 𝍐

## MORCOMBELAKE
Dorset

**S. MOORES BISCUIT FACTORY**
Biscuits have been made in Morcombelake since 1880 and daily ouput here now runs at about 60,000 biscuits. Baking takes place during the morning and this is the best viewing time.

℘ Chideock 029 789 253.
Open: all year Mon–Fri 9–5 (ex BH & 1 week Xmas).
Shop and gallery.

## MORETON CORBET
Shropshire

**MORETON CORBET CASTLE**
Castle with a small 13th-century keep and the ruins of a fine Elizabethan house, captured by Parliamentary forces in 1644.

Open: at all reasonable times.
&
(AM)

## MOUSA ISLAND
*See Shetland*

## MUCH MARCLE
Hereford & Worcester

**WESTONS CIDER WORKS**
The Bounds
A cider and perry works with tours and tastings and products on sale.

℘ 053 184 233.
Open: Mon–Fri 9–1 & 2–4.30. Guided tours available Tue & Thu 2.30. Parties (max 25) by prior arrangement only.

## MUGDOCK
Strathclyde

**MUGDOCK COUNTRY PARK**
Craigallian Rd, Near Milngavie
500 acres of unspoilt countryside encompassing lochs, woods, pasture and moorland as well as the historic castles of Mugdock and Craigend. Mugdock (pre-1372) was primarily a defensive structure, whereas the 19th-century Craigend was principally a status symbol. There are well-established walks and trails through the park. Horse riders, cyclists and orienteers are welcome. There is also a barbeque site (charge), which visitors should book in advance.

℘ 041 956 6100.
Open: Country park accessible at all reasonable times: Information Centre 1–4.30. Guided tours available. Parties should pre-book.
& (part) toilets for the disabled. ⊼

## MUIR OF ORD
Highland

**GLEN ORD DISTILLERY**
Enjoy a friendly guided tour of this old Highland distillery, rounded off with a 'wee dram' of single malt whisky.

℘ 0463 870421.
Open: Mar–Nov Mon–Fri 9–12 & 2–4. Guided tours. Large parties should pre-book. Shop.

## MUIRSHIEL
Strathclyde

**MUIRSHIEL COUNTRY PARK**
(4m NW of Lochwinnoch on unclass road)
Set in wild upland country, with trails and walks. Windy Hill (1036ft) gives fine views. Many woodland and moorland birds can be seen as well as mammals and in June there are fine displays of rhododendrons. The visitor centre has a display of natural history. Guided walks can be arranged, along with map reading and navigation courses.

℘ Lochwinnoch 0505 842803.
Open: park daily, dawn–dusk; visitor centre daily Apr–Sep 9–8.30; Oct–Mar 9–4.30. Coach parties please ring beforehand.
⊼

## MUSSELBURGH
Lothian

**PINKIE HOUSE**
A fine Jacobean building of 1613 and later, incorporating a tower of 1390. Fine painted ceiling in the long gallery. The house now forms part of the Loretto School.

℘ 031 665 2059.
Open: mid Apr–mid Jul & mid Sep–mid Dec, Tue 2–5. ⌘

## NETLEY MARSH
Hampshire

**TOOLS FOR SELF RELIANCE**
Netley Marsh Workshops
Project run by volunteers who collect unwanted handtools and sewing machines and refurbish them, before distributing them cost free, to people in third world countries. Visitors can watch the refurbishment taking place, see the exhibition of strange and beautiful African tools and artefacts, the 100ft mural and the tool warehouse.

℘ 0703 869697.
Open: Mon–Fri 9–5 (closed BHs & first half Aug). Guided tours available. Parties by arrangement only.
& (ground floor only) toilets for the disabled. Shop.

## NEW ABBEY
Dumfries and Galloway

**SHAMBELLIE HOUSE MUSEUM OF COSTUME**
(0.25m N on A710)
A costume collection, made by Charles Stewart of Shambellie, of European fashionable dress from the late 18th century to early 20th century. Mainly women's dress and accessories although some children's and men's clothes; also fancy dress costume.

℘ 038785 375 or 031 225 7534. (National Museums of Scotland). Open: mid May–mid Sep, Thu–Mon 10–5.30, Sun 12–5.30. Donations. Guided tours by prior arrangement.
⌘ (ex guide dogs).

## NEWARK-ON-TRENT
Nottinghamshire

**MILLGATE MUSEUM OF SOCIAL AND FOLK LIFE**
48 Millgate
A trip back in time to Victorian days, with old fashioned street scenes and shop layouts depicting the social and domestic life of bygone days.

℘ 0636 79403.
Open: all year daily, Mon–Fri 10–5, plus weekends Apr–Dec & BH 1–5. Donations welcome. Guided tours for school parties.
⌑ Shop ⌘ (ex guide dogs).

## NEWARK CASTLE

A castle has stood upon this site, which holds a major strategic position guarding the important river crossing, the Fosse Way and the Great North Road, since 1129. The Curtain Wall and the Gate House remain. There is a permanent exhibition in the South West Tower.

✆ 0636 79403.
Open: Mar–Sep, Tue–Wed, Fri–Sun & BH Mon 1–5. Donations. Guided tours available for school parties by prior arrangement.
☴ ♿ (ground floor & gardens) Shop.

## NEWBOROUGH

Staffordshire

**THE PIANO WORKSHOP**
Yoxhall Lane
A 'hospital' for sick pianos, where interested visitors can watch restoration work taking place on old instruments, listen to a music lesson or examine brand new and recycled instruments. Specialist advice is always on hand and Victorian, Edwardian and contemporary sheet music is for sale.

✆ 0283 75 433/655.
Open Wed & Sat 9–5. Guided tours are available.
☕ ☴ ♿ Shop.

## NEWBURY

Berkshire

**NEWBURY DISTRICT MUSEUM**
The Wharf
Situated in the town's two most picturesque buildings – the 17th-century Cloth Hall and the 18th-century Granary. Displays include archaeology, natural history, costume, traditional crafts and games and pastimes. Audio-visual displays tell the story of the Civil War in Newbury and the History of Ballooning. Frequent temporary exhibitions throughout the year.

✆ 0635 30551.
Open: all year; Apr–Sep Mon–Sat 10–

6, Sun & BH 2–6, Oct–Mar Mon–Sat 10–4 (closed Wed all year & winter Suns). Donations requested. Coach parties must book in advance.
♿ (part). Shop.

## NEWCASTLE-UPON-TYNE

Tyne and Wear

**JOHN GEORGE JOICEY MUSEUM**
City Road
Housed in a fascinating historic building just yards from the famous Tyne Bridge, this museum has period rooms, swords, guns, paintings and many other items of local and military history.

✆ 091 232 4562.
Open: all year Tue–Fri 10–5.30, Sat 10–4.30 (Closed Sun & Mon, but open BH Mons). Coach parties not accepted.
☕ Shop.

**LAING ART GALLERY**
Higham Place
Close to the city centre, this premier art gallery in the northeast includes paintings by famous artists, from Gauguin to Stanley Spencer and Burne-Jones. There is a lively new Art on Tyneside display, plus many special exhibitions and activities.

✆ 091 232 7734 or 6989.
Open: all year Tue–Fri 10–5.30, Sat 10–4.30, Sun 2.30–5.30 (Closed Mon, but open BH Mons). Coach parties welcome.
☕ ♿ (part) special displays for the visually impaired. Shop.

**MUSEUM OF ANTIQUITIES**
University Quadrangle
Ideal place to begin a visit to Hadrian's Wall. Models of forts, milecastles etc. Reconstruction of 3rd-century temple to Mithras. World famous prehistoric, Roman and Anglo-Saxon collections.

✆ 091 222 7844 or 222 6000 Ext 7849.
Open: Mon–Sat 10–5. (Closed Good Fri, 24–26 Dec & 1 Jan.) Donations.

Guided tours by prior arrangement.
♿ Shop ♒ (ex guide dogs).

**MUSEUM OF SCIENCE & ENGINEERING**
Blandford House, Blandford Square
The history of the River Tyne, with its shipbuilding heritage and remarkable inventors and engineers. Also the exciting 'hands on' science factory and, due to open spring 1992, the Time Tunnel – a journey through Newcastle's past, present and future.

✆ 091 232 6789.
Open: all year Tue–Fri 10–5.30, Sat 10–4.30 (Closed Sun & Mon, but open BH Mons).
Coach parties welcome, advance booking preferred.
☕ ♿ (step at front, but internal lift) toilets for the disabled, wheelchairs on loan. Shop.

**THEATRE ROYAL**
Grey Street
Tours of the theatre for groups of 10 or more

✆ 091 232 0997.
Open: all year Mon–Sat 10am–11pm.
☕ (Cafeteria 9.30–7, 11 Fri & Sat; licensed restaurant lunches and 5.30 onwards.) ♿ (Lift to upper level restaurant) Shop.

## NEW MILLS

Derbyshire

**NEW MILLS HERITAGE AND INFORMATION CENTRE**
Rock Mill Lane
The Heritage Centre offers information on the local area, with exhibitions on the town's history and past and present industries. Maps, trails and guidebook publications are on sale in the shop.

✆ 0663 46904.
Open: Tue–Fri 10.30–4, Sat–Sun 10.30–5. Guided tours available by prior arrangement only.
☕ ♿ toilets for the disabled. Shop. Parking charge.

## NEWPORT
Dyfed

### PENTRE IFAN BURIAL CHAMBER
(3m SE)
Remains of this chamber comprise capstone and three uprights with semi-circular forecourt at one end. Excavated 1936–37 when found to be part of vanished long barrow.

Open: at all reasonable times. (AM)

## NEWPORT
Gwent

### MUSEUM & ART GALLERY
John Frost Square
Archaeology and history of Gwent including Roman finds from Caerwent and Pontypool; section on Chartist movement of 1838–40. Natural history and geology. Also collection of early English watercolours. John Wait Teapot Collection. The Newport Tourist Centre is housed here. Programmes of special events.

℘ 0633 840064.
Open: Mon–Thu 9.30–5, Fri 9.30–4.30, Sat 9.30–4 (ex public holidays).
& (lifts) Shop ✖ (ex guide dogs).

## NEWTONMORE
Highland

### CLAN MACPHERSON HOUSE AND MUSEUM
Relics and memorials of the Clan Chiefs and other Macpherson families. Prince Charles Edward Stuart relics, including letters to the Clan Chief (1745) and a letter to the Prince from his father (the Old Pretender). Royal Warrants, Green Banner of the Clan, swords, pictures decorations and medals. Also James Macpherson's fiddle, and other interesting historical exhibits.

℘ 05403 332.
Open: May–Sep, Mon–Sat 10–5.30, Sun 2.30–5.30. Other times by appointment. Donations.
& Shop ✖ (ex guide dogs).

## NEWTON STEWART
Dumfries and Galloway

### CREEBRIDGE WEAVING MILLS
(0.5m N, on A714)
Producing high quality mohair products (from the fleece of the Angora goat). Visitors are shown weaving, brushing with natural teasles, and finishing processes for the soft, light and warm wool.

℘ 0671 2868.
Open: all year Mon–Sat 9–5. Guided tours on request.
& Shop.

### KIRROUGHTREE VISITOR CENTRE
Creebridge
(1m off A75 at Newton Stewart)
Run by the Forestry Commission, the Visitor Centre tells the story of the tree-planting programme in Galloway Forest Park. There is a nursery, with potted forest trees for sale, an adventure playground, a centre for cycling and a forest drive (charge).

℘ 0671 2420.
Open: Etr–Oct daily 8–dusk. The Park Ranger will conduct guided tours for large parties.
🛏 🍴 & Forest shop.

## NEWTOWN
Powys

### ORIEL 31 (DAVIES MEMORIAL GALLERY)
The Park
Art gallery exhibiting all aspects of the visual arts: painting, sculpture, photography and textiles as well as display of crafts and applied arts. Changing exhibitions.

℘ 0686 625041.
Open: Mon–Sat 10–5.
& (ground floor & grounds only)
Shop.

### ROBERT OWEN MEMORIAL MUSEUM
The Cross, Broad Street
Museum on the life and work of Robert Owen, born here in 1771. The pioneer of modern British socialism and father of the co-operative movement, Owen was earlier a model employer at the New Lanark Mills, where he built world-famous schools.

℘ 0686 626345.
Open: all year (ex Xmas & New Year), Mon–Fri 9.45–11.45 & 2–3.30, Sat 10–11.30. Donation welcome. Coach parties by prior arrangement. Must be prepared to split into groups. Shop.

### TEXTILE MUSEUM
Commercial Street
Housed in the upper floor workshops of a woollen mill where handloom weavers once worked, the museum has interesting relics from the days when Newtown had a thriving woollen industry. Exhibits include mill machinery, 19th century handlooms, photographs and books.

℘ 0686 626243.
Open: May–Oct, Tue–Sat 10–1 & 2–4.

### W H SMITH (1920S REPLICA SHOP)
24 High Street
This branch of W H Smith is a unique combination of a shop and a museum. The shop has been completely restored to its original state at the time it was first opened in 1927, and on the first floor is the museum. Displays, photographs, models and memorabilia date back to 1792.

℘ 0686 626280.
Open: Mon–Sat 9–5.30, BH Mons 9–12.
& (shop only, toilet).

## NORTHAM BURROWS
Devon

### NORTHAM BURROWS COUNTRY PARK
An opportunity to enjoy activities associated with the seaside and the countryside. In 640 acres of grassy coastal plain which offers 2 miles of safe, sandy beach protected by the natural barrier of Pebble Ridge. Since ancient times the so-called 'Potwallopers' of Northam have

enjoyed the right to graze their stock on the Burrows, and their sheep and horses can be seen on the common. There is also an Exhibition Centre.

✆ 0237 479708.
Open: Country Park accessible at all reasonable times; Information Centre Etr–Sep daily 10–5. Guided tours are available. Toll for vehicles onto common May–Sep.
& (part; access over Pebble Ridge to beach) toilets for the disabled. Shop.

## NORTHAMPTON
Northamptonshire

CENTRAL MUSEUM AND ART GALLERY
Guildhall Road
Reflecting Northampton's standing as Britain's boot and shoe capital, the museum houses the largest collection of boots and shoes in the world. Also on display in four galleries are archaeological artefacts illustrating the history of the town from the Stone Age to 1675, priceless Chinese and English ceramics, Italian art from the 15th–18th centuries and art and sculpture from a variety of periods and cultures.

✆ 0604 39415.
Open: Mon–Sat 10–5 (Thu 10–8), Sun 2–5. Guided tours available by prior arrangement (at least 1 week's notice required). Parties by appointment only.
& toilets for the disabled. Shop.

DELAPRE ABBEY
(0.5m S off A508)
16th- to 19th-century house with fine porch, built on site of Cluniac nunnery. Contains Northamptonshire Record Office and HQ of Northamptonshire Record Society. Details for events in grounds from Parks & Leisure Officer, Northampton Borough Council, Cliftonville House, Bedford Road, Northampton.

✆ 0604 762129.
Abbey grounds, open: all year dawn–

dusk. Walled garden open May to Sep only during daylight. Certain parts of the interior shown Thu only, May–Sep 2.30–5; Oct–Apr 2.30–4.30. Donations. Coach parties accepted by special arrangement only.
& (ground floor of Record Office & grounds only) toilets for the disabled.
✵ (in house).

MUSEUM OF LEATHERCRAFT
60 Bridge Street
A collection of historic and contemporary leatherwork which traces the history of its use all over the world from ancient times to the present day and is housed in the fine building near the city centre which was formerly Northampton's Blue Coat School.

✆ 0604 34881.
Open: Mon–Sat 10–5. Guided tours available by appointment. Parties by prior arrangement.
& (by prior arrangement only, with limited viewing) Shop.

## NORTH BERWICK
Lothian

NORTH BERWICK LAW
(S off B1347)
A conical volcanic peak rising to 613ft to the south of the town and an excellent viewpoint. The summit is crowned by a watch tower dating from Napoleonic times and an archway made from the jawbones of a whale.

Open: accessible at all reasonable times.

NORTH BERWICK MUSEUM
Small museum in former Burgh school with sections on local and natural history, archaeology and domestic life. Exhibitions held throughout the summer.

✆ 0620 3470.
Open: Jun–Sep, Mon–Sat 10–1 & 2–5, Sun 2–5. For opening times outside summer season, please telephone. Donations welcome.
Shop ✵

## NORTH CREAKE
Norfolk

CREAKE ABBEY
(1m N off B1355)
Church ruin with crossing and eastern arm belonging to a house of Augustinian canons founded in 1206.

Open: accessible at all reasonable times.
&
(AM)

## NORTH SHIELDS
Tyne & Wear

STEPHENSON RAILWAY MUSEUM
Middle Engine Lane, Chirton Industrial Estate
The long history of railways, including George Stephenson's *Killingworth Billy* of the early 1800s, the huge 1930s streamliner *Silver Link* and other locomotives and rolling stock are displayed in this developing museum. Steam train rides (charge) link with the Metro at Percy Main. Special events and summer rallies.

✆ 091 262 2627.
Open: May–Oct Wed–Sat 10.30–4.30, Sun 12.30–5 (closed Mon & Tue, but open BH Mons). Coach parties welcome.
⊟ (vending machine) & (part; ramp) Shop (weekends only).

## NORTH WALSHAM
Norfolk

CAT POTTERY
1 Grammar School Road
Visitors can watch life-sized, life-like pottery cats being made in the traditional workshops, then browse around the collection of 'railwayana' in the yard adjacent.

✆ 0692 402962.
Open: Mon–Fri 9–6, Sat 10–1. Guided tours are available. Large parties not accepted.
& (part) Shop.

## NORTH WOOTTON

Somerset

**WOOTTON VINEYARD**
North Town House
A vineyard set in the foothills of the Mendips, 3m from Wells, 9,000 vines specially imported from the Rhine and Alsace. The old farm buildings house a winery where fresh dry white wine is made. Visitors can walk in the vineyards and wines may be purchased direct from the cellar.

✆ Pilton 074989 359.
Open: Mon–Sat 10–1 & 2–5. Coach parties by appointment. Guided group tours by appointment, 25–40 people (charge).
Shop ✻

## NORWICH

Norfolk

**CITY HALL**
St Peter Street
Dating from 1938, the City Hall has a model of the city on show. Visitors can also see the Council Chamber.

✆ 0603 622233.
Open: all year Mon–Fri 9–5. Guided tours charged for (accompanied children free). Special arrangements for group visits are possible.
& (ground floor) toilets for the disabled. Shop.

**GUILDHALL**
Gaol Hill
Civic plate and insignia dating from 1549 is on show.

✆ 0603 666071.
Open: all year Mon–Sat 9.30–6 (5.30 in winter); also summer Suns 9.30–1. Guided tours (charge) summer Mon–Sat 2.30, Sun 10.30, winter Sat 2.30.
& (ground floor only, ramps) toilets for the disabled. Shop.

## NOTTINGHAM

Nottinghamshire

**BREWHOUSE YARD MUSEUM**
Castle Boulevard
Housed in 17th-century buildings on a two-acre site. The museum

depicts daily life in the city in post-medieval times with period rooms and thematic displays. Unusual rock-cut cellars open showing their uses in the past. The museum contains material which can be handled or operated by the public. The cottage gardens contain unusual local plants. Exhibitions of local historical interest changing every two months.

✆ 0602 483504 Ext 3600.
Open: all year daily 10–12 & 1–5. (Closed 25 Dec). Coach parties by prior arrangement. Guided tours by arrangement with Curator.
& (ground floor) toilets for the disabled. ✻ (ex guide dogs).

**CANAL MUSEUM**
(near Broadmarsh Shopping Centre)
On the banks of the Nottingham and Beeston Canal, the museum presents a broad insight into the history of the River Trent, local canals, bridges, floods, natural history and archaeology. Reconstructions of the interior of a canal warehouse and canal office add atmosphere and there are two colourful narrow boats. Audio-visual presentation.

✆ 0602 284602 (Nottingham Industrial Museum).
Open: all year, Etr–Oct Wed–Sat 10–12 & 1–5.45, Sun 1–5; Oct–Etr Wed, Thu & Sat 10–12 & 1–5, Sun 1–5 (closed Xmas Day).
🖨& (limited). Shop.

**GREEN'S SCIENCE CENTRE, MILL & MUSEUM**
Windmill Lane, Sneinton
Restored working 19th-century tower windmill once owned by George Green, mathematical physicist (1793–1841). Museum and science centre tell the story of windmills and Green's life. Interactive exhibits illustrate his contribution to science. Flour on sale.

✆ 0602 503635.
Open: Wed–Sun 10–5 & BH (closed Xmas Day). Donations welcome.

Coach parties by prior arrangement.
& (mill ground floor only) toilets for the disabled. Shop ✻

**INDUSTRIAL MUSEUM**
Courtyard Buildings, Wollaton Park
Housed in an 18th-century stable block are displays illustrating Nottingham's industrial history and in particular the lace and hosiery industries, together with exhibits on the pharmaceutical industry, engineering, tobacco industry and printing. A mid-19th-century beam pumping engine, regularly in steam, and heavy agricultural machinery is also on display. Outside yards display a horse gin from a local coalmine, Victorian street furniture etc.

✆ 0602 284602.
Open: Apr–Sep, Mon–Sat 10–6, Sun 2–6; Oct–Mar, Thu & Sat 10–4.30; Sun 1.30–4.30. (Closed 25 Dec). Admission charge Sun & BH. (Ticket valid for both this and Natural History Museum, Wollaton Hall – see separate entry.)
🖨& (part) toilets for the disabled. Shop ✻ 🎍

**THE LACE CENTRE**
Severns Building, Castle Road
Financed by eight lace firms, this centre, housed in a picturesque 15th-century timber house, tells the story of lace. It has lace hanging in panels from the beamed ceiling and displayed all around in the form of table cloths, mats, lampshades, curtains, bedspreads, souvenir dolls, lingerie, handkerchiefs etc.

✆ 0602 413539.
Open: daily 10–5 (11–4 Jan & Feb) (Closed 25 & 26 Dec). Parties (30 max in 2 groups). Demonstrations of lacemaking by hand Thu 2–4 in summer.
Shop.

**MUSEUM OF COSTUME AND TEXTILES**
43–51 Castlegate
Situated in a row of elegant 18th-century houses, the museum contains fashion displays from 1790

*Costumes at Nottingham*

onwards, in a series of authentically furnished and decorated period rooms. The museum also contains one of the best collections of lace in the country, plus unique map tapestries of 17th-century Nottinghamshire and an extensive collection of accessories, including hats, shoes, bags and fans.

℗ 0602 483504.
Open: daily 10–5. (Closed Xmas Day.)
& (ground floor only) Shop ✖

**NATURAL HISTORY MUSEUM**
Wollaton Hall
Housed in imposing Elizabethan mansion by Robert Smythson, dating from 1580–1588, and situated in large park with deer. Wide range of displays including birds, mammal, mineral and fossil displays. Exhibition programme.

℗ 0602 281333.
Open: Apr–Sep, Mon–Sat 10–7, Sun

2–5; Oct–Mar, Mon–Sat 10–dusk, Sun 1.30–4.30. (Closed Xmas Day.) Admission charge Sun & BH includes Industrial Museum – see separate entry.
旦 & toilets for the disabled. Shop ⊼ ✖

**NOTTINGHAM CASTLE MUSEUM**
The Castle
Nottingham Castle lies in attractive grounds with a network of caves in the rocks beneath. Inside, displays of ceramics, silver, glass and paintings depict the history of the castle while the exhibition programme includes both historical and contemporary shows.

℗ 0602 483504.
Open: Apr–Sep 10–5.45, Oct–Mar 10–4.45. (Closed Xmas Day.) Donations. (Charge for grounds Sun & BHs only.) Guided tours available by prior arrangements.
旦 & (chair lift to all floors, automatic car on requests,

wheelchairs available on loan) toilets for the disabled. Shop.

**NOTTINGHAM STORY**
Tourist Information Centre, 16 Wheeler Gate
A 25-minute audio-visual presentation highlights many of the important characters who have contributed to the city's heritage, including Lord Byron, D H Lawrence and, of course, Robin Hood.

℗ 0602 470661.
Open: all year Mon–Sat 10–4 (programme screened hourly). (Closed Sun & 25–26 Dec).

# NUNEHAM COURTENAY
Oxfordshire

**JOHN MATTOCK ROSE NURSERIES**
An internationally known rose grower with display gardens of hundreds of thousands of roses grown annually from leading rose hybridists.

℗ 086738 265 or 454.
Open: daily Mon–Sat 8.30–5.30, Sun 10.30–5.30. Garden centre all year, rose field & garden Jun–Sep. Guided tours for horticultural societies and/or by special arrangement. Prior notice requested for coach parties.
旦 ⊼ & toilets for the disabled. Garden Centre.

**OXFORD UNIVERSITY ARBORETUM**
(On A423 just S of the village) 50 acres of conifers and broad leaf trees.

℗ 0865 276920 or 276921.
Open: May–Oct Mon–Sat 9–5 & Sun 2–6. Guided tours by prior arrangement (charge). Coach parties by prior arrangement.
& (part) ✖

# NUNNEY
Somerset

**NUNNEY CASTLE**
Small 14th-century castle in the French style, consisting of a central →

block with large round towers at the angles and surrounded by a moat.

Open: at all reasonable times.
(AM)

## NUTBOURNE
West Sussex

**NUTBOURNE MANOR VINEYARD**
(Between A283 and A29)
In a fine wine-growing setting, the 14 acres of German vines include two lakes and ruined mills.

℘ 07983 3554.
Open: Etr–end Oct, Wed–Sun, 9–5. Guided tours (charge). Parties by appointment.
Shop.

## OBAN
Strathclyde

**OBAN DISTILLERY**
Stafford Street
Built in 1794 beneath a massive cliff, the fortress-like stone buildings of Oban Distillery have hardly changed outside since the turn of the century. Inside, the Distillery with its two stills has been re-equipped for modern-day production of Highland malt.

℘ 0631 62110.
Open: all year Mon–Fri & summer Sats 9.30–4.30. Guided tours available Mon–Fri. Parties by appointment only.
Ġ toilets for the disabled. Shop.

## OGMORE
Mid Glamorgan

**OGMORE CASTLE**
On River Ogmore, with inner and outer wards and early 12th-century three-storeyed keep preserving hooded fireplace. West wall 40 ft high, and dry moat around inner ward.

Open: accessible at all reasonable times.
(AM CADW)

## OLD CLEEVE
Somerset

**JOHN WOOD SHEEPSKINS**
Visitors can see sheepskins being processed from their natural state, including tanning, dyeing and the crafting of various sheepskin products.

℘ Washford 0984 40291.
Open: factory tours, Apr–Oct Mon–Fri 10.45 & 11.30, 2.15 & 3.00 (parties by appointment); showroom & shop all year Mon–Fri 9–5; also Sat & BH 10–4.30.
🖵 Ġ Shop ✖ (ex guide dogs).

## OLD WHITTINGTON
Derbyshire

**REVOLUTION HOUSE**
High Street
This former alehouse takes its name from the revolution of 1688. It was here, as history and tradition relate, that three local noblemen met to plan their part in the downfall of James II. Today the cottage contains a display of 17th-century country furniture, a film about the revolution and a programme of changing exhibitions.

℘ 0246 453554.
Open: all year Sat & Sun 10–4, daily mid Apr–Oct 10–4. Coach parties must book in advance. Free guided tours available.
Shop.

## ✦ ORKNEY, ISLES OF ✦

## BIRSAY
Orkney

**EARLS PALACE**
(14m N of Stromness on A967)
Located in windy position on the north-west corner of the Orkney Mainland, this large ruin was the residence of the 16th-century Earls of Orkney. The Palace was constructed around a courtyard with projecting rectangular towers at the corners, except at the northwest.

Open: accessible at all reasonable times.
Ġ
(AM)

## DOUNBY
Orkney

**CLICK MILL**
(NE of village, off B9057)
An example of one of the rare old Orcadian horizontal watermills in working condition.

Open: at all reasonable times.
(AM)

## FINSTOWN
Orkney

**STENNES STANDING STONES**
(3m SW on A965)
Remains of a stone circle, from the second millennium BC. Nearby is the Ring of Brogar (c2000 BC) consisting of a splendid circle of upright stones with a surrounding ditch.

Open: at all reasonable times.
(AM)

## HOY
Orkney

**DWARFIE STANE**
(Off unclass road between Moness Pier and Rackwick)
Located in a remote glen south of Ward Hill, the Dwarfie Stane consists of a great block of sandstone, measuring 28 ft long, 14 ft wide and 8 ft tall, into which a passage has been cut. No other such rock-cut tomb is known in Britain and it is believed to be about 5000 years old.

Open: at all reasonable times.

## KIRKWALL
Orkney

**HIGHLAND PARK DISTILLERY**
(1m S on A961)
Traditional methods are used with peat fires to dry the barley, hand-beaten copper pot stills for distilling and old sherry casks to

mature the finished product. The correct maturing period of at least twelve years is strictly observed. Visitors are shown the complete process of whisky making from the barley store to the warehouses. There is also an audio-visual presentation on the history of Orkney and the distillery.

✆ 0856 4619.
Open: Apr–Sep Mon–Fri 10–4 (open until 7.30pm Jun–Aug), 10–4 also Sat Jun–Aug. For winter opening and guided tour times please telephone in advance. Coach parties should give advance notice
&. (ground floor) Shop ✖

**RENNIBISTER EARTH HOUSE**
(At Rennibister Farm, 4m W off A965)
Excellently preserved earth house, dating from the Iron Age, which can

be reached by descending a short ladder to an underground chamber from which there is an underground passage with supporting pillars.

Open: at all reasonable times. (AM)

## LAMB HOLM
Orkney

**ITALIAN CHAPEL**
(8m S of Kirkwall on A961)
Converted in World War II from a couple of Nissen huts to an ornate chapel, by Italian prisoners of war. These prisoners also helped to build the nearby Churchill Causeways linking the islands of Orkney Mainland, Lamb Holm, Glimps Holm, Burray and South Ronaldsay.

✆ Holm 085678 278.
Open: at all reasonable times.
&. ✖

*Cutting peat for Highland
Park Distillery, Kirkwall*

## PAPA WESTRAY
Orkney

**KNAP OF HOWAR**
(W side of island near Holland House)
Believed to be north-west Europe's oldest standing house. It was built over 5,000 years ago and visitors can see how large flagstones have been used for cupboards, hearths and seating. Other finds in the house have included whalebone mallets and unique stone borers and grinders. There are many other prehistoric monuments on the island.

Open: at all reasonable times. (AM)

## ROUSAY
Orkney

**MIDHOWE BROCH AND TOMBS**
(5.5m W of Island's pier)
Standing on the cliff edge overlooking the small island of Eynhallow, this is a good example of an Iron Age broch with a walled enclosure cut off by a deep rock-cut ditch. Several secondary buildings, which have survived persistent coastal erosion, are dotted around the broch. Nearby is Midhowe Chambered Cairn, considered to be one of the best in Orkney. Its central chamber is almost 75ft long.

Open: at all reasonable times.

## STROMNESS
Orkney

**PIER ARTS CENTRE**

Collection housed in warehouse building on its own stone pier. Also galleries for visiting exhibitions and children's work. Arts library and reading room in adjacent house.

✆ 0856 850209.
Open: all year (ex Xmas–9 Jan approx) Tue–Sat 10.30–12.30 & 1.30–5, Sun Jun–Aug 2–5. Donation welcome.
&. (ground floor only) Shop ✖

## WESTRAY
Orkney

**NOLTLAND CASTLE**
Late 16th-century ruined castle which was never completed. It has a fine hall, vaulted kitchen and a notable winding staircase.

Open: Apr–Sep Mon–Fri 9.30–6, Sun 2–6.
(AM)

## ORPINGTON
Gtr London

**BROMLEY MUSEUM**
The Priory, Church Hill
Housed in an impressive building dating back to medieval times, surrounded by formal and informal gardens. Displays include the archaeology of Bromley and the life and work of Sir John Lubbock. Also a small, but important, geological collection and expanding collections of social history, dress and fine art.

✆ 0689 873826.
Open: all year Mon–Wed, Fri, Sat 9–5. (Closed PH.) Guided tours & coach parties by advance notice in writing. (Car park cannot accept coaches.)
& (ground floor only) ✖

## OSWESTRY
Shropshire

**OLD OSWESTRY HILL FORT**
(0.5m N, accessible from unclass road off A483)
Iron Age hill fort covering 68 acres, with five ramparts and elaborate western portal. Abutted by part of the pre-historic Wat's Dyke.

Open: at all reasonable times. Access via a kissing gate.
(AM)

**OSWESTRY BICYCLE MUSEUM**
11 Arthur Street
The history and development of the bicycle through the ages. In a Georgian listed building, the Museum's creator, David Higman, has amassed a fascinating collection of bicycle memorabilia, such as enamel signs and adverts, posters, and paintings, as well as old bicycles going back to the Penny Farthing, models in period dress, and saddles, tyres and puncture repair kits from the last century.

Open: Mon–Wed, Fri–Sat 9.30–4. Donations. Guided tours are available. Parties accepted (max 15).
& (ground floor only) Shop.

## OUNDLE
Northamptonshire

**BARNWELL COUNTRY PARK**
Country park with picnic meadows, and waterside walks which lead around the edges of lakes and along a backwater of the River Nene, giving picturesque views. No fishing is allowed in the central wildlife refuge but there are opportunities elsewhere in the park (day fishing permits required). Countryside Warden. Countryside event programme.

✆ 0832 73435.
Open: all year, 9.30–6, dusk in winter. Coach parties & coach parking by arrangement. Tours available to pre-booked groups by prior arrangement. Rod licence (available from Anglian water, North St, Oundle) required for day fishing permit.
& (access by paved ramp & path to fishing points; fishing is free for disabled people) toilets for the disabled. 🅿

## OUTWOOD
Surrey

**OUTWOOD ART GALLERY**
Shepheards Hurst House,
Prince of Wales Road
In a converted stable block, this art gallery and sculpture park has permanent displays of fine craft, watercolours, oil paintings and sculpture by contemporary artists. More sculpture is on display in informal gardens.

✆ 034 284 2126.
Open: Feb–Dec, Tue–Sat 10.30–5.30.
& (ground floor only).

## OXFORD
Oxfordshire

Ancient and picturesque University city on rivers Cherwell and Thames, dating back to 8th century. The University, the oldest in Britain, probably dates from c1167 and consists of a large number of colleges built over a period of several centuries, many of which are among the finest buildings of their age. Access to some colleges is restricted to certain times and details may be obtained from the Oxford Information Centre, St Aldate's.

✆ 0865 726871 (Centre).
Open: Mon–Sat 9.30–5, Sun & BH Mon 10.30–1 & 1.30–4 end May–Aug. Guided tours of the city & university (charge, reduced fee for pre-booked groups). Coach parties: pre-booking for tours essential.
& (Centre access through Housing Dept Mon–Fri) Shop.

**ASHMOLEAN MUSEUM OF ART AND ARCHAEOLOGY**
Beaumont Street
The oldest (1683) museum in the country, housed in C R Cockerell's building of 1845 (with later extensions). Its exhibits include archaeological items of British, European, Mediterranean, Egyptian and Near Eastern origins. Also exhibited are coins and medals of all countries and periods, in the Heberden Coin Room; Italian, Dutch, Flemish, French, and English oil paintings, Old Master and modern drawings, watercolours, prints and miniatures; European ceramics; English silver, Chinese and Japanese porcelain; painting and lacquer; Tibetan art; Indian sculpture and paintings; Islamic pottery and metalwork; Chinese bronzes; casts from the antique and objects of applied art. Temporary exhibits throughout the year.

✆ 0865 278000.
Open: all year, Tue–Sat 10–4, Sun 2–4. (Closed Etr & during St. Giles Fair

in early Sep, Xmas period & 1 Jan.)
Donations. Guided tours charged for.
Coach parties divide into groups of
15, each with responsible person.
& (with porter assistance up steps,
toilet.) Shop ✖ (ex guide dogs).

## MUSEUM OF THE HISTORY OF SCIENCE

Old Ashmolean.Building, Broad
Street
Contains the finest collection of
early astronomical, mathematical
and optical instruments in the
world. Housed in the Old
Ashmolean Building, a fine example
of 17th-century architecture which
was originally built to hold the
collection of Elias Ashmole. One of
the most distinguished parts of the
present display is the series of
Islamic and European astrolabes,
once used for astronomical
calculations. Also early
microscopes and other optical
instruments, photographic
apparatus, clocks and watches, air
pumps etc. Of special interest are
the penicillin material, H G J
Moseley's X-ray spectrometer, and
a prototype of Dr C R Burch's ultra
violet reflecting microscope made in
1946. Exhibitions.

✆ 0865 277280.
Open: Mon–Fri 10.30–1 & 2.30–4.
(Closed BH, Xmas and Etr week).
Donations welcome. Guided tours for
small parties by prior arrangement.
Bookstall ✖

## MUSEUM OF OXFORD

St Aldate's
The story of the City and University
from the earliest times to the
present day, through archaeology,
historic documents and
photographs and period open
displays. Free talks and
demonstrations Thursday
lunchtimes.

✆ 0865 815559.
Open: all year, Tue–Sat, 10–5.
(Closed Good Fri & Xmas).
Donations welcome. Coach parties
should pre-book.
Shop ✖

## ST EDMUND HALL

College of Oxford University,
Queen's Lane
This is the only surviving medieval
hall and has a Norman crypt, 17th-
century dining hall, chapel and
quadrangle. Other buildings 18th
and 20th century.

✆ 0865 279007.
Open: all year (ex Etr & Xmas week)
daily during daylight.
& toilets for the disabled. Shop
(bursary) ✖

## UNIVERSITY BOTANIC GARDEN

High Street (by Magdalen
Bridge)
Gardens of great botanical interest,
founded in 1621, and the oldest in
the country.

✆ 0865 276920/1.
Open: all year (ex Good Fri & Xmas
Day) daily 9–5 (4.30 Oct–Mar),
greenhouses 2–4. Guided tours by
prior arrangement (charge).
& (ex toilets) ✖

# PAISLEY
Strathclyde

## COATS OBSERVATORY

Oakshaw Street
Opened to the public in 1883, Coats
Observatory was at that time one of
the best equipped small
observatories in the country. The
array of equipment includes a 10
inch equatorial telescope of 1898
and a 5 inch telescope installed in
1882. In addition to its astronomical
function, it is also a weather station
and the main seismic station for
southwest Scotland.

✆ 041 889 2013.
Open: Mon, Tue & Thu 2–8; Wed, Fri
& Sat 10–5. Coach parties not
accepted.

# PALNACKIE
Dumfries and Galloway

## ORCHARDTON TOWER

A rare example of a circular tower
built originally in the late 15th
century.

Open: Apr–Sep Mon–Fri 9.30–6, Sun
2–6.
(AM)

# PARHAM
Suffolk

### 390TH BOMB GROUP MEMORIAL AIR MUSEUM

Parham Airfield (1m SW Great
Glenham, E of B1116
Hatcheston-Framlingham rd)
Housed in an original World War II
Control Tower, the exhibits include
a fine collection of USAAF uniforms,
decorations, combat records,
equipment, personal items,
memorabilia and wartime
photographs.

✆ 0359 51209.
Open: Mar–Nov Suns & BH Mons 1–6.
Other times by prior arrangement
only. Guided tours are available.
⌨ & (ground floor only) toilets for
the disabled. Shop.

# PENARTH
South Glamorgan

## TURNER HOUSE

A small gallery holding temporary
and travelling exhibitions of
pictures and *objets d'art* from the
National Museum of Wales, and
other sources.

✆ Cardiff 0222 708870.
Open: Tue–Sat & BH Mons, 11–12.45
& 2–5, Sun 2–5. (Closed 24–26 Dec &
1 Jan, Good Fri.) Donations. Parties
by appointment.
& (ground floor only) Shop ✖

# PENCARROW
Cornwall

## PENCARROW GALLERY

Pencarrow House
Gallery of the Cornwall Crafts
Association specialising in high
quality crafts and books.

✆ 020884 465.
Open: Etr–mid Oct, Sun–Thu & BH,
1.30–5 (11–5 Jun–mid Oct).
& toilets for the disabled. Small
garden centre.

## PENMACHNO
Gwynedd

### PENMACHNO WOOLLEN MILL
Local weavers are still working at this centuries-old mill, set in a peaceful Welsh Valley by a waterfall. Power looms were introduced in the last century which weave soft lightweight tweeds and rugs. The mill shop stocks beautiful co-ordinated knitwear and other crafts. The mill contains a wool exhibition and the Weaver's Loft café.

✆ Betws-y-Coed 0690 710545.
Open: daily from Etr–mid Nov, 9–5.30, Sun 11–4.30. Weaving, Mon–Fri. (Closed Sun mornings early & late season.)
⌨ Shop ✖

## PENMON
Gwynedd

### PENMON PRIORY
There has been a religious settlement here since the 6th century. The Priory church and adjacent ruins date from the 12th century, and have the best Romanesque detail in North Wales. North of the church is the holy well where St Seiriol is said to have baptised converts. On the opposite side of the road is a 1,000-hole dovecote dating from about 1600 and crowned with an open hexagonal lantern.

Open: at all reasonable times. (AM)

## PENNARTH FAWR
Gwynedd
(3.5m NE of Pwllheli, off A497)
Part of a house built probably in the early 15th century, preserving hall, buttery and screen.

Open: at all reasonable times. (AM CADW)

## PERTH
Tayside

### BLACK WATCH REGIMENTAL MUSEUM
Balhousie Castle, Hay Street

Treasures of the 42nd/73rd Highland Regiment from 1725 to the present day, including, paintings, silver, colours and uniforms.

✆ 0738 21281 Ext 30.
Open: Mon–Fri 10–4.30 (winter 3.30); Sun & BHs Etr–Sep 2–4.30. Other times & parties 15+ by appointment. Donations.
Shop ✖ (ex guide dogs).

### DEWAR'S SCOTCH WHISKY
J. Dewar & Sons, Inveralmond
A fascinating tour showing the scale of an operation that fills over 300,000 bottles with Scotch Whisky every day.

✆ 0738 21231.
Open: guided tours all year, Mon–Thur 10, 11.15, 2 & 3.15, Fri 10 & 11.15. (Closed company holidays). Parties must book in advance. Children under 8 not admitted.
✖ Shop.

### FAIR MAID'S HOUSE
North Port
Situated near the historic North Inch where the battle of the Clans was fought in 1392. In the 14th century it became the home of Simon Glover, a glovemaker whose daughter Catherine was the heroine of Sir Walter Scott's 'Fair Maid of Perth'. The house was a guildhall for over 150 years. It was renovated

in the 19th century and is now a centre for Scottish crafts. A recently uncovered wall is said to be the oldest one visible in Perth.

✆ 0738 25976.
Open: all year, Mon–Sat 10–5.
& (ground floor only).

### PERTH MUSEUM AND ART GALLERY
78 George Street
Purpose-built to house collections of fine and applied art, social and local history, natural history and archaeology. Frequent special events.

✆ 0738 32488.
Open: Mon–Sat 10–5.
& (ground floor only) toilets for the disabled. Shop ✖

### QUARRYMILL WOODLAND PARK
Isla Road
Quarrymill Park is 27 acres of attractive woodland, crisscrossed by a network of pleasant paths. Walkers can follow the burn as it flows through the den and cascades over weirs and waterfalls. The birds of Quarrymill include woodland and waterside species such as dippers, grey wagtails, mallards and the occasional heron, mandarin duck and kingfisher. Wild flowers abound.

✆ 0738 33890.
Open: Park accessible at all reasonable times (car park open 9am–9pm summer, closes at 5 in winter); Visitor Centre Apr–Oct 9–5,

*Fair Maid's House, Perth*

winter check with Centre Manager. Guided tours are available. Parties by prior arrangement. 🏃 toilets for the disabled. Shop 🍴

## PETERBOROUGH
Cambridgeshire

**CITY OF PETERBOROUGH MUSEUM AND ART GALLERY**
Priestgate
Displays include local geology, archaeology, natural history, social history and articles from former French prisoners' jail at Norman Cross. The museum also has an extensive programme of temporary exhibitions.

✆ 0733 43329.
Open: Tue–Sat 10–5. (Closed Good Fri & Xmas.) Guided tours and parties by prior arrangement.
🏃 (ground floor only) Shop 🐾

## PETERHEAD
Grampian

**ARBUTHNOT MUSEUM AND ART GALLERY**
St Peter Street
Specialises in local exhibits, particularly those relating to the fishing industry with Arctic and whaling specimens. Also a British coin collection.

✆ 0779 77778.
Open: all year, Mon–Sat 10–12 & 2–5. (Closed PH.)
Guided tours can be booked in advance.
Shop 🐾 (ex guide dogs).

## PETERSFIELD
Hampshire

**THE BEAR MUSEUM**
38 Dragon Street
The first of its kind to open in Britain, the museum houses a large collection of Teddy Bears from 1903 onwards. Among the displays are a Bear's house and a Teddy Bear's Picnic, as well as a large collection of antique dolls.

✆ 0730 65108.
Open: all year Mon, Tue & Thu–Sat

10–5 (closed Wed, Sun & 2 weeks in July). Coach parties up to 30 max accepted with advance booking.
🖨 🍴 🏃 (part). Shop.

**FLORA TWORT GALLERY**
Churchpath Studio, 21 The Square
Display of charming pictures by local artist, Flora Twort.

✆ 0730 60756.
Open: summer Tue–Sat 10–5; telephone for winter opening times.

## PITLOCHRY
Tayside

**BLAIR ATHOLL DISTILLERY**
(Off A9 S of Pitlochry)
Guided tour of the distillery.

✆ 0796 2234.
Open: Mon–Sat 9.30–5, Sun (Etr–Oct) 12–5 (last tour 4.30). Parties by advance appointment.
🖨 🏃 toilets for the disabled. Shop.

**FASKALLY**
(2m NW)
This Forestry Commission site incorporates woodland and lochside parking, with picnic area and forest walk.

✆ Dunkeld 03502 284.
Open: daily Apr–Sep, dawn–dusk.
🍴 🏃 toilets for the disabled.

## PITSEA
Essex

**NATIONAL MOTORBOAT MUSEUM**
Wat Tyler Country Park
(See separate entry below.)
The first museum in the world dedicated to the history of the motorboat, highlighting the major advances in design and manufacture over the last 100 years. A wide variety of motor boats are exhibited. Reference library, restoration workshop and video studio.

✆ 0268 550077.
Open: Thu–Mon 10–4 (ex Xmas). Guided tours available for parties only.

🖨 🏃 (ramped access) toilets for the disabled. Shop 🍴

**WAT TYLER COUNTRY PARK**
(1m S of A13/A132 junction)
Once part of the Pitsea Hall Estate and then owned by explosives firms and the Ministry of Defence, the site is today a country park emphasising conservation, walking, nature study and local wildlife.

✆ Basildon 0268 550088.
Open: all year 9–dusk. Guided tours are available.
🖨 (11–3 or 11–6 on summer weekends, school & public holidays.)
🏃 toilets for the disabled. Shop 🍴

## PITSFORD
Northants

**PITSFORD WATER**
Holcot Road, Nr Brixworth
One of the East Midlands' largest reservoirs, with pleasant landscaped grounds, picnic areas and walks. There is a large Nature Reserve, trout fishing by day permit and sailing (club).

✆ 0604 781350.
Open: accessible at all reasonable times. Guided walks by arrangement in Nature Reserve (charge).
🍴 🏃 (ramp & boat for disabled anglers) Shop.

## PLAXTOL
Kent

**OLD SOAR MANOR**
(1m E)
Fine example of a late 13th-century knight's residence, with solar (over a vaulted undercroft) and chapel. Exhibition.

✆ 0732 810622.
Open: daily Good Fri–30 Sep 10–6. Parking limited.

## PLYMOUTH
Devon

**CITY MUSEUM AND ART GALLERY**
Drake Circus
Collections of paintings and drawings, ceramics (Oriental and →

English porcelain), silver; local and Egyptian archaeology and local history. Cottonian collection of Old Master drawings, engravings and early printed books. Natural history and bee observatory. Lively changing art exhibitions.

✆ 0752 668000 Ext 4878.
Open: all year Tue–Sat 10–5.30, Sun 2–5. (Closed Mon, ex BH Mons, Good Fri & 25, 26 Dec.) Guided tours and parties by prior arrangement.
🚹 (access from rear, lift to first floor) Shop ⊗

## PONSANOOTH
Cornwall

KENNALL VALE NATURE RESERVE
(4m NW Falmouth)
A 20-acre broad-leaved plantation with some ancient Oak wood and of considerable industrial archaeological interest. For details of 33 other reserves throughout Cornwall, some with wheelchair access and some with charge payable, contact Cornwall Trust for Nature Conservation, Five Acres, Allet, Truro, TR4 9DT.

✆ 0872 73939.
Open: all year, daily ex 3rd Mon in Feb.

## PONTEFRACT
West Yorkshire

PONTEFRACT CASTLE AND VISITOR CENTRE
Romantic ruins are all that remain of this once formidable royal fortress, whose history is vividly displayed on graphic panels in the Visitor Centre.

✆ 0977 797289.
Open: grounds all year daily, Mon–Fri 8.30–7 (dusk Nov–Mar), Sat & Sun 10.30–7 (or dusk). Visitor Centre Apr–Oct daily 10.30–12.30 & 1.30–4.30, Nov–Mar 2–4. Coach parties & guided tours by prior arrangement only.
🚹 (grounds) disabled parking at Castle Gates, toilets for the disabled. Shop.

## PONTYPRIDD
Mid Glamorgan

THE GROGG SHOP
Models of miners, hill farmers, coracle men, as well as sculptured figures from Welsh folklore and Welsh rugby characters and other 'groggs' are made here in an individual style. Visitors can watch John Hughes (the sculptor) and his team at work.

✆ 0443 405001.
Open: all year Mon–Fri 9–5, Sat 10–5, Sun 2–4; BH weekends & Mon 11–4.30. (Closed Xmas.)

## POOLE
Dorset

POOLE PARK
(Off Parkstone Road)
Opened in 1890, 100 acres of parkland and lakes with numerous facilities. Wildlife abounds and there is a zoo.

✆ 0202 675151 Ext 3500.
Open: all year. Closed to vehicles 6–10am.
🍴 (9–5 (6 peak season, 4.30 winter)). 🚹 (park virtually flat) toilets for the disabled. Shop.

POOLE POTTERY
The Quay
Potters and painters demonstrate their skills in the Crafts Centre, along with other local craftspeople. There is an exhibition of pottery-making over the years, and a museum showing some of the early pieces – pottery has been made at Poole Quay for over a century. The showroom is the largest in the south; personalised pottery is available.

✆ 0202 668681.
Open: Showroom daily 10–5 (ex Xmas); exhibition, museum, craft centre Mar–Xmas.
🍴 🚹 (showroom & tearoom only) Shop.

## PORTHMADOG
Gwynedd

FFESTINIOG RAILWAY MUSEUM
Located in Harbour Station the museum includes old four-wheeled hearse converted from quarryman's coach, one of the original steam locomotives (1863), historic slate wagon, model steam engine (1869), and maps and diagrams illustrating history of the well-known narrow-gauge railway.

✆ 0766 512340.
Open: Late Mar–Oct, 9.30–4 (later on busy days).
🍴 (licensed) 🚹 toilets for the disabled. Shop.

## PORTREATH
Cornwall

CORNISH GOLDSMITHS
Tolgys Mill
Visitors can see jewellery being made to order in the workshops. The showroom holds possibly the largest display of gold jewellery in the country.

✆ 0209 218198.
Open: all year daily 9.30–5.30 (closed 25 Dec). Coach parties welcome.
🍴 (licensed) 🅿 🚹 toilets for the disabled. Shop.

## PORT SUNLIGHT
Merseyside

LADY LEVER ART GALLERY
Numerous exhibits including 18th and 19th-century English paintings with particularly good collection of pre-Raphaelites, 17th and 18th-century English furniture, Wedgwood pottery and Chinese porcelain, Greek vases, antique Roman and Edwardian sculpture. Tapestry, needlework and English watercolours are also represented. The collection was formed by the first Lord Leverhulme.

✆ 051 645 3623.
Open: daily Mon–Sat 10–5, Sun 2–5. Donations.
🍴 🚹 (ground floor, lift to enter building and cafeteria) Shop.

## PRESCOT
Merseyside

**PRESCOT MUSEUM OF CLOCK AND WATCHMAKING**
34 Church Street
Displays on the local clock and watchmaking industry, plus a programme of temporary exhibitions. 'Hands-on' sessions for the blind.

✆ 051 430 7787.
Open: all year Tue–Sat 10–5, Sun 2–5. Coach parties must book in advance. Donation box.
⌂ (by arrangement). Shop.

## PRESTONPANS
Lothian

**SCOTTISH MINING MUSEUM**
Prestongrange
One of two sites which make up the Scottish Mining Museum (the other is at Newtongrange). Together they offer guided tours, powerful machines and informative exhibitions which bring history to life. Steam days on first Sunday of each summer month. 'Talking Tableaux' at Lady Victoria Colliery.

✆ 031 663 7519.
Open: Etr Sun–Sep daily 11–4. Guided tours and parties by prior arrangement.
&. (ground floor only) toilets for the disabled. ✸ (ex guide dogs) Shop.

## PRESTWICH
Gt Manchester

**HEATON HALL**
Heaton Park (on A665)
The finest neo-classical house in the north, surrounded by extensive parkland. Designed by James Wyatt for the Earl of Wilton, the house has magnificent decorated interiors with period furnishings and paintings. Unique circular Pompeiian Room and Music Room with original organ in working order. Exhibition programme and occasional Sunday afternoon concerts.

✆ 061 773 1231 (summer only). Open: details under review –

telephone 061 236 5244 for information. Donations. Parties by arrangement.
⌂ (licensed) &. (ground floor only) toilets for the disabled. Shop ✸

## PRICKWILLOW
Cambs

**PRICKWILLOW ENGINE MUSEUM**
Main Street
A collection of old diesel engines from 1919, formerly used in land drainage in the Fens. Prize exhibit is a 1922 Mirrlees Bickerton and Day diesel, still in working order. There is also a display of old tools and implements associated with the drainage of the Fens, and a wealth of old photographs. The system of drainage dykes and ditches can be seen stretching for miles from the back of the museum. On four or five special days during the summer visitors can see the engines working. Telephone for details.

✆ 035 388 230.
Open: Apr–Oct daily, dawn–dusk. Donations. Guided tours by arrangement.
⌂ (by arrangement).

## QUEEN'S VIEW
Tayside

**QUEEN'S VIEW CENTRE**
Loch Tummel, Pitlochry
This Forestry Commission Centre has exhibits which show changes in the Tummel Valley since Queen Victoria's visit in 1866. Audio-visual programmes, forest walks and information desk. There is a charge for parking.

✆ 03502 284.
Open: Etr Oct daily 10–5.30. Donations requested. Guided tours (charge).
⌂ ㆓ &. toilets for the disabled. Shop ✸ (ex guide dogs).

## QUINTRELL DOWNS
Cornwall

**NEWQUAY PEARL**
(At crossroads of A392 Newquay–Bodmin road and A3058)

Demonstrations of the jewellers' art by resident craftspeople plus the largest collection of pearl jewellery in the West Country.

✆ 0637 872991.
Open: all year daily 9.30–5.30 (open until 9pm late May–late Aug Mon–Fri). Coach parties welcome.
⌂ &.

## RADCLIFFE
Gt Manchester

**RADCLIFFE TOWER**
Tower Street, off Church Street East
Remains of medieval tower once part of a larger hall occupied by the Radcliffe family. Adjacent to medieval parish church.

✆ 061 705 5871 (Bury Reference Library).
Open: at all reasonable times.
&.

## RAMSEY
Cambridgeshire

**ABBEY GATEHOUSE**
A 15th-century Benedictine ruin.

Open: daily, Apr–Oct 10–5 (or dusk). Donations box.
(NT)

**RAMSEY RURAL MUSEUM**
Wood Lane
This fascinating museum is housed in a number of barns and buildings where the atmosphere of bygone days is expertly created. A walk around the mini village discloses the Ramsey stores, with its old shop fittings, scales and packaging, a Victorian schoolroom, the kitchen and washroom of a typical Fenland home in pre-electric days, collections of old agriculture machinery and tools and much more.

✆ 0487 813223.
Open: Apr–Sep Thu & Sun 2–5. (Other times by appointment.) Donations. Guided tours available. Parties 35 max.
⌂ ㆓ &. (ground floor only) toilets for the disabled.

## RAMSGATE

Kent

### RAMSGATE MUSEUM AND ART GALLERY

Ramsgate Library, Guildford Lawn

A display of objects, pictures and documents illustrating the history of Ramsgate.

✆ Thanet 0843 593532.
Open: all year Mon–Wed 9.30–6, Thu & Sat 9.30–5, Fri 9.30–8. (Closed BH.) Groups up to 30 accepted.
& ⌘

## RAWTENSTALL

Lancashire
### ROSSENDALE MUSEUM
Whitaker Park

Set in pleasant parkland with moorland views, the museum is housed in a former Victorian mill owner's mansion, and many of the rooms recall the grandeur of a wealthy industrialist's home. Apart from special temporary exhibitions throughout the year, there is a varied collection of permanent exhibits of fine arts and furniture, and industrial domestic artefacts.

✆ Rossendale 0706 217777/226509.
Open: all year Mon–Fri, 1–5; Sat 10–12 & 1–5 (Sun, 1–5 Apr–Oct, 1–4 Nov–Mar.) (Closed 25, 26 Dec & 1 Jan). Guided tours and parties at other times by prior arrangement.

## READING

Berkshire
### BLAKE'S LOCK MUSEUM
Gas Works Lane

In an attractive Victorian building, the museum illustrates the history of industrial and commercial life in Reading, with a section on its waterways. There are reconstructions of a family bakery, a gentlemen's hairdressers and a printers workshop. A special attraction is a highly decorated traditional gypsy caravan.

✆ 0734 390918.
(Reading Museum & Art Gallery).

Open: Tue–Fri 10–5 Sat, Sun 2–5. Parties by prior arrangement.
⌂ & toilets for the disabled. Shop ⌘

### MUSEUM AND ART GALLERY
Blagrave Street

Noted especially for its exceptional collection of exhibits from Roman Silchester and finds from the River Thames area, including a splendid Bronze Age torc from Moulsford, and displays of local natural history. Please note that during renovation changing exhibitions from the Museum's collections and the museum shop will be in the restored areas of the Town Hall adjacent. Telephone for details.

✆ 0734 55911 Ext 2242.
Open: all year Mon–Fri 10–5.30 & Sat 10–5, Sun 2–5. Shop ⌘

## REAY

Highland
### DOUNREAY PUBLIC EXHIBITION
Dounreay Nuclear Power Station

Information panels, models, participatory displays and charts relating to fast reactors and nuclear energy generally. Housed in a former airfield control tower overlooking the plant which is conspicuous for its 135ft sphere and the prototype fast reactor.

✆ Thurso 0847 802121 Ext 2235.
Open: mid Apr–Sep Tue–Sun 10–4. Groups and tours of the reactor by prior arrangement.
⌂ & (lower floor only)

## REDCAR

Cleveland
### THE ZETLAND LIFEBOAT MUSEUM
Esplanade/5 King Street

Built in 1800 by Henry Greathead, the Zetland lifeboat saved over 500 lives before being taken out of service in 1880. She now forms the centrepiece of the museum, surrounded by a display of photographs, models and other exhibits associated with the history

of sea rescue in the North of England. Upstairs is a display of lifesaving equipment, past and present, and a reconstruction of a fisherman's cottage. Also upstairs is the Lawie Picknett Gallery, which contains a display of photographs and postcards of old Redcar, a selection of model ships and a collection of Redcar crested china.

✆ 0642 479060.
Open: May–Sep daily 11–4. Donation box. Guided tours by arrangement only.
& (ground floor only) Shop.

## REIGATE

Surrey
### PRIORY MUSEUM
Bell Street

Contained in house, originally founded in 1235, and converted into Tudor mansion, of which the hall fireplace is the finest surviving relic. Palladian stucco changed the face of the building in 1779, and the painted staircase by Verrio (about 1710) is a notable example. The house is now used as a school and a part is a small museum with changing displays.

✆ 0737 245065.
Museum open: Wed in term time only 2–4.30 & first Sat in month 11–4. Conducted tours and groups by prior arrangement.
& (ground floor only) Special 'hands on' exhibits for the blind and mentally handicapped.
Shop ⌘

## REIGATE HEATH

Surrey
### OLD WINDMILL

Mill dating from 1750 which was converted into a church in the 1880s. Services (visitors are welcome) held 3pm on third Sun of each month between May and Oct.

Open: most daylight hours. If not, apply to adjoining Golf Clubhouse for key.
& ⌘

## RICHMOND
North Yorkshire

### SWALEDALE POTTERY
Low Row
Hand-thrown pottery is produced and sold here, including an extensive range of stoneware, tableware and terracotta ware.

✆ 0748 86377.
Open: Mar–Oct Mon–Sat 9–5.
Coaches parties welcome.
& Shop.

## RICHMOND-UPON-THAMES
Gt London

### RICHMOND PARK
Charles I enclosed the park area as part of a royal estate in 1637 and successive monarchs shaped the land to suit their hunting needs. Sometimes described as 'wild countryside' on London's doorstep, it nowadays has large numbers of red and fallow deer roaming unharmed. With other kinds of wildlife in evidence, the park is a favourite haunt for naturalists and tourists alike. The formal gardens at Pembroke Lodge and the various plantations show a wealth of exotic shrubs and wild flowers. A popular part is the Isabella Plantation, now a woodland garden with rhododendrons, azaleas, and a running brook. Eighteen-acre Pen Ponds have been specially built for angling (a fishing permit is required). Adam's Pond, where the deer are seen to drink, is also used for model sail boats.

✆ 081 948 3209.
Open: (summer) 7am till dusk; (winter) 7.30–dusk.
⌨ &

## ROCHESTER
Kent
### GUILDHALL MUSEUM
High Street
A major portion of the building dates from late 17th-century and has magnificent decorated plaster ceilings. The collections include local history, archaeology, arms and armour, dolls, toys and Victoriana, models of local sailing barges, fishing vessels. Shorts flying-boats and Napoleonic prisoner-of-war work. The museum also houses the civic plate and regalia of the city.

✆ Medway 0634 848717.
Open: daily 10–5.30. (Closed 1 Jan, Good Fri & 25–26 Dec.) Groups and short talks for schools on specific topics by prior arrangement only.
& (ground floor only) Shop ✀ (ex guide dogs).

## ROTHERHAM
South Yorkshire

### ART GALLERY
Brian O'Malley Central Library and Arts Centre, Walker Place Continuous programme of temporary exhibitions including, at times 19th- and 20th-century paintings from the museum collections, and Rockingham pottery.

✆ 0709 382121 Ext 3621.
Open: Tue–Sat 10–5. (Closed Sun, Mon & BHs.) Donations. Guided tours available for groups by appointment only. Parking charge.
⌨ (licensed) & toilets for the disabled. Shop ✀ (ex guide dogs).

### CLIFTON PARK MUSEUM
Clifton Lane
Late 18th-century mansion reputedly designed by John Carr of York. Contains 18th-century furnished rooms, family portraits, and period kitchen. Displays of Victoriana, local history, local Roman antiquities, numismatics, glass and glass-making, church silver, and 19th- and 20th-century paintings. Also British ceramics including Rockingham, local geology and natural history. Temporary exhibitions.

✆ 0709 382121 Ext 3635.
Open: Mon–Thu & Sat 10–5, Sun 2.30–5 (4.30 Oct–Mar). Donations. Guided tours occasionally available for groups by arrangement.

⛫ & (ground floor & grounds; toilets accessible) Shop ✀ (ex guide dogs).

## ROTHER VALLEY COUNTRY PARK
South Yorkshire
(10m E Sheffield, 9m S Rotherham. Signposted from junctions 30 & 31 of M1, & from Swallownest, Eckington, Killamarsh & Mosborough) Parkland, straddling the South Yorkshire and Derbyshire boundaries, created from restored opencast coal workings and including 3 lakes in an attractive landscaped setting with over 350,000 newly-planted trees. Extensive footpath and cycle network (cycles can be hired). Nature Reserve and Ranger service. Visitor Centre based on an historic complex of buildings at Bedgreave Mill. Fishing and watersport facilities (charge). Special events programme.

✆ 0742 471452.
Open: daily 8.30–dusk. (Closed Xmas Day.) Guided tours available for organised groups by prior arrangement. Parking charge weekends & BHs.
⌨ (10–5) ⛫ & toilets for the disabled. Shop.

## ROTHES
Grampian

### GLEN GRANT DISTILLERY
Established in 1840. The whisky produced here is regarded as one of the best, and is used in many first-class blends as well as being sold as a single Glen Grant Malt. Traditional malt whisky methods of distillation are used together with the most modern equipment.

✆ 03403 494.
Open: Apr–Sep, Mon–Fri 10–4.
Guided tours, groups by appointment.
& (ground floor only) Shop & Bar ✀ (ex guide dogs).

## ROTHESAY
*See Bute, Isle of*

*Checking the fermenting process at Glen Grant*

museum traces their growth from 1810 to the present day, with original letters, books and papers. The display also traces the life of Dr Henry Duncan, the founder of savings banks. The 7th-century preaching cross which now stands in Ruthwell church was restored by him, and the museum also contains drawings and other documents relating to the cross.

## ROUSAY
### See Orkney

## ROYSTON
Hertfordshire

### ROYSTON MUSEUM
Lower King Street
Former chapel schoolroom, which contains a local history museum with displays depicting the history of the town. Regular temporary
· exhibitions.

℘ 0763 242587.
Open: Wed, Thu & Sat 10–5. Tours and groups by prior arrangement. Donations box.
Ġ (ground floor only). Shop ✖

## RUBERY
West Midlands

### WASELEY HILLS COUNTRY PARK
Gannow Green Lane
In all around 150 acres of pasture and woodland. The view from Windmill Hill takes in the Malverns and the Cotswolds, as well as Birmingham landmarks such as the University clock tower and Post Office building. The North Worcestershire Path crosses the Park, whose Information Centre is housed in an ancient timber-framed barn. Events programme. Crafts displays and demonstrations every Sunday and bank holiday.

℘ Romsey 0562 710025.
Open: all year, daily 8–dusk. Donations. Limited parking for large

vehicles. Guided walks programme.
▱ (wkdays 10–5, wkends 9–5) ☶
Ġ (ground floor & grounds; smooth walkways/wheelchair routes to cafe & toilets) parking & toilets for the disabled. Shop.

## RUFFORD
Nottinghamshire

### RUFFORD CRAFT CENTRE AND COUNTRY PARK
(On A614 2m S of Ollerton)
Within the Country Park, the Craft Centre has a full year's programme of exhibitions on all arts and crafts. A diverse collection of sculpture is permanently displayed within an attractive formal garden to the rear of the Craft Centre, which is housed in a converted stable block once part of a 17th-century country estate. The Country Park, which comprises woodland, open parkland and a beautiful lake with a variety of wildfowl, once formed a large part of the estate.

℘ 0623 822944.
Open: Country Park accessible at all reasonable times; Craft Centre: Mar–Dec daily 10–5. Parties should pre-book refreshments.
▱ ☶ Ġ (ramps, suitable paths & wheelchair hire) toilets for the disabled. Shop.

## RUTHWELL
Dumfries & Galloway

### SAVINGS BANKS MUSEUM
Housed in the building where savings banks first began, the

℘ Clarencefield (038787) 640.
Open: daily, 10–1, 2–5; Closed Sun & Mon in winter. Tours and parties by appointment.
Ġ Objects can be handled by visitors with sight disabilities.

### RUTHWELL CROSS
(Off B724)
One of Europe's most famous carved crosses resting in the parish church in an apse built specially for it. The date is probably late 7th century and the 18ft-high cross is richly carved with Runic characters showing the earliest form of English in Northumbrian dialect.

Open: Apr–Sep Mon–Fri 9.30–6, Sun 2–6.
(AM)

## SAFFRON WALDEN
Essex

### FRY ART GALLERY
Bridge End Gardens, Castle Street
Collection of works by the artistic community which flourished around the village of Great Bardfield at the time of the Second World War, including Bawden, Ravilius, Ayrton, Aldridge and Rothenstein. The gallery is set in a Victorian landscaped garden which is also open to the public.

Open: Etr–Oct Sat, Sun & BHs 2.45–5.30. Donation welcome. Guided tours for parties of all ages by prior arrangement, donation expected. Shop.

**SAFFRON WALDEN MUSEUM**
Museum Street
Built in 1834, the museum houses
collections of ethnographical,
geographical, botanical,
ornithological and archaeological
material.

Open: Apr–Sep, Mon–Sat 11–5, Sun &
BH 2.30–5, Oct–Mar, Mon Sat 11–4,
Sun & BH 2.30–5. (Closed Good Fri
and 24 & 25 Dec.)
⚹ (ground floor & gardens only)
Shop ✿

## ST ABBS
Borders

**ST ABBS HEAD NATURE RESERVE**
(N from B6438)
This exposed headland north of
Eyemouth, now a National Nature
Reserve, has fine cliffs rising to
300ft. It is an important site for cliff
nesting seabirds. Kittiwakes and
guillemots are the most numerous
with smaller numbers of fulmars,
shags, razorbills, herring gulls and
puffins. The headland is a good
landfall site for autumn migrants
and a number of rarities have been
recorded.

✆ Coldingham 08907 71443.
Open: accessible at all reasonable
times; Visitor Centre Apr–Oct daily
10–5. (NTS). Parking free at car park
at southern end; charge at other car
park (disabled drivers free).
🖥 (11–5.30 Apr–May weekends only,
Jun–Sep daily).

## ST ANDREWS
Fife

**CRAWFORD ARTS CENTRE**
93 North Street
The Centre has a programme of
changing art exhibitions, children's
workshops and theatre which takes
place in the galleries and studio.

✆ 0334 74610.
Open: Mon–Sat 10–5; Sun 2–5.
(Closed 2 weeks Xmas.) (Admission
charge for theatre and workshops;
Galleries free, but donations
welcome.)
⚹ (main gallery) Shop.

## ST AUSTELL
Cornwall

**ENGLISH CHINA CLAYS**
John Keay House
Tours can be arranged by
telephoning Mrs Sue Ryder, giving
at least a week's notice.

✆ 0726 74482 Ext 3293.
Open: all year Mon–Fri tours at 10am
& 2pm. All tours guided and by
appointment only. Coach parties max
40–45.
⚹

## ST BEES
Cumbria

**ST BEES HEAD NATURE RESERVE**
(On public footpath N of car
park on seafront)
Sandstone cliffs rising to almost
300ft with wide views to the Isle of
Man and Dumfries and Galloway. On
the headland there is a large
seabird colony with guillemots,
razorbills and puffins. A cliff path
runs between St Bees and
Whitehaven.

Open: at all reasonable times.

## ST DOGMAELS
Dyfed

**ST DOGMAELS ABBEY**
Standing near the centre of the
village, the ruined Abbey was
founded in the 12th century by
monks of the French order of Tiron.
The north and west walls of the
nave still rise to almost their
original height. Open-air
Shakespeare productions are held
here in August.

✆ Cardigan 0239 613230.
Open: at all reasonable times.
⚹
(AM)

## ST HELENS
Merseyside

**PILKINGTON GLASS MUSEUM**
(On Prescot Road, A58 1m
from town centre)
Four thousand years of

glassmaking. Outstanding collection
of antique glass, plus displays on
the current applications of glass in
building, transport and technology.
Various temporary exhibitions
throughout the year.

✆ 0744 692499 or 692014.
Open: all year Mon–Fri 10–5, Sat, Sun
& BH 2–4.30. (Closed: Xmas–New
Year.)
⚹ (Stair lift) Shop ✿

**ST HELENS MUSEUM**
College Street
Displays of local history, art and
wildlife, with period rooms, videos
and new exhibitions.

✆ 0744 24061.
Open: all year Tue–Fri 10–5, Sat 10–4.
Donation requested. Guided tours by
prior arrangement (charge).
⚹ Shop.

## ST HILARY
South Glamorgan

**OLD BEAUPRÉ CASTLE**
(1m SW)
Ruined manor house, rebuilt in 16th
century, with notable Italianate
gatehouse and porch. Three-
storeyed porch displays Basset
arms.

Open: at any reasonable time.
(Closed Sun.)
(AM CADW)

## ST IVES
Cambridgeshire

**NORRIS MUSEUM**
The Broadway
A comprehensive collection of
Huntingdonshire local history,
including fossils, archaeology and
bygones, water-colours of local
features, work in bone and straw by
French prisoners at Norman Cross.
Also Huntingdonshire lacemaking.

✆ 0480 65101.
Open: May–Sep, Tue–Fri 10–1 & 2–5,
Sat 10–12 & 2–5, Sun 2–5; Oct–Apr
Tue–Fri 10–1 & 2–4, Sat 10–12.
(Closed: BHs.) Donations welcome.
Shop.

## ST NICHOLAS
Dyfed

**TREGWYNT WOOLLEN MILL**
(1.5m SW)
Woollen mill in 18th-century building where yarns have been made for 200 years. Visitors can see the mill in operation and some of the processes like twisting, cone winding, warping and weaving. Products include tapestry bed covers woven in various designs.

☏ 03485 225.
Open: all year Mon–Fri 9–5.
🍴 (Mon–Fri 9.30–4.30) 🚻 Shop (Mon–Sat 9–5).

## ST OLAVE'S
Norfolk

**ST OLAVE'S PRIORY**
(5.5m SW of Gt Yarmouth on A143)
Remains of small Augustinian priory of c1216 with exceptional early example of brickwork in the undercroft to the south cloisters. Also a single-aisled church.

Open: any reasonable time.
Keykeeper.
♿ (ground floor & grounds only).
(AM)

## SALCEY FOREST
Northamptonshire/ Buckinghamshire

(W of B526 on Harlwell road about 8m S of Northampton) Owned and managed by the Forestry Commission since the 1920s, this ancient forest produces quality timber and provides a home for many animals and plants. There are three circular trails, named after the three kinds of woodpecker found there; with luck visitors may catch sight of them, or some of the other varied wildlife. A leaflet is available in the car park.

Open: accessible at all reasonable times.
🚻 ♿ (surfaced forest walks) toilets for the disabled.

## SALFORD
Gt Manchester

**ORDSALL HALL MUSEUM**
Taylorson Street
Half-timbered manor house, with later brick-built wing (1639), includes Tudor Great Hall, Star Chamber with 14th-century features and Victorian farmhouse kitchen. On upper floor are local and social history displays.

☏ 061 872 0251.
Open: Mon–Fri 10–12.30 & 1.30–5, Sun 2–5. (Closed Good Fri, 25–26 Dec & 1 Jan.) Donations box.
♿ (ground floor only) Shop 🎁

**SALFORD MINING MUSEUM**
Buile Hill Park, Eccles Old Road
This museum of the Lancashire coal industry uses imaginative displays to relate the history of coal mining from Roman times to the present day. Covering all aspects of mining, the galleries are well illustrated and items on display include a horse winding gin c1820, a colliery cage and sections of an Anderton Shearer Loader Coalcutter.

☏ 061 736 1832.
Open: all year Mon–Fri 10–12.30 & 1.30–5, Sun 2–5 (closed Sat, 25 & 26

*The Lesser Spotted Woodpecker, an inhabitant of Salcey Forest*

Dec, 1 Jan & Good Fri). Donation requested. Coach parties must book in advance.
🚻 Shop.

**SALFORD MUSEUM AND ART GALLERY**
Peel Park, The Crescent
The ground floor displays a period street scene typical of a northern industrial town at the turn of the century. The first-floor art galleries house a large collection of works by L S Lowry, as well as a regular series of temporary art exhibitions and displays of decorative arts.

☏ 061 736 2649.
Open: Mon–Fri 10–5, Sun 2–5. (Closed Good Fri, 25–26 Dec & 1 Jan.) Donations.
🍴 (Mon–Fri 11.30–3.30, Sun 2–4.30).
♿ Shop 🎁

## SALTCOATS
Strathclyde

**NORTH AYRSHIRE MUSEUM**
A museum in an 18th-century parish church with classic Scottish architecture. Exhibits portray local historical items, and early 19th century interiors.

☏ 0294 64174.
Open: Jun–Sep Mon, Tue, Thu–Sat 10–1 & 2–5, Oct–May Tue, Thu–Sat 10–1 & 2–5.
♿ (gardens & ground floor only) toilets for the disabled. 🎁

## SANCREED
Cornwall

**CARN EUNY ANCIENT VILLAGE**
(1.25m SW off A30)
Iron-Age village site with characteristic Cornish 'fogou' (subterranean hiding hole), 66ft long with circular chamber. Small site exhibition.

Open: any reasonable time.
(AM)

## SANDOWN
*See Wight, Isle of*

## SAUNDERSFOOT

Dyfed

**SAUNDERSFOOT POTTERY AND CRAFT SHOP**
Wogan Street
Hand-thrown ceramicware. A range of decorative and small colourful pottery is on display and frequent demonstrations of all processes can be seen. The shop also has a good selection of craft goods.

✆ 0834 812406.
Open: Mon–Sat, Apr–Oct, 10–5.30; demonstrations on most summer evenings between 8 & 10.
ሌ Shop.

## SCALLOWAY
*See Shetland*

## SCUNTHORPE

Humberside

**MUSEUM AND ART GALLERY**
Oswald Road
Displays of local history, archaeology and natural science. New Natural Science Gallery due to open in spring of 1992. Programme of temporary exhibitions.

✆ 0724 843533.
Open: Mon–Sat 10–5, Sun 2–5. (Closed Xmas.)
ሌ (ground floor only). Shop
🐕 (ex guide dogs).

**NORMANBY HALL COUNTRY PARK**
Normanby (5m N of Scunthorpe on B1430)
Surrounding a Regency mansion, now a museum of local argricultural history, are 350 acres of formal and informal gardens, parkland and countryside. The park contains red and fallow deer, wild and ornamental birds, trails and walks. Special events also take place. There is a charge for parking.

✆ 0724 720588.
Open: park all year daily dawn to dusk; Hall & museum Apr–Oct daily, Mon–Fri 11–5, Sat & Sun 1–5. Donation requested. Coach parties must book in advance. Free guided walks available.

🍴 (cafe open during season 11–5, restaurant by arrangement) 🚻 ሌ (part; ramps into Hall) toilets for the disabled. Shop.

## SEAFORD

East Sussex

**SEVEN SISTERS COUNTRY PARK**
Exceat (1.5m E)
The country park occupies 692 acres of attractive Sussex downlands, chalk cliffs, shingle beach and wetlands beside the Cuckmere River. Wide variety of birds and salt loving plants, the downland is noted for its orchids and is grazed in the summer by Southdown sheep. At Exceat there is an Information Centre and a nature trail.

✆ Eastbourne 0323 870280.
Open: Good Fri–last weekend Oct 10.30–5.30, otherwise 11–4 weekends only. Admission charge for Living World Exhibition ✆ 0323 870100. Donation requested. Guided tours (donation). Coach parties please give warning.
🚻 ሌ (part) toilets for the disabled. Shop.

## SEDBERGH

Cumbria

**YORKSHIRE DALES NATIONAL PARK CENTRE**
72 Main Street
Visitor centre with interpretative display. Maps, walks, guides and local information available.

✆ (05396) 20125.
Open: daily, Apr–Oct 9.30–5.

**PENNINE TWEEDS**
Farfield Mill (1m from Sedbergh on A684 Hawes road)
Visitors are welcome to look round the Victorian mill which uses machinery dating back to the 1930s. A range of the company's products is displayed in the showroom.

✆ 05396 20558.
Open: all year daily (ex Suns Nov–Mar, 25–26 Dec & 1 Jan) 9.30–5.30.

Coach parties & guided tours by prior arrangement.
ሌ Shop.

## SEETHING

Norfolk

**STATION 146 WORLD WAR II CONTROL TOWER**
(10m SE Norwich off B1332 Bungay road or A146 Loddon road)
This USAAF control tower houses the 448th Bomber Group collection of memorabilia, personal diaries, stories and an extensive collection of photographs of the men who were based here. A model room and roll of honour. Special open day September 6 1992 to commemorate the 50th Anniversary of the arrival of the 2nd Air Division.

✆ 0508 50787.
Open: 10–5, first Sun in each month May–Oct. Donation box.
🍴 (10–5) ሌ (ground floor only). Shop.

## SELBORNE

Hampshire

**THE MALLINSON COLLECTION OF RURAL RELICS**
Selborne Cottage Shop
A small and evocative collection of country bygones displayed with descriptive captions from the writings of rural authors in a building once belonging to Gilbert White, and standing next to the Gilbert White Museum.

✆ 042 050 307 (505 outside opening times).
Open: Mar–Oct, Sat–Thu 10.30–1 & 2–5.30. Other times by appointment. Donation box. Guided tours available. Parties (20 max) by appointment. Shop.

**SELBORNE HILL**
(From car park signed in Selborne village.)
The wooded slopes of Selborne Hill rise steeply to 700 ft to the west of Selborne, home of Gilbert White, the 18th-century naturalist. There are many fine walks through the →

beech woods, although care should be taken in wet weather as paths become very slippery and muddy.

✆ Open: at all reasoanble times. (NT)

## SELKIRK
Borders

**HALLIWELLS HOUSE MUSEUM**
Halliwells Close, Market Place
Housed in Selkirk's oldest surviving dwelling, the museum recreates the building's former role as a home and ironmonger's shop. Upstairs galleries depict the history of the town, using some audio visual techniques to enhance the displays.

✆ 0750 20096.
Open: mid Mar–Oct Mon–Sat 10–5, Sun 2–4; Nov–mid Dec daily 2–4. Donations requested. Coach parties must book in advance. Guided tours for groups of more than 10 (charge). ＆ (part) toilets for the disabled. Shop.

## SELLAFIELD
Cumbria

**SELLAFIELD VISITORS CENTRE**
(Signposted from A595)
An informative insight into the world of nuclear power for visitors of all ages, using life-sized models, computer games and audio-visual displays, situated just outside the Sellafield site.

✆ 09467 27027.
Open: daily Apr–Oct 10–6, Nov–Mar 10–4. (Closed Xmas Day.) Guided tours of the plant by arrangement; guided coach tours around the site available (no notice required). Parties accepted by arrangement. ⌨＆ toilets for the disabled. Shop.

## SEVERN BORE
Avon/Gloucestershire

The Bore is a tidal wave that occurs on the River Severn when the moon and the sun exert their maximum influence, causing a difference of 30–34ft between high and low tide in

the estuary. This occurs on at least 35 days a year. The tide enters the narrowing estuary at Sharpness and forces its way in a series of waves, until it levels out in the Gloucester area.

The best places to see the Bore are at Stonebench on the east bank, 3m SW of Gloucester, off B4008, and at Minsterworth on the west bank, 5m W of Gloucester, on the A48.

## SHAP
Cumbria

**SHAP ABBEY**
(1.5m W on bank of River Lowther)
An abbey of the Premonstratensian order, dedicated to St Mary Magdalene. Most of the buildings are 13th century, but there is also a striking 16th-century west tower.

Open: at all reasonable times.
＆
(AM)

## SHEFFIELD
South Yorkshire

**CITY MUSEUM**
Weston Park
A regional museum of geology, natural sciences, archaeology and Sheffield area trades, including cutlery, plate, ceramics and clocks. Educational facilities for schools and colleges.

✆ 0742 768588.
Open: all year, Tue–Sat 10–5, Sun 11–5. (Closed: 24–26 Dec.) ＆ (ground floor only) Shop ❦ (ex guide dogs).

**SHEPHERD WHEEL**
Whiteley Woods
An early water-powered cutlers' grinding establishment which has been on this site for over 400 years.

✆ 0742 367731.
Open: all year, Wed–Sat 10–12.30 & 1.30–5, Sun 11–12.30 & 1.30–5. (Nov–Feb 4pm closing.)
＆

## SHERBORNE
Dorset

**SHERBORNE ABBEY**
Abbey Close
Superb example of Perpendicular style set in magnificent medieval town. It contains a wealth of fine furnishings and monuments and the Lady Chapel has a reredos by Whistler.

✆ 0935 812452 (Parish Office).
Open: all year daily 9–6 (9–4 winter). Donation welcome. For information on guided tours contact Head Guide, Parish Office (£5 charge). Prior booking essential for coach parties. ＆ (wheelchair available; portable ramp to Lady Chapel).

## SHERE
Surrey

**SILENT POOL**
(0.5m W on A25)
Shaded by trees with footpath around, this crystal clear water is formed by a strong spring. Legend states King John watched a local girl bathing here and that she drowned herself in a fit of shame.

Open: at all reasonable times.

## SHERINGHAM
Norfolk

**HENRY RAMEY UPCHER LIFEBOAT**
Sheringham Promenade
One of the last six rowing and sailing lifeboats in the country still on show and in its original house. Sheringham had a private lifeboat from 1838 to 1935, the RNLI came in 1867. Private and RNLI boats were side by side for 68 years, probably unique in the country.

Open: May–Sep daily 2.30–4.30. Donation welcome. Talks can be arranged for school parties.

## SHERINGHAM, UPPER
Norfolk

**SHERINGHAM PARK**
(Signed from A148 Cromer–Holt road)

An historic landscaped park with gazebo, way-marked woodland walks, cliffs and coastal scenery, and rhododendron drive (at its best in May and June).

℘ 0263 823778.
Open: Park all year daily dawn–dusk. April to September. Donation welcome. Parking charge (NT members free). Coach parties by reservation (charge for non-NT members). Occasional guided walks, see NT literature. 𝍐 ㅎ (toilets, wheelchairs, including an electric wheelchair, available). (NT)

## ✦ SHETLAND ISLES ✦

## LERWICK
Shetland

**CLICKHEINEN**
(0.5m S of Lerwick)
A prehistoric settlement which was occupied for over 1,000 years. Remains include a partially demolished broch.

Open: Late Mar–Sep weekdays 9.30–7, Sun 2–7; Oct–late Mar closes 4pm. (AM)

**FORT CHARLOTTE**
(Overlooking harbour)
Artillery fort begun in 1665 to protect Sound of Bressay in Anglo-Dutch War, renovated in 1781 during American War of Independence.

Open: Late Mar–Sep weekdays 9.30–7, Sun 2–7; Oct–late Mar closes 4pm. (AM)

**SHETLAND MUSEUM**
Lower Hillhead
A museum of the Shetland Islands from pre-history to the present day. Displays of folk life, shipping, archaeology, art and textiles.

℘ 0595 5057.
Open: all year Mon–Wed & Fri 10–7. Thu & Sat 10–5. (Closed Sun.) Exhibitions all year round.

## MOUSA ISLAND
Shetland

**MOUSA BROCH**
The best-preserved late prehistoric drystone tower in Scotland. It rises to a height of 40ft and, uniquely, is almost fully intact. Reached by boat from Leebottom on Mousa Sound.

Open: Apply keeper. Late Mar–Sep weekdays 9.30–7, Sun 2–7; Oct–late Mar closes 4pm. (AM)

## SCALLOWAY
Shetland

**SCALLOWAY CASTLE**
Erected by Patrick Stewart, Earl of Orkney c1600, designed on the two-stepped plan.

Open: Apr–Sep Mon–Fri 9.30–6, Sun 2–6.
(AM)

## SHOREHAM-BY-SEA
West Sussex

**MARLIPINS MUSEUM**
High Street
A Norman and later flint building with interesting façade and internal timbering, possibly built as a customs warehouse, now a maritime, industrial and local history museum.

℘ 0273 462994.
Open: May–Sep, Tue–Sat 10.30–4.30 Sun 2–4.30. Guided tours available by prior written application and subject to a guide being available. Coach parties accepted (max 50). Donations.
Shop ⌀ (ex guide dogs).

## SHREWSBURY
Shropshire

**BEAR STEPS**
St Alkmund's Square
The Bear Steps is a range of 14th-15th century timber-framed buildings completely restored and in daily use. Art and craft exhibitions mainly by local artists are held from Feb to Dec.

℘ 0743 356511.
Open: all year Mon–Fri (Sat by prior arrangement) 10–4. Donations requested. Tour guides are available on a donation basis.
ㅎ (ground floor only). Shop.

## SIDMOUTH
Devon

**THE DONKEY SANCTUARY**
(3m E off A3052)
Visitors can see the many donkeys taken into care, from geriatrics to the very young. Many donkeys have suffered neglect and ill-treatment and the sanctuary's aim is to provide care for them for the rest of their lives.

℘ 0395 516391 or 578222.
Open: all year 9-dusk.
ㅎ toilets for the disabled.

## SILCHESTER
Hampshire

**CALLEVA MUSEUM**
Dealing with the Roman town of *Calleva Atrebatum*, this small museum includes panels of photographs, maps and other illustrative materials as well as actual objects excavated here, in order to present a brief account of life in the nearby walled Roman town (see also Reading Museum). Recently excavated amphitheatre. The 12th-century Church of St Mary is within a short walk of the amphitheatre.

℘ 0734 700362 (mid-day, evenings & weekends).
Open: accessible daily 9 sunset. ⌀

## SIRHOWY VALLEY
Gwent

**SIRHOWY VALLEY COUNTRY PARK**
(6m NW Newport, take A467 from junction 28 M4 & follow signs for Risca & Brynmawr. From Full Moon roundabout follow Country Park signs)
The 1,000-acre park stretching four miles along the picturesque Sirhowy valley is one of the largest country parks in Wales. There is a →

visitor centre, purpose-built barbecue and picnic areas, children's play area, many attractive way-marked walks areas, and guided walks and, more unusually, a fitness training circuit and orienteering routes. There is a programme of special events.

✆ Ynsddu 0495 270991 (Full Moon Information Centre) or 200113 (Ynys Hywel Countryside Centre). Open: at all times to pedestrians; car parks open 9–5.30 (4.30 in winter). Coach parties must give advance notice.
⚞⚟ ♿ (valley floor along disused railway line accessible).

## SIZEWELL B
Suffolk

**SIZEWELL INFORMATION CENTRE**
Single storey exhibition centre. Reception, exhibition hall, conference room and lecture room (available for pre-booked visits). Viewing tower during open hours.

✆ 0728 642139.
Open: Oct–Apr Mon–Sat 10–4, May–Sep daily. Guided tours at set times or by prior arrangement. Coach parties accepted.
▱ (vending machine) ⚞⚟ ♿ (ground floor) toilets for the disabled. Shop.

## SKENFRITH
Gwent

**SKENFRITH CASTLE**
(7m NW of Monmouth on B4521)
13th-century Marcher keep within a towered curtain wall, the work of Hubert de Burgh. One of the three 'trilateral' castles at Gwent.

Open: at all reasonable times. (CADW & NT)

## SKIPTON
North Yorkshire

**CRAVEN MUSEUM**
Town Hall, High Street
Contains collection dealing especially with the Craven district.

There are important exhibits of folk life, lead mining and prehistoric and Roman remains.

✆ 0756 794079.
Open: Apr–Sep, Mon, Wed–Fri 11–5, Sat 10–12 & 1–5, Sun 2–5; Oct–Mar, Mon, Wed–Fri 2–5, Sat 10–12 & 1.30–4.30. Open some BH, phone to check. Donations box.

## SNETTERTON
Norfolk

**INTERNATIONAL LEAGUE FOR THE PROTECTION OF HORSES**
Ann Culvin House
Telephone for directions.

✆ 0953 498682.
Open: all year Wed & Sun (ex Xmas Day) 2.30–4. Donations welcomed. Guided tours by arrangement. Group visits limited to 12 persons.

## SOUTHAMPTON
Hampshire

**CITY ART GALLERY**
Civic Centre, Commercial Road
At the time of our research, the Art Gallery was closed for refurbishment, but is due to re-open in September 1992. It contains 18th- to 20th-century English paintings. Continental Old Masters from 14th to 18th century. Modern French paintings. Collection of sculpture and ceramics. Of special interest are paintings and drawings of the 'Camden Town Group'. Particularly good collection of contemporary British painting and sculpture. Temporary exhibitions.

✆ 0703 231375 for recorded information.

**SOUTHAMPTON MARITIME MUSEUM**
The Wool House, Town Quay
This 600-year-old building, once a wool house, has buttressed stone walls and old roof timbering. Houses an interesting maritime museum. There is a permanent exhibition on the *Titanic* and engravings of French prisoners of war from the Napoleonic Wars in the roof beams.

✆ 0703 223941 & 224216.
Open: all year Tue–Fri 10–1 & 2–5, Sat 10–1 & 2–4, Sun 2–5. (Closed BH, 25–27 & 31 Dec.)
♿ (ground floor only) Shop ⚞ (ex guide dogs)

**TUDOR HOUSE MUSEUM**
Bugle Street, St Michael's Square
A restored, half-timbered 16th-century house, containing a museum of antiquarian and historical interest, social and domestic history, some costume and jewellery. Tudor garden reached through the museum.

✆ 0703 332513.
Open: all year Tue–Fri 10–5, Sat 10–4; Sun 2–5. Closed 12 noon 1pm for lunch. (Closed 25–27 & 31 Dec & BH Mon.)
♿ (ground floor & garden with help) Shop ⚞ (ex guide dogs).

## SOUTHEND-ON-SEA
Essex

**PRITTLESWELL PRIORY MUSEUM**
Priory Park
A medieval priory and private house standing in 40 acres of parkland near the heart of the town and housing a collection of radio, television, printing and writing equipment, natural history exhibits and a display of medieval religious life.

✆ 0702 342878.
Open: Tue–Sat, 10–1 & 2–5. Donation box. Guided tours and parties by appointment.
♿ (ground floor with staff assistance and grounds) Shop ⚞ (ex guide dogs).

**SOUTHCHURCH HALL MUSEUM**
Southchurch Hall Gardens
A medieval timber-framed manor house in moated gardens, close to the seafront, including period settings and displays of medieval life.

✆ 0702 467671.
Open: Tue–Sat, 10–1 & 2–5.

Preference given in mornings to pre-booked school parties in term time. Donation box. Guided tours & group visits by appointment. ঠ (ground floor through separate entrance by arrangement) Shop.

**SOUTHEND CENTRAL MUSEUM AND PLANETARIUM**
Victoria Avenue
The human and natural history of Southeast Essex from the Ice Ages to the 20th century told by objects, pictures and audio guides. The Planetarium (charge) gives 40-minute shows on the hour.

℘ 0702 330214.
Open: Mon 1–5, Tue–Sat 10–5; Planetarium 10–4. Donation box. Guided tours and parties by appointment only.
ঠ Shop.

**SOUTH MOLTON**
Devon

**SOUTH MOLTON MUSEUM**
Town Hall, Broad Street
Part of the Guildhall, a stone-fronted building of c1743, entered through open arcaded frontage. Local history, old charters, weights and measures, pewter, old fire engines, giant cider press. Monthly art, craft and educational exhibitions.

℘ 07695 2951.
Open: Feb–Nov Tue, Thu & Fri 10.30–1 & 2–4; Wed & Sat 10.30–12.30.
ঠ (ground floor only) ✖ (ex guide dogs).

**SOUTHPORT**
Merseyside

**ATKINSON ART GALLERY**
Lord Street
Oil paintings, watercolours, drawings and prints of the 19th and 20th centuries, 20th-century sculpture. Also visiting exhibition programme.

℘ 0704 533133 Ext 2110.
Open: all year, Mon, Tue, Wed & Fri 10–5, Thu & Sat 10–1.
Shop ✖

**BOTANIC GARDENS MUSEUM**
Churchtown (situated in public park)
Collections of local history, natural history, 18th- and 19th-century china. Also Ainsdale National Nature Reserve display, reconstructed Victorian parlour and Cecily Bate collection of dolls. Lifeboat display.

℘ 0704 27547.
Open: all year, Tue–Fri & BH Mon 11–3; Sat & Sun 2–5. (Closed Mon & Good Fri, also Fri following BH, 25 & 26 Dec & 1 Jan.)
ঠ (ground floor only) Shop ✖

**SOUTH SHIELDS**
Tyne & Wear

**ARBEIA ROMAN FORT AND MUSEUM**
Baring Street
Roman fort at the eastern-most end of the Hadrianic frontier, displaying fort defences, stone granaries, gateways, headquarters building, tile kilns and latrine. Museum contains site finds and interpretation. Full-scale simulation of a Roman gateway with interior scenes of life at the fort in Roman times.

℘ 091 456 1369.
Open: May–Sep, Tue–Fri 10–5.30, Sat 10–4.30 & Sun 2–5; Oct–Apr, Tue–Fri 10–4 & Sat 10–12. (Closed Sun).
ঠ (ground floor and gardens only) Shop ✖

**SOUTHWOLD**
Suffolk

**SOUTHWOLD MUSEUM**
Bartholomew Green
Formerly known as Dutch Cottage Museum, it contains local artefacts, pitcures and ephemera; also relics of Southwold light railway.

Open: daily Spring BH–Sep. Also Etr & May Day BH, 2.30–4.30. Donations welcome.

**SPEAN BRIDGE**
Highland

**SPEAN BRIDGE WOOLLEN MILL**
Visitors can see hand loom weaving

here and a demonstration of the original skills of the weaving process (the latter apparently requires rain, so an ideal wet-weather outing!). The adjacent mill shop has a range of Scottish goods.

℘ 039781 260.
Open: all year 9–5.30 (10–4.30 Nov–Apr) (Closed Sun Nov–Apr). Coach parties welcome.
⌸ (licensed) 🚻 ঠ (part) Shop.

**SPEY BAY**
Grampian

**TUGNET ICE HOUSE**
The largest ice house in Scotland, built in 1830. It contains exhibitions on the history and techniques of commercial salmon fishing on the River Spey; the geography, wildlife and industries of the Lower Spey area including ship building at nearby Kingston. There is also an audio-visual on the 'Spey from source to mouth'.

℘ Forres 0309 73701.
Open: Jun–Sep, daily, 10–4.
ঠ toilets for the disabled. Shop ✖ (ex guide dogs).

**STAFFORD**
Staffordshire

**ART GALLERY**
Lichfield Road
Art gallery showing temporary exhibitions of contemporary art craft and photography. Craft shop selling a wide range of work from British craftsmen. There is a programme of workshops and lectures throughout the year.

℘ 0785 57303.
Open: all year, Tue–Fri 10–5, Sat 10–4.
Shop ✖ (ex guide dogs).

**STAFFORD CASTLE**
Ruined castle dating from 12th century with inner and outer bailey, demolished by Parliamentary forces in 1643. Partly rebuilt c1800 in Gothic style.

Open: at all reasonable times.

## STANMER PARK

East Sussex

**STANMER RURAL MUSEUM**
(3m Brighton off A27 Lewes Rd)
This small museum of domestic and agricultural bygones is run voluntarily by members of the Stanmer Preservation Society. It stands in the 5000-acre Stanmer Park, near to the 19th-century church and estate village, which are now protected by a conservation order.

℘ 0273 552170.
Open: Etr Sun–Oct, Suns and BHs 2.30–5. Donation Box. Guided tours available on weekdays for school parties by prior arrangement. Parties (15–20 max) by appointment.
♿ (ground floor & grounds) Parking 100 yds. Shop.

## STAPLEHURST

Kent

**IDEN CROFT HERBS**
Frittenden Road (Signposted from A229 S of Staplehurst).
In quiet country in the heart of Kent, the farm has hundreds of varieties of herbs and aromatic plants. Over an acre of large aromatic herb gardens and walled garden.

℘ 0580 891432.
Open: all year Mon–Sat 9–5, Apr–Sep Sun & BH 11–5. Donations welcome.
♿ (2 wheelchairs on site) toilets for the disabled. Shop.

## STARSTON

Norfolk

**CRANES WATERING FARM AND SHOP**
(Off A140 Dickleburgh to Harleston rd)
Visitors are welcome to look round the working farm. A tour takes a minimum of 30 minutes and there is a pleasant area with wild flowers for picnicking. Milking can be seen 4–5pm. The farm shop sells home-produced dairy and other products and handicrafts. Children's Quiz available. Strong shoes or boots advised.

℘ 0379 852387.
Open: all year, Tue–Fri 10–5.30, Sat 10–5, Sun 10–12 (10–5 Jul–Aug). (Closed Mon, ex Spring & Summer BH, plus some dates in Dec & Jan). Pre-booked parties may be charged a small fee if extra staff have to be brought in. Guided tours if someone is available, otherwise map for DIY tour.
♿ (ex some farm buildings) Shop.

## STEVENAGE

Hertfordshire

**STEVENAGE MUSEUM**
St George's Way
This museum, in the undercroft of the parish church of St George, tells the story of Stevenage from the earliest times to the present day. Temporary exhibitions. Monthly Saturday events.

℘ 0438 354292.

Open: all year, Mon–Sat 10–5. (Closed Xmas.)
♿ Shop ✂

## STICKFORD

Lincolnshire

**ALLIED FORCES MILITARY MUSEUM**
Main Road (On A16 between Spilsby & Boston)
A large private collection of Second World War British, American and post-war vehicles and exhibits of badges, uniforms, aeronautica and equipment.

℘ Boston 0205 480317.
Open: all year Mon–Fri 9–5, weekends by appointment. Guided tours. Coach parties by appointment.
♿ (no toilets).

## STIRLING

Central

**MAR'S WARK**
Broad Street
A partly ruined Renaissance mansion with a gatehouse enriched by sculptures. Built by the Regent Mar in 1570.

Open: Apr–Sep Mon–Fri 9.30–6, Sun 2–6.
(AM)

**STIRLING SMITH ART GALLERY AND MUSEUM**
40 Albert Place, Dumbarton Road
Lively programme of exhibitions throughout the year, featuring

contemporary and historical art, local and social history.

✆ 0786 71917.
Open: Apr–Oct, Tue–Sat 10.30–5, Sun 2–5; Nov–Mar, Tue–Fri 12–5, Sat 10.30–5 & Sun 2–5.
☕ ♿ toilets for the disabled. Shop 🐕

## STOCKTON-ON-TEES

Cleveland

**Preston Hall Museum**
Yarm Road (2m S on A135)
Museum illustrates Victorian social history, and collections include costume, arms, armour and period rooms. Also 19th-century reconstructed street with working blacksmiths and farrier. At weekends a draper's shop is open, with material for sale.

✆ 0642 781184.
Open: all year, Mon–Sat 9.30–5.30, Sun 2–5.30. Last admission 5.
☕ ⛩ ♿ (ground floor only) toilets for the disabled. Shop 🐕 (ex guide dogs). Parking charge.

## STOKE-ON-TRENT

Staffordshire

**City Museum and Art Gallery**
Bethesda Street, Hanley
Exhibits include a large collection of ceramics, with the emphasis on Staffordshire pottery and porcelain. There is also a programme of temporary exhibitions.

✆ 0782 202173.
Open: all year Mon–Sat 10–5, Sun 2–5. (Closed Xmas week & Good Fri.)
☕ (licensed) ♿ toilets for the disabled. Shop 🐕

**Coalport Craft Centre**
Park Street, Fenton
World famous for its fine bone china tableware, figurines, floral studies, cottages and hand painted collector's pieces. The company was established in 1750 in Shropshire and moved to Stoke-on-Trent in 1926, becoming a member of the Wedgwood Group in 1967. The craft centre provides an opportunity to see the making and hand painting of fine bone china.

✆ 0782 45274.
Open: Mon–Thu 9.30–4.30, Fri 9.30–12.30. Factory tours are chargeable & by prior appointment only. (Children must be aged 14 and over to tour factory.)
☕ ♿ toilets for the disabled. Shop.

**Etruria Industrial Museum**
Lower Bedford Street, Etruria
Britain's only surviving steam-powered potter's mill – Jesse Shirley's Etruscan Bone and Flint Mill – was built to grind materials for the agricultural and pottery industries. The mill contains gear room, grinding pans, boiler and 1820's beam engine which is steamed one weekend a month.

✆ 0782 287557.
Open: Wed–Sun 10–4. Donations welcome.

**Ford Green Hall**
Ford Green Road, Smallthorne (On the B5051 Leek–Newcastle-under-Lyme road)
Timber-framed yeoman's farmhouse dating from c1580–1600, with 18th-century additions. Contains appropriate period furnishings.

✆ 0782 534771.
Open: daily 1–5. Facilities for small groups and school parties.
☕ Shop.

**Minton Museum**
Minton House, London Road
The museum has a stunning collection of ceramics dating from 1793.

✆ 0782 744766.
Open: all year Mon–Fri, 9–12.30 & 2–4.30. (Closed factory holidays).
Shop 🐕 (ex guide dogs).

**Moorcroft Pottery**
Sandbach Road, Burslem
Pottery factory shop built around an original bottle oven with a new museum displaying pieces dating from 1897.

*Stoke-on-Trent: decorating a Coalport China figure*

✆ 0782 214323.
Open: all year Mon–Fri 10–5, Sat 9.30–4.30. Guided tours by prior arrangement (charge).
♿ Shop.

**Sir Henry Doulton Gallery**
Nile Street, Burslem
Royal Doulton's own collection of ceramics with exhibits from 1815. A highlight is the collection of out-of-production Royal Doulton figures. Admission to the museum is free, factory tours are charged for.

✆ 0782 575454.
Open: all year Mon–Fri 9–4.30. (Closed factory holidays).
☕ (restaurant for pre-booked parties 9–4.30) Shop 🐕 (ex guide dogs).

## STOKE-SUB-HAMDON

Somerset

**Stoke-sub-Hamdon Priory**
A 15th-century Ham-Hill stone house, once a chantry and retaining original screens and part of great hall. →

℘ 0935 823584.
Open: daily 10–6.
(NT)

## STONEHAVEN
Grampian

**STONEHAVEN TOLBOOTH**
Old Pier, The Harbour
Once a 16th-century storehouse of
the Earls Marischal, later used as a
prison. Now a fishing and local
history museum.

℘ Peterhead 0779 77778.
Open: Jun–Sep, Mon, Thu, Fri & Sat
10–12 & 2–5, Wed & Sun 2–5.
⅃ (ground floor only) Shop
⅋ (ex guide dogs).

## STOURBRIDGE
West Midlands

**EDINBURGH CRYSTAL FACTORY
SHOP AND MUSEUM**
Dennis Hall, King William
Street, Amblecote
Set in the coach house of the
grounds at Dennis Hall, the
museum contains a fascinating
variety of glassware, including
superb examples of the work of
artists and craftsmen such as
George and Thomas Woodall,
William Fritsche, Jules Barbe, John
Thomas Fereday and many others.
The shop sells first and second
quality crystal.

℘ 0384 392521.
Open: all year Mon–Fri 9–4.30, Sat
9.30–4.30, Sun 10.30–4.30. Closed 25
Dec–2 Jan (provisional). Coach
parties accepted.
⅃ ⅃ toilets for the disabled. Shop.

**ROYAL DOULTON CRYSTAL (UK)**
High St, Amblecote (off A491)
Conducted tours show at close
quarters the production of fine
crystal tableware and giftware.

℘ 0384 440442.
Open: Mon–Fri 10 and 11.15 (Tours),
Mon–Sat 9–5.30 (Shop). Parties
accepted.
⅃ (with assistance) Shop ⅋ (on
tours).

## STREET
Somerset

**THE SHOE MUSEUM (C & J CLARK
LTD)**
High Street
The museum is housed in the
oldest part of the factory and
contains shoes from Roman times
to the present, Georgian shoe
buckles, caricatures and engravings
of shoemakers, costume
illustrations and fashion plates,
shoe machinery, hand tools,
advertising material, and 19th-
century documents and
photographs illustrating the early
history of the firm from the
founding in 1825 by Cyrus Clark.

℘ 0458 43131 Ext 2169.
Open: Etr Mon–Oct, Mon–Fri 10–4.45,
Sat 10–4.30; winter months by
appointment only.
Shop ⅋

## STROMNESS
### See Orkney

## STROUD
Gloucestershire

**STROUD DISTRICT (COWLE)
MUSEUM**
Lansdown
The exhibits cover geology,
archaeology, local crafts, industrial
archaeology (including local mills
and houses), and farmhouse
household equipment. A full-length
model of the dinosaur
Megalosaurus is on display. Branch
museum nearby with displays of
local crafts and industries.

℘ 0453 763394.
Open: all year Mon–Sat 10.30–1 & 2–
5. (Closed BHs.)
Shop.

## SUNDERLAND
Tyne and Wear

**GRINDON CLOSE MUSEUM**
Grindon Lane
Edwardian period rooms, including
chemist's shop and dentist's
surgery.

℘ 091 512 84042.
Open: all year Mon–Wed & Fri 9.30–
12.30 & 1.30–6 (5pm Tue), Sat 9.30–
12.15 & 1.15–4; Jun–Sep also Sun 2–
5. (Closed Thu, BH and preceding
Sat.)
⅋

**MUSEUM AND ART GALLERY**
Borough Road
The wildlife and geology of the
North East. The history of
Sunderland and its industries,
particularly glass, pottery and
shipbuilding. Period rooms, silver,
paintings and a wide range of
temporary exhibitions.

℘ 091 514 1235.
Open: all year Tue–Fri 10–5.30, Sat
10–4, Sun 2–5, BH Mon 10–5.30.
(Closed Mon, Good Fri, 25–26 Dec &
1 Jan.)
⅃ (10–4.45 Mon–Fri, 10–12 Sat).
⅃ Shop ⅋

**MONKWEARMOUTH STATION
MUSEUM**
North Bridge Street
Land transport museum in station
built in 1848. The booking office,
platform areas and footbridge have
all been restored and there is also
rolling stock. Displays inside the
museum deal with transport in
northeast England with a display
showing the evolution of steam
locomotives.

℘ 091 567 7075.
Open: all year Tue–Fri & BH 10–5.30,
Sat 10–4.30, Sun 2–5. (Closed Good
Fri, 25–26 Dec & 1 Jan.)
⅃ Shop ⅋

## SWANAGE
Dorset

**DURLSTON COUNTRY PARK**
Over 260 acres of countryside and
coastland in the southeast corner
of the Isle of Purbeck. There are
clifftop and downland walks and a
series of guided walks led by Park
Wardens. Also visit the Great Globe,
built in 1887, and see the world as it
was then!

℘ 0929 424443.

Open: Park Display and Information
Centre Etr–Oct 10.30–5.30. Organised
groups welcome by prior
arrangement. Parking charge. Guided
walks (charge); walks/events leaflet
on request.
🍽 (licensed) 🚻 ♿ (ground floor)
Shop.

## SWANSEA
West Glamorgan

### GLYNN VIVIAN ART GALLERY AND MUSEUM
Alexandra Road
Works by British and French
masters and contemporary British
artists. Collections of Continental
and Swansea porcelain and pottery.
Major contemporary exhibitions
and Summer Festival Exhibition,
also education service and craft
outlet.

✆ 0792 655006.
Open: daily 10.30–5.30. (Closed 25–
26 Dec & 1 Jan.)
♿ (ground floor & sculpture court)
toilets for the disabled. Shop ✧

### MARITIME AND INDUSTRIAL MUSEUM
South Dock
Contains complete working woollen
mill in continuous production.
Displays relating to the industry and
the Port of Swansea and its
environment. Transport exhibits,
maritime and agriculture sections.

✆ 0792 650351.
Open: daily 10.30–5.30. (Closed 25–
26 Dec & 1 Jan.) Donations box.
♿ Shop ✧

## SWARTHMOOR
Cumbria

### SWARTHMOOR HALL
Former home of George Fox,
founder of the Quakers. This
Elizabethan and later house is now
administered by the Society of
Friends.

✆ Ulverston 0229 53204.
Open: mid Mar–mid Oct, Mon–Wed &
Sat 10–12 & 2–5. Donation.

## SWINDON
Wiltshire

### LYDIARD HOUSE
Lydiard Park (1m N of M4 junc
16 on unclass road)
Fine Georgian mansion set in
pleasant park, together with the
adjoining parish church of St Mary,
which contains memorials to the St
John family. Visitor Centre in
grounds of Park.

✆ 0793 770401.
Open: daily, Mon–Sat 10–1 & 2–5.30.
Sun 2–5.30. (Closed Good Fri &
Xmas.) Donations. Tours available for
organised parties if staff available by
pre-arrangement (charge). Prior
booking requested for coach parties.
🍽 🚻 ♿ (ground floor & grounds)
toilets for the disabled in Visitors
Centre. Shop.

### MUSEUM AND ART GALLERY
Bath Road
Contains a small collection of items
of local interest and the Swindon
Art Collection of 20th-century
British pictures and ceramics.

✆ 0793 26161 Ext 3129.
Open: all year Mon–Sat 10–6, Sun 2–
5. (Closed Good Fri & 25–26 Dec.)
Handling table and tape cassettes for
visually handicapped.
Shop ✧

### RICHARD JEFFERIES MUSEUM
Coate Farm (off A345)
Birthplace in 1848 of Richard
Jefferies, the nature writer, and now
a museum exhibiting literature
relating to local wildlife written by
Jefferies and Alfred Owen Williams.

✆ 0793 26161 Ext 3130.
Open: Etr–Oct Wed, Sat & Sun 2–5.
Shop ✧

## TARDEBIGGE
Hereford and Worcester

### TARDEBIGGE LOCKS
(Between Tardebigge and
Stoke Pound)
Tardebigge Locks on the Worcester
and Birmingham Canal were built by
John Woodhouse between 1812 and

1815 and are the largest flight of
locks in the country. In a little over
two miles the canal is raised 217ft.
The top lock is much deeper than
the rest because in 1808 an
experimental boat lift was installed,
however it was soon decided that it
would not stand up to constant
rough treatment. A deep lock was
constructed in its place. A towpath
runs along the eastern bank of the
canal.

Open: accessible at all reasonable
times on towpath.

## TENBY
Dyfed

### TENBY POTTERY
Upper Frog Street
All processes of pottery making can
be seen from the showroom:
throwing, firing, decorating, glazing
and kilnpacking. Everything is hand
thrown and individually decorated
ranging from thimbles to large plant
pots.

✆ 0834 2890.
Open: Mon–Fri 10.15–1 & 2.15–5.30.
Sat 10.15–1. School demonstrations
by arrangement.
♿ (ground floor only) Shop.

## THETFORD
Norfolk

### ANCIENT HOUSE MUSEUM
White Hart Street
15th-century, timber-framed house
with fine carved ceilings. Displays of
Thetford and Breckland life.

✆ 0842 752599.
Open: Mon–Sat 10–5 (Mon closed 1–
2), Sun 2–5. (Closed Good Fri, 24–26
Dec & 1 Jan). Free mid Sep–early Jul,
otherwise a charge is made. Donation
Box. Guided tours for parties by prior
arrangement.
Shop.

### THETFORD CASTLE
One of the original motte and bailey
castles, at 80 ft perhaps the largest
still in existence. The earliest form
of castle, before masonry was
added.  →

*Tiverton Museum*

Open: daily (ex Xmas Day), Visitor Centre 10–5. Guided walks by prior arrangement. Special events. ☎ (051 648 4959) ⊼ ♿ (ground floor & grounds).

## TILLICOULTRY
Central

**CLOCK MILL HERITAGE CENTRE**
Upper Mill Street
The Clock Mill has been converted into a heritage centre and also includes a Tourist Information Centre. There are displays from the past and several craft workshops.

✆ Stirling 0786 75019.
Open: Apr–mid Oct daily 10–5. (Closes at 6 Jul & Aug). Groups and tours available.
♿ (ground floor only) toilets for the disabled. Shop.

## TIVERTON
Devon

**TIVERTON MUSEUM**
St Andrew Street, near Town Hall. (Entrance from public car park)
Comprehensive museum housed in a restored 19th-century school containing numerous local exhibits, a Victorian laundry, two waterwheels, costume gallery, industrial gallery covering the Grand Western Canal and local trades, natural history and wartime rooms. Heathcoat Lace gallery featuring 19th-century lace-making machine and other relics of Heathcoat Lace Making Factory. Agricultural section includes a collection of farm wagons and a complete smithy. A large railway gallery houses the GWR locomotive No 1442, and other railway relics. New display of Tiverton's recently-discovered Roman Fort.

✆ 0884 256295.
Open: Mon–Sat 10.30–4.30. (Closed 19 Dec–1 Feb.) Groups and tours by prior arrangement.
♿ (ground floor only; ramp access from museum yard) Shop ✖ (ex guide dogs).

Open: accessible at all reasonable times.

**WARREN LODGE**
(2m W of town, off B1107)
Remains of a two-storeyed hunting lodge in 15th-century flint with stone dressings.

Open: at all reasonable times. (AM)

## THIRSK
North Yorkshire

**TRESKE LIMITED**
Station Works
Visitors can watch craftsmen at work here, making a wide range of furniture to designs by some of Britain's leading designers. The finished articles are on display in fine old maltings.

✆ 0845 522770.
Open: all year daily 10–5. Coach parties welcome. Shop.

## THURSTASTON
Merseyside

**WIRRAL COUNTRY PARK**
(Visitor Centre, Station Rd)
The abandoned West Kirby to Hooton railway line forms the basis of this country park. The old 12-mile line ran close to the Dee Estuary and embankments offer views across the Dee to the Welsh hills. The Visitor Centre provides a Ranger Service and information on study areas, walks, fishing and horseriding, children's events and wildlife cruises.

✆ 051 648 4371/3884.

## TOLPUDDLE
Dorset

### TOLPUDDLE MARTYR'S MUSEUM
James Loveless Cottage (on A35, approx 7 miles NE of Dorchester).
The museum tells the story of six agricultural labourers from Tolpuddle who were transported to Australia in 1834 for forming a Trade Union. Other related sites in the village include the Martyr's Tree, under which the men met, and the grave of one of them – James Hammett.

✆ 0305 848237.
Open: all year daily 10–5.30. (Closed 24 Dec–1 Jan. Donation requested. Coach parties must book in advance. ﯼ (part) Shop.

## TOMINTOUL
Grampian

### TOMINTOUL MUSEUM
The Square
Reconstructed farm kitchen and blacksmith's shop, Harness displays, local landscape and wildlife displays.

✆ Forres 0309 73701.
Open: 13 Apr–May & Oct, Mon–Sat 9–5.30; Sun 2–5.30; closes at 6 Jun & Sep; 7 Jul & Aug.
ﯼ Shop ⌾

## TOMNAVOULIN
Grampian

### TOMNAVOULIN-GLENLIVET DISTILLERY
(On B9008 6.5m N of Tomintoul)
A video presentation is followed by a tour where visitors will see the process of whisky making, followed by whisky sampling in the hospitality lounge. Picnic area by the River Livet.

✆ Glenlivet 08073 442.
Open: Etr–Oct, tours 9.30–4.30; last tour 3.45. Groups by arrangement.
⊓ ﯼ (ground floor only) toilets for the disabled. Shop.

## TONBRIDGE
Kent

### TONBRIDGE CASTLE AND GROUNDS
Castle Street
Norman Motte and Bailey Castle situated in delightful grounds by the River Medway. The Gatehouse is due to reopen at Easter 1992 with a new exhibition.

✆ Tourist Information Centre 0732 770929.
Open: grounds open all year daily. Audio tours (charge £1, ch & pen 50p) available from the Tourist Information Centre. Coach parties by arrangement with Tourist Information

Centre.
ﯼ toilets for the disabled. Shop (in Tourist Information Centre).

## TONDU
Mid Glamorgan

### GLAMORGAN NATURE CENTRE
(1m W)
A small nature reserve in open countryside, headquarters of Glamorgan Wildlife Trust. Exhibition area in centre building, giving an introduction to the wildlife of the county and the work of the Trust. Waymarked trail. The Centre can provide details of the other 46 nature reserves throughout Glamorgan.

✆ Aberkenfig 0656 724100.
Open: Mon–Fri 9–1. Groups and tours by arrangement.
⊓ ﯼ (excellent access) toilets for the disabled.

## TORQUAY
Devon

### BABBACOMBE POTTERY
Babbacombe Road
See both traditional and modern methods of pottery manufacture, including hand painting, and try your hand on the potter's wheel. →

*The impressive gateway of Tonbridge Castle*

There are ornamental gardens, a fishpond and dovecote.

✆ 0803 323322.
Open: all year Mon–Fri 9–5 (daily 9am–10pm in summer).
🚐 🅿 ♿ Shop.

## TORRINGTON
Devon

**TORRINGTON MUSEUM**
The Town Hall
Museum and Tourist Information Centre in the Town Hall. Special exhibitions include the Devon County Council Project, the Tarka Trail and the Coronation robes and coronets of the Earl and Countess Orford.

✆ 0805 24324.
Open: May–Sep, Mon–Fri 10.15–12.45, & 2.15–4.45, Sat 10.15–12.45.
Donation requested. Coach parties of 20 max accepted.

## TREFRIW
Gwynedd

**TREFRIW WOOLLEN MILL**
Visitors can watch the weaving of tapestry bedspreads and tweeds at the mill, which also generates its own electricity and the turbine house can also be seen. The large shop sells mill products, plus Welsh crafts and knitwear.

✆ Llanrwst 0492 640462.
Open: Mon–Fri 9–5.30 (Winter 5pm); also weekends Spring BH–Aug, Sat 10–4, Sun 2–5. (Closed BH).
🚐 ♿ Shop ⌘ (in mill).

## TUNBRIDGE WELLS
Kent

**TUNBRIDGE WELLS MUSEUM AND ART GALLERY**
Civic Centre
Local and natural history, and Tunbridge ware. Collections of toys, dolls and domestic bygones. Regularly changing art gallery exhibitions.

✆ 0892 26121.

Open: Mon–Sat 9.30–5 (Closed Sun & BH). Donations welcome. Parties by arrangement.
⌘

## TUTBURY
Staffordshire

**GEORGIAN CRYSTAL**
Silk Mill Lane
Visitors can watch demonstrations of glass-blowing and decorating.

✆ 0283 814534.
Open: all year (ex Xmas–New Year), Mon–Sat 9–5. Parties by prior arrangement.
♿ (Ground floor only) Shop.

## TWICKENHAM
Gt London

**ORLEANS HOUSE GALLERY**
Riverside
Site of Orleans House, in which Louis Phillippe, Duc d'Orléans, King of the French 1830–48, lived in exile in the early 19th century. It was demolished in 1927. Surviving Grade I listed octagonal room, designed by James Gibbs in about 1720, has exquisite plasterwork. The adjacent art gallery shows temporary exhibitions.

✆ 081 892 0221.
Open: all year Tue–Sat 1–5.30 (4.30pm Oct–Mar) Sun & BH 2–5.30 (Oct–Mar 2–4.30). (Closed 25–26 Dec and Good Fri.) Woodland gardens open all year, daily 9–dusk. Donations welcome. Groups and tours by arrangement.
♿ (partial) toilets for the disabled. Shop ⌘ (ex guide dogs).

## UFFFINGTON
Oxfordshire

**CASTLE AND WHITE HORSE**
Iron Age hill fort situated on the ancient Ridgeway at a height of more than 700ft on the Berkshire Downs. Below it, cut in the chalk, is the famous White Horse.

Open: accessible at any reasonable time.

## ULEY
Gloucestershire

**ULEY LONG BARROW (HETTY PEGLER'S TUMP)**
Neolithic burial mound of earth about 180ft long, surrounded by a dry-built reveting wall and containing a central passage of stone with three burial chambers.

Open: any reasonable time.
(AM)

## UPMINSTER
Gt London

**TITHE BARN AGRICULTURAL AND FOLK MUSEUM**
Hall Lane
15th-century thatched timber building containing large selection of old agricultural implements, craft and farm tools, domestic bygones and items of local interest.

✆ 04024 47535.
Open: Apr–Oct, first weekend in each month, 1.30–6. Advise telephoning to check before visit.
♿ Shop ⌘

## UPTON
Dorset

**UPTON COUNTRY PARK**
Over 100 acres of parkland, gardens and woodland on the edge of Poole Harbour. Nature trails, Countryside Heritage Centre.

Open: all year daily. Guided tours by arrangement with Wardens. Coach parties not accepted at weekends.
🚐 (tearooms 10.30–5 summer, may be closed in winter). 🅿 ♿ (ground floor & grounds) toilets for the disabled. Shop.

## VENTNOR
*See Wight, Isle of*

## VOGRIE COUNTRY PARK
Lothian

(On B6372 between Dewarton & Newlandrigg, 12m S of Edinburgh, signposted from A7 at Gorebridge & A68 just before Pathhead) A 19th-century estate with a house, park, farmland and woods. There is a large field, adventure playground and barbeque site free for public use, though the field and barbeque facilities should be booked in advance. There are several formal gardens and countryside walks. Visitor facilities are available in Vogrie House, and an exhibition with details of the natural and social history of Vogrie. Ranger Service.

✆ Gorebridge 0875 21990. Open: all year daily dawn–dusk. Guided walks during summer, or private parties by arrangement with Countryside Rangers. Limited parking for coaches. 大 ᵬ (ground floor & grounds) toilets for the disabled.

## WAEN-Y-LLYN
Clwyd

**WAEN-Y-LLYN COUNTRY PARK**
(Off A541 Mold–Wrexham) A small country park situated on Hope Mountain near Wrexham. There are a variety of wildlife habitats, including moorland, heathland and a small lake. Ideal for birdwatching and walking, with extensive views of Cheshire, Merseyside and the Clwydian Range.

✆ 035285 614. Open: all year, daily.

## WAKEFIELD
West Yorkshire

**WAKEFIELD ART GALLERY**
Wentworth Terrace Important collection of 20th-century paintings and sculpture. Special rooms devoted to locally-born Barbara Hepworth and Henry Moore. Also temporary exhibitions.

✆ 0924 375402. Open: all year, Mon–Sat 10.30–5, Sun 2.30–5 all BHs during spring & summer months. ᵬ (ground floor only by prior arrangement) ✀

**WAKEFIELD MUSEUM**
Wood Street Archaeology and history of Wakefield from prehistoric times to recent past. Waterton Collection of exotic birds and animals. Temporary exhibitions.

✆ 0924 295351. Open: all year Mon–Sat 10.30–5; Sun & all BHs spring and summer months 2.30–5. ᵬ (ground floor only by arrangement).

## WALLSEND
Tyne & Wear

**WALLSEND HERITAGE CENTRE**
Salisbury House, 2 Buddle Street Relates the rich history of the town, formerly Roman *Segedunum*, at the eastern end of Hadrian's Wall. Also shipbuilding and mining history of the area, plus a programme of special events and exhibitions.

✆ 091 262 0012. Open: May–Oct Thu–Sat 10.30–12 & 12.30–4.30. Coach parties welcome. ᵬ toilets for the disabled.

## WALSALL
W Midlands

**MUSEUM AND ART GALLERY**
Lichfield Street Garman Ryan collection including important works by Blake, Degas, Van Gogh and Epstein. Regular loan exhibitions. Local history museum.

✆ 0922 653135. Open: Mon–Fri 10–6 & Sat 10–4.45. (Closed Sun, Xmas & BHs.) ᵬ Shop ✀ (ex guide dogs)

**WALSALL LEATHER CENTRE MUSEUM**
56–57 Wisemore A working museum in the capital of the British saddlery and leathergoods trade. Demonstrations every Tuesday, Wednesday and Saturday by leather workers. Products on sale. Attractive ground.

✆ 0922 721153.

Open: all year, Tue–Sat 10–5, Sun 12–5 (Nov–Mar 4pm). Open BHs, closed Xmas. Guided tours subject to availability. Coach parties max 40. 且 大 ᵬ toilets for the disabled. Shop.

## WALTHAM ABBEY
Essex

**EPPING FOREST DISTRICT MUSEUM**
39–41 Sun Street A social history museum situated in two 16th and 17th century timber-framed houses in this historic town. Exhibits include Tudor oak panelling, a rural life collection and and temporary exhibitions of arts and crafts. Annual community festival in May.

✆ 0992 716882. Open: all year Fri–Mon 2–5, Tue 12–5; Wed, Thu closed (ex group bookings). Guided tours for pre-booked parties. ᵬ (ground floor only) Shop.

**LEE VALLEY PARK COUNTRYSIDE CENTRE**
Abbey Farmhouse, Crooked Mile Visitor Centre with information and displays about the area and the Lee Valley Park. It also provides an extensive programme of events for the casual visitor, environmental programmes for schools and talks for groups and societies.

✆ 0992 713838. Open: all year daily 10–5, please telephone for winter hours which may be restricted. Coach parties please given prior notice. ᵬ (ground floor & grounds) toilets for the disabled. Shop.

**WALTHAM ABBEY GATEHOUSE, BRIDGE AND ENTRANCE TO CLOISTERS**
14th-century gatehouse with separate carriage and pedestrian entrances. Harold's Bridge is also probably 14th century. Cloister entrance dates from 12th century. In the historic Norman and later Abbey Church nearby is an undercroft museum.                →

Open: at any reasonable time.
(AM)

## WANDLEBURY RING
Cambridgeshire

(4m SE of Cambridge off
A1307)
On the summit of the low Gog
Magog Hills, the remains of an Iron
Age hill-fort which once comprised
a double rampart and ditch, 1,000ft
in diameter; about 110 acres of the
hills have been protected by the
Cambridge Preservation Society.

℘ 0223 248706.
Open: daily. Donation of £1
requested.
🎋 Shop

## WANTAGE
Oxfordshire

VALE AND DOWNLAND MUSEUM
CENTRE
The Old Surgery, Church
Street
A lively museum centre with
displays on the geology,
archaeology and local history of the
Vale of the White Horse and the
town of Wantage. Temporary
exhibitions and local craft
demonstrations occasionally.

℘ 02357 66838.
Open: all year Tue–Sat 10.30–4.30 &
Sun 2.30–5. (BH Mon check in
advance.)
🖳 ᵬ (ground floor only) Shop.

## WARRINGTON
Cheshire

RISLEY MOSS NATURE PARK
Ordnance Ave (Junc 11 M62
motorway)
One of the few remaining
mosslands, now open as a country
park and nature reserve with picnic
area and birdwatching hides.
Information on the area and display
in Visitors Centre.

℘ 0925 824339.
Open: all year, summer Mon-Thu 9–5,
Sat, Sun & BH 10–6; winter Mon–Thu
10.30–4.30, Sat Sun & BH 9–5.

(Closed Fri & 25 Dec). Parties by
advance booking only.
ᵬ toilets for the disabled.

SOUTH LANCASHIRE REGIMENT
(PWV) REGIMENTAL MUSEUM
Peninsula Barracks, O'Leary
Street, Orford
Military museum of South
Lancashire Regiment from 1717
onwards.

℘ 0925 33563.
Open: all year, Mon–Fri 9–2.30
(ex PH), also for parties evenings &
weekends by arrangement.
🦮

## WARWICK
Warwickshire

ST JOHN'S HOUSE
Coten End (junction of A429
and A445 E of town)
Fine 17th-century house rebuilt by
the Stoughton family on the site of
an old hospital. It is now a branch
of the County Museum (domestic
scenes, costume, and other
changing displays), Victorian
schoolroom. Includes the museum
of the Royal Warwickshire
Regiment.

℘ Leamington Spa 0926 412132 or
412500. For Regimental Museum 0926
491653.
Open: all year Tue–Sat & BH 10–12.30
& 1.30–5.30; May–Sep also Sun 2.30–
5. Donations welcome.
ᵬ (ground floor only) Shop.

WARWICKSHIRE MUSEUM
Market Place
17th-century market hall now a
museum displaying the geology,
history and natural history of
Warwickshire. Notable for the
Sheldon tapestry map of
Warwickshire, habitat displays and
giant fossil plesiosaur. Temporary
exhibitions throughout the year and
children's holiday activities in
summer and at Christmas.

℘ 0926 410410 Ext 2500.
Open: all year Mon–Sat 10–5.30; Sun
(May–Sep only 2.30–5). Donations
welcome. Shop.

WARWICKSHIRE YEOMANRY
MUSEUM
The Court House, Jury Street
Display of military exhibits, includes
uniforms, medals, militaria and
weapons dating from 1794 to 1945.
Also selected items of silver from
the Regimental collection. There is
a very fine display of paintings and
pictures covering the same period.

℘ 0926 492212.
Open: Good Fri–end Sep, Fri, Sat, Sun
& BH 10–1 & 2–4.
Shop 🦮 (ex guide dogs).

## WASHINGTON
West Sussex

CHANCTONBURY RING
(1.5m SE) Reached by footpath
Situated on the South Downs Way,
Chanctonbury Ring consists of a
clump of beech trees planted in
1760, situated within the remains of
an Iron Age fort. Excavations have
revealed remains of two Roman
buildings and prehistoric barrows.
There are good views from the
summit.

Open: accessible at all reasonable
times.

## WATFORD
Hertfordshire

WATFORD MUSEUM
194 High Street
Museum describing the history of
the Watford area from earliest times
to the present day. There are
special features on brewing and
printing together with a display of
wartime Watford based on the
'Dad's Army' series written by
Jimmy Perry from his Watford
experience. A good art gallery and a
constantly changing programme of
exhibits.

℘ 0923 32297.
Open: all year Mon–Sat 10–5. (Closed
25–26 Dec.)
ᵬ toilets for the disabled & some
special parking. Shop 🦮 (ex guide
dogs).

*West Bretton: 'Knife Edge'
Sculpture by Henry Moore*

## WAYLAND'S SMITHY
Oxfordshire
(1m S off the B4507 Compton
Beauchamp turning near end of
unclass road)
A well-preserved megalithic long
barrow in a copse close to the
Ridgeway path. The long barrow
was excavated in 1919–1920 and
revealed eight Stone Age skeletons.
Wayland the Smith figures in
Scandinavian mythology as a maker
of invincible weapons.

Open: accessible at all reasonable
times.
(AM)

## WEETING
Norfolk

### WEETING CASTLE
A ruined 11th-century fortified
manor house, situated in a

rectangular moated enclosure and
preserving slight remains of three
storeyed cross-wing.
Open: at all reasonable times.
(AM)

## WELLINGBOROUGH
Northamptonshire

### WELLINGBOROUGH HERITAGE
CENTRE
Croyland Hall, Burystead Place
An exhibition of local history from
earliest times including local
industries and a 1940s kitchen.
Temporary exhibitions are held in
the Regency drawing-room
overlooking the lake.

℘ 0933 276838.
Open: Tue–Sat 10–4.30, Sun 2–4.30.
(Closed Xmas & Mon, but open BH).
Donation Box. Guided tours and
parties by prior arrangement.
&. toilets for the disabled.

## WELSHPOOL
Powys

### COCKPIT
New Street
During the 18th century
cockfighting was a keenly followed
sport and this Grade II listed
cockpit has been recently restored
to its original state.

Open: Apr–Sep, Mon–Fri 10–4.
&. (ground floor only).

### ORIEL 31 ART GALLERY
High Street
The largest collection of original
prints in mid-Wales are contained in
this gallery which also shows all the
print processes of lithography,
woodcraft and screen printing.
Every month there are changing
exhibitions with a wide range of
subjects from sculpture and
photography to textiles and
painting.

℘ 0938 552990.
Open: all year Mon–Sat 11–5.
Donations box. Shop.

### POWYSLAND MUSEUM AND
MONTGOMERY CANAL CENTRE
Canal Wharf
Museum of archaeology and local
history.

℘ 0938 554656.
Open: all year weekdays (ex Wed)
11–1 & 2–5, summer weekends 10–1
& 2–5, winter Sat 2–5. (Closed Wed &
winter Suns).
Shop ✖ (ex guide dogs).

### SEVERN FARM POND
(East of town off B4381)
Nature reserve with pond, wetland,
scrub and meadow habitats. Bird
observation hide.

℘ 0686 624751.
Open: all year daily. Guided tours
available to parties by prior
arrangement.
&. (Bird observation hide & surfaced
paths suitable for disabled visitors.)

## WEMBLEY
Greater London

### FRYENT COUNTRY PARK
Countryside in Brent. A network of
paths of varied type and distance
lead through woodland, parkland,
meadow and to hilltops and historic
ponds.

℘ 081–900 5016 (Countryside
Rangers).
Open: all year. Guided tours are
sometimes available.
&. (access path available at certain
times).

## WEST BRETTON
West Yorkshire

### YORKSHIRE SCULPTURE PARK
Bretton Hall
Set in beautiful grounds, this park
is the country's leading outdoor
exhibition centre of contemporary
sculpture, including works by Henry
Moore and Barbara Hepworth.
There is a programme of changing
exhibitions, educational activities
and events.

℘ 0924 830302.                    →

Open: daily, summer 10–6; winter 10–4. (Closed 25–26 Dec & 1 Jan.) Donations. Guided tours. Coach parties by prior arrangement. 🖳🗇 (sculpture trail) (toilets and motorised scooters for the disabled. Shop.

## WESTCLIFF-ON-SEA
Essex

**BEECROFT ART GALLERY**
Station Rd (opposite Cliffs Pavilion)
Eight galleries, with magnificent views of the Thames estuary, mounting 20 or more exhibitions a year and with an extensive permanent collection. Annual Essex 'Open Exhibition' in July and Aug.

✆ 0702 347418.
Open: all year Mon–Sat 9–5. (Closed BH). Donation box. School parties and groups welcome.
🗇 (ground floor only).

## WEST MALLING
Kent

**ST LEONARD'S TOWER**
(On unclass road W of A228)
Fine early Norman tower, probably built c1080 by Gundulf, Bishop of Rochester.

Open: at all reasonable times.
🗇 (grounds only).
(AM)

## WESTON-SUPER-MARE
Avon

**WOODSPRING MUSEUM**
Burlington Street
The museum is housed in the old workshops of the Edwardian Gaslight Company. Around a central courtyard are displays of the Victorian Seaside Holiday, an old chemist's shop, a dairy, a lion fountain with Victorian pavement mosaic and a gallery of wildlife in the district. Other exhibits include Mendip minerals and mining, local archaeology, costume rooms, transport including bicycles, cameras and the Dentist in 1900. Display featuring 'The Weston-super-Mare Story'. Changing

exhibitions held in the Temporary Exhibition Gallery. Adjoining is Clara's Cottage, a Westonian's home of the 1890s with period rooms, kitchen, parlour, bedroom and backyard. Also a room for the display of Peggy Nisbet dolls.

✆ 0934 621028.
Open: all year Mon–Sat, 10–5. (Closed Good Fri, Xmas & New Year.)
🖳🗇 (ground floor only) toilets for the disabled., hearing loop. Shop
🐕 (ex guide dogs)

## WETHERAL SHIELDS
Cumbria

**ANIMAL'S REFUGE & HOSPITAL**
Oak Tree Farm (Exit 42 from M6, signposted from B6263 beyond village of Cumwhinton)
Animal welfare centre set in farm buildings, housing dogs, cats, rabbits, birds, ponies, donkeys, sheep and goats.

✆ 0228 560082.
Open: all year Mon–Sat 9.30–5. Donations welcome. Free guided tours for parties & coaches by prior arrangement.
🖳🗇 Shop.

## WEYBRIDGE
Surrey

**WEYBRIDGE MUSEUM**
Church Street
Local exhibits of archaeology, social history, natural history and costume. Changing displays and exhibitions.

✆ 0932 843573.
Open: all year weekdays (ex Wed) 2–5, Sat 10–1 & 2–5 (Aug Mon–Sat 2–5). Donation welcome.
🗇 (service lift; difficult but staff will help; advance notice requested) Shop.

## WEYMOUTH
Dorset

**RADIPOLE LAKE**
Situated in the corner of Swannery Car Park, Weymouth. Nature

Reserve famous for its wintering and breeding wildlife and breeding reedbed and scrub birds. Three observation hides and viewing facilities in Visitor Centre. New RSPB Birdshop. Full facilities for disabled.

✆ 0305 773519/778313.
Open: all year daily 9–5 (Closed Xmas week, but open 1 Jan). Parking charge varies according to season; special rate for members. Guided tours (charge). Coach parties by prior arrangement.
🗇 sound system, top rail for visually handicapped).

## WHISTON
Merseyside

**STADT MOERS COUNTRY PARK**
Pottery Lane
Over 200 acres of Parkland reclaimed from industrial use. Facilities include picnic area, nature conservation area and Visitor Centre.

✆ 051 443 3682 (Ranger Service).
Open: all year, daily. Guided tours available. Parties accepted.
🗇 toilets for the disabled. Shop.

## WHITBY
North Yorkshire

**WHITBY ARCHIVES**
1st Floor, 17–18 Grape Lane
Constantly changing exhibition of historical local photographs, press cuttings etc. Heritage shop and gallery, local history and genealogical records.

✆ 0947 600170.
Open: all year daily 10.30–4.30 (Closed 10 days over Xmas/New Year). Donation box. Coach parties welcome.
Shop.

## WHITEHAVEN
Cumbria

**WHITEHAVEN MUSEUM AND ART GALLERY**
Civic Hall
The permanent collection includes local industries, maritime history

and archaeology. There are also around 12 temporary exhibitions each year. Videos of local interest can be viewed on request. A programme of lectures usually takes place on the first Tuesday of each month, commencing at 7.30pm. Local history publications and photographic reference collection also available.

𝒫 0946 693111 Ext 307.
Open: all year Mon–Sat 10–4.30. (Closed Sun & BHs). Donation requested. Guided tours on request subject to staff availability.
🍽 (Mon–Fri 12–4) ♿ (toilets, not restaurant) Shop.

## WHITSTABLE
Kent

**WHITSTABLE MUSEUM**
Foresters' Hall, Oxford St
A new museum specialising in this unique coastal community and the seafaring traditions of the area. A recently opened picture gallery displays the growing collection of ship portraits.

𝒫 0227 276998.
Open: Thu–Sat, Mon–Tue 10.30–1 & 2–4. Parties accepted by prior arrangement.
♿ Shop.

## WHITTINGTON
Staffordshire

**WHITTINGTON BARRACKS, STAFFORDSHIRE REGIMENT MUSEUM**
An interesting museum displaying details of the Regiment's battle honours; captured trophies, weapons old and new, uniforms past and present, and a special display of medals.

𝒫 0543 021311 Ext 3240/3229.
Open: all year Mon–Fri 9–4. (Closed BH).
♿ Shop.

## WICK
Highland

**CASTLE OF OLD WICK**
A four-storeyed ruined square

tower known also as Castle Oliphant, probably of 12th century.

Open: Apr–Sep Mon–Fri 9.30–6, Sun 2–6.
(AM)

## WIDNES
Merseyside

**PEX HILL COUNTRY PARK**
Cronton (1.5m NW off the A5080)
A country park of remnant heathland on a sandstone outcrop with a viewpoint across the Mersey estuary to North Wales. A Visitor Centre with exhibitions of the history and natural history of the site is staffed by the Knowsley Countryside Ranger service. Facilities are provided for walking, riding, cycling, rock climbing and picnicking, and there is a lively programme of special events.

𝒫 051 495 1410.
Open: Park all year, Visitor Centre Apr–Sep Thu–Sun 2–7.30; Oct–Mar Sat & Sun 1–4.30; BH 1–8. Free guided tours. Coach parties should book one week in advance.
🚻 ♿ (ramped access points) Shop.

## ✦ WIGHT, ISLE OF ✦

## CHILTON CHINE
Isle of Wight

**ISLE OF WIGHT PEARL**
(On the A3055 which runs along the SW coast of the island)
Visitors can see experienced craftspeople who design and make jewellery here. Showroom has a huge display of pearl jewellery.

𝒫 0983 740352.
Open: all year daily, Jun–Aug Mon–Fri 9–9, Sat & Sun 10–5.30, Sep–May daily 10–5.30. Coach parties welcome. Guided tours available out of season.
🍽 ♿ toilets for the disabled. Shop.

## COWES
Isle of Wight

**MARITIME MUSEUM AND PUBLIC LIBRARY**
Beckford Road
Ship models, photographs, paintings, books and other items showing the island's maritime past.

𝒫 0983 293341.
Open: Mon–Fri 9.30–6, Sat 9.30–4.30. (Closed Sun, BH and Sat before BH.)
🍽

**SIR MAX AITKEN MUSEUM**
83 High Street
Housed in the old Ratsey and Lapthorn sail-loft, the museum has numerous half models and full models, including many of Sir Max Aitken's own yachts. Pictures and items from Nelson's day as well as yacht furniture are just some of the museum's fascinating exhibits.

𝒫 0983 295144.
Open: Jun–Oct Mon–Fri 10–2. Guided tours available. Parties 12 max.
♿ (access and lift by appointment).

## SANDOWN
Isle of Wight

**MUSEUM OF ISLE OF WIGHT GEOLOGY**
Sandown Library, High Street
This museum, situated in the local library, houses a collection of fossils and exhibits of the island's geology.

𝒫 0983 404344.
Open: Mon–Fri 9.30–5.30, Sat 9.30–4.30.
Shop 🍽

## VENTNOR
Isle of Wight

**BOTANIC GARDENS**
Fine range of plants, palms, trees and exotic shrubs. Also Museum of Smuggling.

𝒫 0983 855397.
Open: gardens only daily 24hrs.    →

*Botanic Gardens, Ventnor*

telephone if travelling long distance). ♿ (ground floor) Shop.

## WINCHCOMBE
Gloucestershire

**WINCHCOMBE POTTERY**
(Off B4632 Winchombe–
Broadway road)
Pottery producing a wide range of hand-thrown stoneware pots for domestic use. Visitors are welcome to look round the showroom and at most times the workshop. A furniture-maker, sculptor and decorative painter also work on the premises.

✆ 0242 602462.
Open: all year, daily May–Sep, Mon–Fri 8–5, Sat 9–4, Sun 12–4. (Closed Sun Oct–Apr.) Guided tours available for groups (charge) by appointment. Coach parties by appointment. Shop.

## WINCHESTER
Hampshire

**THE GREAT HALL AND QUEEN ELEANOR'S GARDEN**
Winchester Castle
The Great Hall is the only visible remaining part of Winchester's medieval castle, a fortress and royal residence used regularly by the Kings of England throughout the Middle Ages. At the west end is the legendary Round Table of King Arthur. Queen Eleanor's Garden is a reconstructed 13th-century garden with plants valued at that time for their beauty, scent, medicinal and household uses.

✆ 0962 846476.
Open: daily 10–5 (10–4 weekends Nov–Mar). (Closed 25–26 Dec & Good Fri). Donation requested.
♿ Shop.

**GUILDHALL GALLERY**
Broadway
On show are local topographical views. Temporary exhibitions of paintings, crafts and sculpture.

Admission charge to Temperate House. Parking charge. Guided tours by arrangement with Curator (charge). 🍴 (cafe & restaurant/bar) ♿ (partial access to gardens) toilets for the disabled. Shop.

## WILBURTON
Cambs

**THE HERB GARDEN**
Nigel House, High Street
Features herbs in culinary, aromatic, medicinal, Biblical, Shakespearian, astrological dye bed collections etc. Plants, dried herbs, pot pourri and oils are on sale.

✆ (0353) 740824.
Open: May–Sep most days (phone to check) 10–7. Donations (for cancer charity). Free guided tours are available.
♿ strong 'pusher' needed as the paths are grassy.

## WILLENHALL
West Midlands

**WILLENHALL MUSEUM**
A museum about the people of Willenhall and their town, the capital of the British lock industry.

✆ Walsall 0902 634542.
Open: all year Mon–Sat 10–5 (last admission 4pm) (Closed BH.)
Shop 🚫 (ex guide dogs).

## WILMINGTON
East Sussex

**THE LONG MAN**
(0.5m S on footpath)
The exact date of this 231ft chalk cut figure on Windover Hill is unknown, but it may date from the 6th century. The figure holds an upright staff in each hand. During the 19th century the figure was renovated, having been almost lost from sight.

Open: accessible at all reasonable times.

## WIMBORNE MINSTER
Dorset

**WILLIAM WALKER GLASS STUDIO**
77 High Street
Delicately coloured handmade glass in English Crystal. Visitors to the studio can see glass being blown.

✆ 0202 880940.
Open: Mon–Sat 9–5 (please

℘ 0962 68166 Ext 2296 or 0962 52874.
Open: during exhibitions, Tue–Sat 10–5, Sun & Mon 2—5. (Closed Mon in winter.) Subject to alteration.
▱ ♿ ✾ (ex guide dogs).

**PILGRIMS' HALL (SCHOOL)**
The Close
Its name is derived from the pilgrims who came to the shrine of St Swithun of Winchester (Bishop 852–862). Its most notable feature is the 14th-century hammerbeam roof. Today the hall is used by the Cathedral choir school.

℘ 0962 54189.
Open: daily 9.30–9.30 (except when in use by the school for concerts, examinations etc).

**ROYAL HAMPSHIRE REGIMENT MUSEUM AND MEMORIAL GARDEN**
Serle's House
This fine Baroque 18th-century house incorporates the Royal Hampshire Regiment Museum and Memorial Gardens.

℘ 0962 863658.
Open: all year Mon–Fri 10–12.30, 2–4; Etr–Oct Sat, Sun, BH 12–4. Donation Box. Guided tours available. Parties by prior arrangement.
♿ (ground floor and garden only) Shop.

**WINCHESTER CITY MUSEUM**
The Square
Winchester's history from its prehistoric past to the present day, including Roman mosaics, Saxon silver and reconstructions of Victorian shops and an Edwardian bathroom.

℘ 0962 848269.
Open: Apr–Sep Mon–Sat 10–5, Sun 2–5; Oct–Mar Tue–Sat 10–5, Sun 2–4.
Guided tours for school parties by arrangement.
♿ (ground floor only) Shop.

**THE WINCHESTER GALLERY**
Park Avenue
The Winchester School of Art Gallery featuring a different

exhibition each month of contemporary art, craft and design.

℘ 0926 842500.
Open: generally academic year Sep–Jun, Mon–Thu 10–5, Fri 10–4.30, Sat in term time 9–12. (Closed Sun.)
Guided tours for parties by prior arrangement. Coach parties should give notice if parking is required.
▱ (9–4.30 in term time) ♿

**WINDSOR**
Berkshire
**HOUSEHOLD CAVALRY MUSEUM**
Combermere Barracks, St Leonard's Road
One of the finest military museums in Britain. Uniforms, weapons, horse furniture and armour of the Household Cavalry from 1660 to the present.

℘ (07535 868222 Ext 203.
Open: all year Mon–Fri (ex BH) 10–1 & 2–5. Donation.
♿ Shop ✾

**WINDSOR CASTLE**
Perhaps the largest fortress of its kind in the world, Windsor Castle has belonged to the sovereigns of England for over 900 years and is by far the oldest residence still in regular use. Two precincts of the Castle are open free of charge. (Admission is charged to see the State Apartments, exhibition of the Queen's presents and royal carriages and Queen Mary's Doll's House.)

℘ 0753 868286, pre-recorded information (0753) 831118.
Open: all year, times vary through the year. Guided tours in precincts only, contact Tourist Information 0753 867443.
♿ toilets for the disabled. Shop.

**WINKLEIGH**
Devon
**INCH'S CIDER CO LTD**
Western Barn

℘ 0837 83560.
Open: all year (ex Xmas). Mon–Sat

10–4. (Charge for museum.) Parties by appointment only.
Shop.

**WINSTER**
Derbyshire
**MARKET HOUSE**
Stone-built market house dating from the 17th or 18th century.

℘ Thorpe Cloud 033 529 245.
Open: most summer weekends.
Shop ✾
(NT)

**WISBECH**
Cambridgeshire
**WISBECH AND FENLAND MUSEUM**
Contains fine collection of ceramics, objets d'art, archaeology, natural history and articles which illustrate Fenland life.

℘ (0945) 583817.
Open: all year Tue–Sat 10–5 (4pm Oct–Apr).
Museum library and archives available by appointment only.
Guided tours by appointment. Coach parties by prior arrangement.
Shop ✾ (ex guide dogs).

**WITCOMBE, GREAT**
Gloucestershire
**WITCOMBE ROMAN VILLA**
(0.5m S of reservoir in Witcombe Park)
A large courtyard Roman villa in which a hypocaust and several mosaic pavements are presented.

Open: at all reasonable times. (Keys at farmhouse adjoining.) Enquiries to English Heritage, Bridge House, Sion Place, Clifton, Bristol. ℘ 0272 734472.
♿ (part).
(AM)

**WOLVERHAMPTON**
West Midlands
**BANTOCK HOUSE MUSEUM**
Bantock Park, Bradmore Road
This 18th- and 19th-century house contains important collections of English enamels, japanned tin and →

papier-mâché products of the Midlands. Also shown are early Worcester porcelain, pottery, English and foreign dolls and toys and the Thomas Balston collection of Staffordshire portrait figures.

✆ 0902 312132.
Open: Mon & Thu 10–7, Tue, Wed & Fri 10–5, Sun 2–5. (Closed Good Fri, Etr Sun, Xmas & New Year's Day.) Free guided tours. Children's holiday activities.
& (ground floor & grounds only)
✤ (guide dogs permitted on ground floor only).

**CENTRAL ART GALLERY**
Lichfield Street
18th- and 19th-century English water colours and oil paintings. Modern paintings, sculpture and prints. Fine Oriental collections. Wolverhampton Room with artefacts and memorabilia of the town. Full programme of temporary exhibitions.

✆ 0902 312032.
Open: Mon–Sat 10–6. (Closed BH.)
⊡ & Shop ✤ (in house, ex guide dogs).

## WOLVERLEY
Hereford & Worcester

**KINGSFORD COUNTRY PARK**
Blakeshall Lane (Signposted from B4189 at Wolverley)
Two hundred acres of mixed woodland including pine, beech and oak. The park is adjacent to the National Trust's Kinver Edge and offers fine views of the Clent Hills, Clee Hill and some of the loveliest countryside in the area. Two long-distance footpaths, the Worcester Way and the North Worcestershire Path, begin at Kingsford. There are some interesting rock caves, still used as domestic dwellings up till the 1960s.

✆ 0562 851129.
Open: all year. Donation welcome. Occasional guided walks.
☔ & (easy access trail) toilets for the disabled.

## WOODBRIDGE
Suffolk

**PHOENIX TRAIL**
Tangham
The great storm of October 1987 devastated Rendlesham Forest, one of Britain's most attractive pinewoods. The Phoenix Trail has been created to show how foresters are rebuilding an even better woodland. Conditions underfoot are usually good. Allow 1½ to 2 hours for the full trail. There is a pig-rearing area and a number of archaeological sites.

✆ 0394 450214.
Open: all year daily in daylight. Coach parties by prior arrangement.
☔ & toilets for the disabled.

## WOODHENGE
Wiltshire

(1m N of Amesbury)
Neolithic henge monument of c2300 BC, consisting of six rings of timber posts, now marked by concrete stumps, within a ditch, and entered by a causeway. The long axis of the rings, which are oval, points to the rising sun on Midsummer's Day.

Open: accessible at all reasonable times.
&
(AM)

## WOODSTOCK
Oxfordshire

**OXFORDSHIRE COUNTY MUSEUM**
Fletcher's House
Situated in a fine town house, this permanent exhibition illustrates the Story of Oxfordshire from early times to the present day. There are temporary exhibits and demonstrations throughout the year.

✆ 0993 811456.
Open: Oct–Apr Tue–Fri 10–4, Sat 10–5, Sun 2–5; May–Sep Mon–Fri 10–5, Sat 10–6, Sun 2–6. (Closed Good Fri & 25–26 Dec.)
⊡ ☔ & (ground floor and grounds only) Shop.

## WORCESTER
Hereford and Worcester

**CITY MUSEUM AND ART GALLERY**
Foregate Street
Temporary art exhibitions from local and national sources. Natural history and geology displays. 19th-century chemist's shop. Also collections of Worcestershire Regiment and Worcestershire Yeomanry Cavalry.

✆ 0905 25371.
Open: all year Mon, Tue, Wed & Fri 9.30–6, Sat 9.30–5.
⊡ & Shop ✤

**DYSON PERRINS MUSEUM OF WORCESTER PORCELAIN**
Severn Street
The largest collection of Worcester porcelain in the world, with a display of pieces dating from 1751 to the present day.

✆ 0905 23221.
Open: all year Mon–Fri 9.30–5 & Sat 10–5. Donations welcome. (Tours of works Mon–Fri by prior arrangement; prices on application.)
⊡ (licensed) & Shop ✤

**GUILDHALL**
High Street
The Guildhall has a fine early Georgian frontage and during the summer months heritage displays portray Worcester's history and personalities, with a very varied display featuring such people and places as Edward Elgar, Woodbine Willie, Vesta Tilley and the Music Halls. Also shown are the seven ages of Worcester.

✆ 0905 723471.
Open: all year Mon–Thu 9.30–5, Fri 9.30–4.30.
& (ground floor only) ✤ (ex guide dogs).

**TUDOR HOUSE**
Friar Street
500-year-old timber-framed house, with a squint and an ornate plaster ceiling. Now a museum of local life featuring social and domestic history, including children's room,

Edwardian bathroom and World War II Home Front displays. Large agricultural exhibits are displayed in yard at rear.

✆ 0905 25371.
Open: all year Mon–Wed & Fri–Sat 10.30–5.
& (ground floor only) Shop 🐾

## WORDSLEY
West Midlands

**STUART CRYSTAL**
Red House Glassworks
The Redhouse Cone and surrounding site has been created as a museum representing 200 years of glassmaking history. Glass repair and engraving service on site.

✆ Brierly Hill 0384 71161 Ext 274.
Redhouse Cone, Museum and Factory Shop, Open: daily 9–5.
🛏 & (ground floor and gardens only) Shop 🐾

## WORKINGTON
Cumbria

**HELENA THOMPSON MUSEUM**
Park End Road
Costume, furniture and other decorative art and local history in 18th-century house. Temporary exhibitions in former stable block.

✆ 0900 62598.
Open: all year Mon–Sat, Apr–Oct 10.30–4, Nov–May 11–3. Parties by prior arrangement.
& (ground floor & garden only) 🐾 (ex guide dogs).

## WORKSOP
Nottinghamshire

**IBTE MUSEUM OF TELECOMMUNCATIONS**
Queen St
Preserves and displays the development of telecommunications with particular reference to the Worksop area. Visitors are encouraged to use the equipment on display.

✆ 0909 483680.

Open: all year, by appointment. Donation box. Parties of 30 max. Guided tours available.
🛏 & Shop.

**WORKSOP PRIORY CHURCH AND GATEHOUSE**
Church has unique Norman west front with twin towers and 12th-century Transitional nave, with 20th-century additions. 14th-century scroll ironwork on doors in south porch. Remarkable 14th-century double archway with large upper room which from 1623 housed the earliest elementary school in county. Elaborate façade with statues, and 16th-century wayside shrine and chapel.

Open: Etr–Sep Mon–Fri 9–4, Sat–Sun 9–5. (Closed Tue, lunch 1–2.) Coach parties & guided tours by special arrangement.
& (ground floor & grounds).

## WORTHING
West Sussex

**WORTHING MUSEUM AND ART GALLERY**
Chapel Road
Archaeology, Downland display, history of Worthing, pictures, pottery, toys and dolls. Large costume collection. Frequent exhibitions.

✆ 0903 39999 Ext 121, Sat only 0903 204229.
Open: Mon–Sat 10–6 Apr–Sep, 10–5 Oct–Mar. Donations box.
& (wheelchair available on request). Shop.

## WREXHAM
Clwyd

**BERSHAM INDUSTRIAL HERITAGE CENTRE**
Bersham (2m SW)
An Interpretative Centre housed in a Victorian school building which is situated along an eight-mile industrial history trail. Exhibitions on John Wilkinson, the Bersham iron-works, the Davies Brothers,

gatesmiths of Croes Foel and a reconstructed forge.

✆ 0978 261529.
Open: Etr–Oct, Tue–Sat & BH 10–12.30 & 1.30–4, Sun 2–4; Nov–Etr, Tue–Fri 10–12.30 & 1.30–4, Sat 12.30–3.30.
& Shop 🐾

**TY-MAWR COUNTRY PARK**
Cae Gwilym Lane, Cefn Mawr
(On the River Dee at Cefn Mawr off A483)
Thirty-five acres of grassland sloping down to the riverside. Magnificient views of the Cefn viaduct and Pontcysyllte aqueduct. Riverside walks, picnic areas, abundant wildlife and farm animals. The Visitor Centre is housed in a converted sandstone barn.

✆ 0978 822780.
Open: all year daily in daylight. Visitor Centre daily Apr–Sep, weekends Oct–Mar. Donation welcome. Guided tours by prior arrangement (donation accepted). Special events.
🚻 & toilets for the disabled. Shop.

## YARMOUTH, GREAT
Norfolk

**MUSEUM EXHIBITION GALLERIES**
Central Library, Tolhouse Street
Travelling and local art exhibitions.

✆ 0493 858900.
Open: all year Mon–Fri 9.30–5.30; Sat 9.30–1, 2–5.30. (Closed Good Fri, late May & Aug BH wknds, 24–26 Dec & 1 Jan.)
🐾

**TOLHOUSE MUSEUM AND BRASS RUBBING CENTRE**
Tolhouse Street
History of Great Yarmouth in former courthouse with prison cells in the dungeons. Brass rubbing centre with range of replica brasses.

✆ 0493 858900.
Open: all year Mon–Fri 10–1 & 2–5.30; also open Sun in summer. (Closed Good Fri, 24–26 Dec & 1 Jan.) Charge for brass rubbing. Shop 🐾

## YELVERTON
Devon

**PAPERWEIGHT CENTRE**
4 Buckland Terrace, Leg O'Mutton
Exhibition of over 800 beautiful pieces of antique and modern glass. Millefiori, faceted, diamond-cut dated and signed 'investment' paperweights, many for sale.

℘ 0822 854250.
Open: Apr–Oct Mon–Sat (also Sun end May–mid Sep) 10–5; winter Wed 1–5, Sat 10–5; 1 Dec–Xmas Mon–Sat 10–5. Parties over 25 by appointment. & (ramp on request) Shop.

## YEOVIL
Somerset

**MUSEUM OF SOUTH SOMERSET**
Hendford Manor Hall
Local history and archaeology and specialised collections of costumes and firearms.

℘ Mon–Sat 0935 24774.
Open: Tue–Sat 10–4, Sun 2–4 (Closed Mon, for party visits only, but open BH Mons). Donations welcome. & (ground floor only).

## YORK
North Yorkshire

**BORTHWICK INSTITUTE OF HISTORICAL RESEARCH**
St Anthony's Hall, Peasholme Green
Originally a late 15th-century guildhall, it has served in turn as poor-house, hospital, armoury, and Blue-Coat school. Now the Borthwick Institute of Historical Research, part of York University, with a collection of ecclesiastical archives. Exhibition of documents.

℘ 0904 642315.
Hall open: all year Mon–Fri 9.30–12.50 & 2–4.50. (Closed Xmas, Etr & PH.)

**CITY ART GALLERY**
Exhibition Square
A treasure-house of European and British paintings spanning seven centuries, plus the unrivalled Milner-White collection of stoneware pottery and an exciting programme of temporary exhibitions, workshops, lectures and events.

℘ 0904 623839.
Open: all year daily Mon–Sat 10–5, Sun 2.30–5 (last admission 4.30). (Closed Good Fri, 25 & 26 Dec and 1 Jan). Coach parties must book in advance.
🖵 (vending machine) & (entrance ramp, stairlift) toilets for the disabled. Shop.

**KING'S MANOR**
Exhibition Square
Formerly the home of the Abbot of St Mary's Abbey, King's Manor was later the stopping place of James VI of Scotland on way to become James I of England, and of Charles I at time of Civil War. It was much altered in early 17th century, and was fully restored to become part of university in 1964.

℘ 0904 430000.
Courtyards open: daily 9–5 (ex 25 Dec). Principal rooms open on certain days only during spring & summer. Check with porter. Donations requested.
🖵 (Mon–Fri 10–4) & (ground floor & courtyard) toilets for the disabled.

# IEWPOINTS

A full lists of AA Viewpoints, which provide excellent panoramas of the surrounding countryside, is given below.

## ENGLAND

**AVON**
**Portishead** 1m W of Portishead
**CORNWALL**
**Pendennis Head** 1m SE of Falmouth
**DERBYSHIRE**
**Highoredish** 3m E of Matlock
**DORSET**
**Bulbarrow** 5m S of Sturminster Newton
**ESSEX**
**One Tree Hill** 0.25m NW of A13/B1420 junction 1.5m S of Basildon
**GLOUCESTERSHIRE**
**Leckhampton Hill** 1m S of Cheltenham on B4070
**Robinswood Hill** 2m S of City Centre in Robinswood Hill Country Park
**Symonds Yat** 3m N of Coleford off B4432
**HEREFORD & WORCESTER**
**Clent Hills** S of A456, 2m SW of Halesowen
**Windmill Hill** Waseley Country Park 3.5m S of Halesowen
**ISLE OF WIGHT**
**Bembridge Down** 2m ENE of Sandown
**KENT**
**Farthing Corner** on Farthing Corner service area M2
**LEICESTERSHIRE**
**Beacon Hill** 2m SW of Loughborough
**OXFORDSHIRE**
**Wittenham Clumps** 1.5m off A4130 Nr Brightwell
**SHROPSHIRE**
**Clee Hills** 6m E of Ludlow
**SOMERSET**
**Dunkery Beacon** between Luccombe and Wheddon Cross
**Wellington Monument** 2.5m S of Wellington
**STAFFORDSHIRE**
**Central Forest Park** Stoke-on-Trent
**W SUSSEX**
**Duncton Hill** 5m SW of Petworth
**WARWICKSHIRE**
**Magpie Hill** in Burton Dassett Hills Country Park
**WILTSHIRE**
**Barbury Castle** in country park 5m S of Swindon

**N YORKSHIRE**
**Sutton Bank** 5m E of Thirsk
**W YORKSHIRE**
**Holme Moss** 1m SW of Holme to East of A6024

## WALES

**ANGLESEY**
**South Stack** in RSPB Reserve 3m W of Holyhead
**Waun-y-Llyn** 5m SE of Mold in country park
**DYFED**
**Foel Eryr** 13m NE of Haverfordwest 0.5m W of B4329
**GWENT**
**Sugar Loaf** 3m NW of Abergavenny
**GWYNEDD**
**Great Orme's Head** on top of Great Orme, Llandudno
**POWYS**
**Montgomery Town Hill** 0.5m SW of Montgomery, off B4385 via unclassified road

## SCOTLAND

**BORDERS**
**Scott's View** 3m E of Melrose
**CENTRAL**
**David Marshall Lodge** 1m N of Aberfoyle
**Queen's View, Auchineden** 6m N of Bearsden
**HIGHLAND**
**Bealach Na Ba'** *(Pass of the Cattle)* 5m SE of Applecross
**Glen Garry** On A87 7.25m from A82 at Invergarry
**Knockan Cliff** 8m NE of Ullapool
**Struie Hill** 6m SE of Bonar Bridge
**LOTHIAN**
**Blackford Hill** Edinburgh City Centre W of Royal Observatory
**Cockleroy** Beecraigs Country Park, 2m S of Linlithgow
**STRATHCLYDE**
**Lyle Hill** 2m E of Greenock, between A78 & A770
**TAYSIDE**
**Queen's View** 6m E of Tummel Bridge on B8019

# NDEX

## D

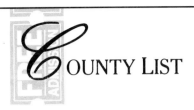

# COUNTY LIST

This list has been compiled to help you find all the places to visit in your vicinity, and is arranged in the order: England, Channel Islands, Isle of Man, Scotland, Scottish Islands, Wales. Under each county heading is a list of the towns in that county which feature in the book, and alongside them the establishments you will find there. The main directory of the book is in alphabetical order of towns.

## ENGLAND

### AVON

**Bath**
Botanic Gardens
Victoria Art Gallery

**Bristol**
Ashton Court Estate
Avon Gorge & Leigh Woods
Blaise Castle Estate
Bristol Industrial Museum
City Museum & Art Gallery
Maritime Heritage Centre
Oldbury Court Estate
Red Lodge
St Nicholas Church Museum
The Georgian House
University Botanic Garden

**Clevedon**
Clevedon Craft Centre

**Severn Bore**

**Weston-super-Mare**
Woodspring Museum

### BEDFORDSHIRE

**Ampthill**
Houghton House

**Bedford**
Bedford Museum

**Luton**
Cecil Higgins Art Gallery & Museum
Museum & Art Gallery

### BERKSHIRE

**Arborfield**
Royal Electrical & Mechanical Engineers
Museum

**Elcot**
Elcot Park Hotel

**Newbury**
Newbury District Museum

**Reading**
Blake's Lock Museum
Museum & Art Gallery

**Windsor**
Household Cavalry Museum
Windsor Castle

### BUCKINGHAMSHIRE

**Aylesbury**
Buckinghamshire County Museum

**High Wycombe**
Wycombe Local History & Chair Museum

**Salcey Forest**

### CAMBRIDGESHIRE

**Buckden**
Buckden Palace

**Cambridge**
Fitzwilliam Museum
Kings College Chapel
Scott Polar Research Institute
Sedgewick Museum of Geology
University Museum of Archaeology &
Anthropology
University Botanic Garden

**Huntingdon**
Cromwell Museum
Hinchingbrooke Country Park

**March**
March & District Museum

**Peterborough**
City of Peterborough Museum & Art Gallery

**Prickwillow**
Prickwillow Engine Museum

**Ramsey**
Abbey Gatehouse
Ramsey Rural Museum

**St Ives**
Norris Museum

**Wandlebury Ring**

**Wilburton**
The Herb Garden

**Wisbech**
Wisbech & Fenland Museum

### CHESHIRE

**Burwardsley**
Cheshire Candle Workshops Ltd

**Chester**
Chester Visitor Centre
Grosvenor Museum

**Macclesfield**
Macclesfield Riverside Park
West Park Museum

**Warrington**
Risley Moss Nature Park
South Lancashire Regiment (PWV)
Regimental Museum

*CLEVELAND*

**Hartlepool**
Gray Art Gallery & Museum
Hartlepool Maritime Museum
**Middlesbrough**
Dorman Museum
Middlesbrough Art Gallery
Tees (Newport) Bridge
**Redcar**
The Zetland Lifeboat Museum
**Stockton-on-Tees**
Preston Hall Museum

*CORNWALL*

**Fowey**
St Catherine's Castle
**Helston**
Helston Folk Museum
**Launceston**
Lawrence House Museum
**Madron**
Lanyon Quoit
**Pencarrow**
Pencarrow Gallery
**Ponsanooth**
Kennall Vale Nature Reserve
**Portreath**
Cornish Goldsmiths
**Quintrell Downs**
Newquay Pearl
**St Austell**
English China Clays
**Sancreed**
Carn Euny Ancient Village

*CUMBRIA*

**Ambleside**
Hayes Garden World
**Armathwaite**
Eden Valley Woollen Mill
**Carlisle**
Guildhall
**Grizedale**
Grizedale Forest Park
**Hadrian's Wall**
**Hardknott Castle Roman Fort**
**Keswick**
Castlerigg Stone Circle
**Maryport**
Maritime Museum
**St Bees**
St Bees Head Nature Reserve
**Sedbergh**
Yorkshire Dales National Park Centre
Pennine Tweeds
**Sellafield**
Sellafield Visitors Centre

**Shap**
Shap Abbey
**Swarthmoor**
Swarthmoor Hall
**Wetheral Shields**
Animal's Refuge & Hospital
**Whitehaven**
Whitehaven Museum & Art Gallery
**Workington**
Helena Thompson Museum

*DERBYSHIRE*

**Arbor Low**
Arbor Low Henge
**Ashbourne**
Derwent Crystal
**Bamford**
High Peak Garden Centre
**Buxton**
Grin Low/Buxton Country Park
Pavilion Gardens
**Chesterfield**
Peacock Information & Heritage Centre
**Derby**
Derby Museum & Art Gallery
**Elvaston**
Elvaston Castle Country Park
**Hayfield**
Sett Valley Trail
**Heanor**
Shipley Country Park
**Ilkeston**
Erewash Museum
**Matlock**
John Smedley Ltd
**New Mills**
New Mills Heritage & Information Centre
**Old Whittington**
Revolution House
**Winster**
Market House

*DEVON*

**Ashburton**
Ashburton Museum
**Axminster**
Axminster Carpets Ltd
**Barnstaple**
St Anne's Chapel & Old Grammar School
Museum
**Brixham**
Berry Head Country Park
**Capton**
Prehistoric Hill Settlement Museum
**Dartington**
Dartington Cider Press Centre
**Dartmouth**
Bayard's Cove Fort
**Exeter**
Devonshire Regimental Museum
Guildhall
Quay House Interpretation Centre

Royal Albert Memorial Museum
St Nicholas Priory
**Honiton**
Honiton Pottery
**Lydford**
Lydford Castle
**Lynmouth**
Watersmeet Estate
**Modbury**
Woodturners Craft Centre
**Northam Burrows**
Northam Burrows Country Park
**Plymouth**
City Museum & Art Gallery
**Sidmouth**
The Donkey Sanctuary
**South Molton**
South Molton Museum
**Tiverton**
Tiverton Museum
**Torquay**
Babbacombe Pottery
**Torrington**
Torrington Museum
**Winkleigh**
Inch's Cider Co Ltd
**Yelverton**
Paperweight Centre

## DORSET

**Badbury Rings**
**Blandford Forum**
Royal Signals Museum
**Bournemouth**
The Shelley Rooms
**Broadwindsor**
Broadwindsor Craft Centre
Earthworks
**Cerne Abbas**
Cerne Giant
**Christchurch**
Christchurch Castle & Norman House
Christchurch Priory
Highcliffe Castle Ground
**Corfe Castle**
Corfe Castle Museum
**Dorchester**
Maiden Castle
Old Crown Court
**Knowlton**
Knowlton Circles
**Milton Abbas**
Milton Abbey Church
**Morcombelake**
S Moores Biscuit Factory
**Poole**
Poole Park
Poole Pottery
**Sherborne**
Sherborne Abbey
**Swanage**
Durlston Country Park

**Tolpuddle**
Tolpuddle Martyr's Museum
**Upton**
Upton Country Park
**Weymouth**
Radipole Lake
**Wimborne Minster**
William Walker Glass Studio

## CO DURHAM

**Barnard Castle**
Egglestone Abbey
**Bowes**
Bowes Museum
**Chester-le-Street**
Ankers House Museum
**Darlington**
Art Gallery
Darlington Museum
**Durham**
St Aidan's College Grounds

## ESSEX

**Aveley**
Belhus Woods Country Park
**Basildon**
Langdon Hills Country Park
**Billericay**
Cater Museum
**Brentwood**
Thornden Country Park
Weald Country Park
**Broadley Common**
Ada Cole Memorial Stables
**Canvey Island**
Dutch Cottage Museum
**Chelmsford**
Chelmsford & Essex Museum
**Colchester**
Hollytrees Museum
Natural History Museum
Olivers Orchard
Trinity Museum
Tymperleys Clock Museum
**Dagenham**
Ford Motor Company
**Danbury**
Danbury Country Park
**East Bergholt**
Bridge Cottage
**East Mersea**
Cudmore Grove Country Park
**Finchingfield**
Finchingfield Guildhall & Museum
**Grays**
Thurrock Museum
**Greensted**
St Andrews Church
**Hadleigh**
Hadleigh Castle
Hadleigh Castle Country Park

**Harlow**
　　Harlow Museum
　　Mark Hall Cycle Museum & Gardens
**Harwich**
　　The Playhouse Gallery
　　The Guildhall
**Maldon**
　　Maldon Maritime Centre
**Mistley**
　　Mistley Towers
**Pitsea**
　　National Motorboat Museum
　　Wat Tyler Country Park
**Saffron Walden**
　　Fry Art Gallery
　　Saffron Waldon Museum
**Southend-on-Sea**
　　Prittleswell Priory Museum
　　Southchurch Hall Museum
　　Southend Central Museum & Planetarium
**Waltham Abbey**
　　Epping Forest District Museum
　　Lee Valley Park Countryside Centre
　　Waltham Abbey
**Westcliffe-on-Sea**
　　Beecroft Art Gallery

## GLOUCESTERSHIRE

**Berkeley**
　　Berkeley Nuclear Power Station
**Birdlip**
　　Crickley Hill Country Park
**Cheltenham**
　　Art Gallery & Museum
　　Gustav Holst Birthplace Museum
**Cirencester**
　　Cirencester Park
　　Brewery Court
**Cranham**
　　Prinknash Abbey & Pottery
**Deerhurst**
　　Odda's Chapel
**Fairford**
　　St Mary's Church
**Gloucester**
　　City Museum & Art Gallery
　　Folk Museum
　　Gloucester Antique Centre
　　Gloucester Docks
**Severn Bore**
**Stroud**
　　Stroud District (Cowle) Museum
**Uley**
　　Uley Long Barrow (Hetty Pegler's Tump)
**Winchcombe**
　　Winchcombe Pottery
**Witcombe, Great**
　　Witcombe Roman Villa

## GREATER LONDON

**Bexley**
　　Bexley Museum

**Enfield**
　　Forty Hall Museum
**Hampton Court**
　　Bushey Park
**London**
**E2**　　Bethnal Green Museum of Childhood
　　　　Geffrye Museum
**E6**　　East Ham Nature Reserve
**E15**　Passmore Edwards Museum
**E16**　North Woolwich Old Station Museum
**E17**　Vestry House Museum
　　　　William Morris Gallery
**EC1**　Mount Pleasant Letter District Office
　　　　Museum of the Order of St John
　　　　National Postal Museum
**EC2**　Bank of England Museum
　　　　Guildhall
　　　　Museum of London
**EC3**　London Metal Exchange
**EC4**　Middle Temple Hall
　　　　St Brides Church
　　　　The Story of Telecommunications
**N17**　Bruce Castle Museum
**N22**　Alexandra Palace & Park
**NW1**　Cecil Sharpe House
　　　　Regents Park
**NW3**　Keats House
　　　　Kenwood, Iveagh Bequest
**NW4**　Church Farm House Museum
**NW8**　Primrose Hill
**NW10** Grange Museum of Community History
**SE1**　The Museum of Garden History
**SE3**　Rangers House
**SE5**　South London Art Gallery
**SE9**　Eltham Palace
　　　　Winter Gardens
**SE10**　Greenwich Park
　　　　Royal Naval College Painted Hall & Chapel
**SE15**　Livesey Museum
**SE17**　Cuming Museum
**SE18**　Museum of Artillery in the Rotunda
　　　　Royal Artillery Regimental Museum
**SE23**　Horniman Museum
**SW1**　Design Centre
　　　　Green Park
　　　　Houses of Parliament
　　　　Westminster Hall
　　　　St James's Park
　　　　Tate Gallery
**SW3**　National Army Museum
**W1**　　Agnew's Galleries
　　　　Museum of Mankind
　　　　Wallace Collection
**W2**　　Hyde Park
**W3**　　Gunnersbury Park Museum
**W4**　　Hogarth's House
**W8**　　Commonwealth Institute
　　　　Kensington Gardens
**W14**　Leighton House
**WC1**　British Museum
　　　　Jewish Museum
　　　　Percival David Foundation of Chinese Art

**WC2** Africa Centre
Contemporary Applied Arts
London Silver Vaults
National Gallery
National Portrait Gallery
The Photographer's Gallery
Public Record Office Museum
Sir John Soan's Museum
**Orpington**
Bromley Museum
**Richmond-upon-Thames**
Richmond Park
**Twickenham**
Orleans House Gallery
**Upminster**
Tithe Barn Agricultural & Folk Museum
**Wembley**
Fryent Country Park

## GREATER MANCHESTER

**Ashton-under-Lyne**
Museum of the Manchesters
Portland Basin Industrial Heritage Centre
**Bolton**
Tonge Moor Textile Museum
Warburtons
**Bury**
Bury Art Gallery & Museum
**Manchester**
Castlefield Urban Heritage Park
City Art Galleries
Fletcher Moss Museum & Art Gallery
Fletcher Moss Botanical Gardens
Gallery of English Costume
Greater Manchester Police Museum
John Rylands University Library
Manchester Craft Centre
Manchester Museum
Whitworth Art Gallery
Wythenshawe Horticultural Centre
**Prestwich**
Heaton Hall
**Radcliffe**
Radcliffe Tower
**Salford**
Ordsall Hall Museum
Salford Mining Museum
Salford Museum & Art Gallery

## HAMPSHIRE

**Aldershot**
Queen Alexandra's Royal Army Nursing
Corps Museum
Royal Army Dental Corps Historical Museum
Royal Corps of Transport Museum
**Alton**
Curtis Museum & Allen Gallery
**Andover**
Andover Museum
**Basingstoke**
Viables Craft Centre
Willis Museum & Art Gallery

**Bransgore**
MacPenny's
**Danebury Ring**
**Eastleigh**
Eastleigh Museum
**Fawley**
Calshot Crafts Centre
**Fordingbridge**
Alderholt Mill
**Havant**
Havant Museum
**Maybush**
Ordnance Survey
**Moors Valley Country Park**
**Netley Marsh**
Tools for Self Reliance
**Petersfield**
The Bear Museum
Flora Twort Gallery
**Selborne**
The Mallinson Collection of Rural Relics
Selborne Hill
**Silchester**
Calleva Museum
**Southampton**
City Art Gallery
Southampton Maritime Museum
Tudor House Museum
**Winchester**
The Great Hall & Queen Eleanor's Garden
Guildhall Gallery
Pilgrims' Hall (School)
Royal Hampshire Regiment Museum &
Memorial Garden
Winchester City Museum
The Winchester Gallery

## HEREFORD & WORCESTER

**Church Lench**
Annard Woollen Mill
**Hereford**
Hereford City Museum
**Leominster**
Queen's Wood Country Park & Arboretum
**Much Marcle**
Westons Cider Works
**Tardebigge**
Tardebigge Locks
**Wolverley**
Kingsford Country Park
**Worcester**
City Museum & Art Gallery
Dyson Perrins Museum of Worcester
Porcelain
Guildhall
Tudor House

## HERTFORDSHIRE

**Berkhamsted**
Berkhamsted Castle
**Elstree**
Aldenham Country Park

**Hertford**
Hertford Castle
**Hitchin**
Hitchin Museum & Art Gallery
**Letchworth**
First Garden City Heritage Museum
Letchworth Museum & Art Gallery
**Royston**
Royston Museum
**Stevenage**
Stevenage Museum
**Watford**
Watford Museum

## HUMBERSIDE
**Beverley**
Art Gallery & Museum
**Blacktoft**
South Farm Craft Gallery
**Bridlington**
Park Rose Pottery & Leisure Park
**Burton Agnes**
Burton Agnes Manor House
**Flamborough Head & Bempton Cliffs**
**Hull**
Ferens Art Gallery
Hull & East Riding Museum
Town Docks Museum
Wilberforce & Georgian Houses
**Scunthorpe**
Museum & Art Gallery
Normanby Hall Country Park

## KENT
**Ashford**
Intelligence Corps Museum
**Aylesford**
Kit's Coty House
**Biddenden**
Baby Carriage Collection
Biddenden Vineyards
**Broadstairs**
North Foreland Lighthouse
**Brook**
Wye College Museum of Agriculture
**Canterbury**
Royal Museum & Art Gallery
**Chatham**
Capstone Farm Country Park
**Cranbrook**
Cranbrook Union Mill
**Dungeness**
'A' Power Station
**Folkestone**
Museum & Art Gallery
Rowlands Confectionery
**Leeds**
Kent Garden Costume Dolls & Country Wines
**Maidstone**
Museum & Art Gallery
Tyrwhitt-Drake Museum of Carriages

**Minster-in-Thanet**
Minster Abbey
**Plaxtol**
Old Soar Manor
**Ramsgate**
Ramsgate Museum & Art Gallery
**Rochester**
Guildhall Museum
**Staplehurst**
Iden Croft Herbs
**Tonbridge**
Tonbridge Castle & Grounds
**Tunbridge Wells**
Tunbridge Wells Museum & Art Gallery
**West Malling**
St Leonard's Tower
**Whitstable**
Whitstable Museum

## LANCASHIRE
**Beacon Fell**
Beacon Fell Country Park
**Blackburn**
Lewis Museum of Textile Machinery
Museum & Art Gallery
**Blackpool**
Coronation Rock Company
Grundy Art Gallery
**Burnley**
Towneley Hall Art Gallery & Museum
**Fence**
Slate Age (Fence) Ltd
**Heysham**
Heysham Nuclear Power Station
**Lancaster**
Ashton Memorial & Williamson Park
City Museum
**Rawtenstall**
Rossendale Museum

## LEICESTERSHIRE
**Leicester**
John Doran Museum
University of Leicester Botanic Gardens

## LINCOLNSHIRE
**Billinghay**
Old Vicarage Museum & Craft Workshop
**Bransby**
Bransby Home of Rest for Horses
**Fulbeck**
Manor Stables Craft Workshops
**Heckington**
The Pearoom Craft Centre
**Lincoln**
Hatsholme Country Park
Lincoln Cathedral
**Stickford**
Allied Forces Military Museum

## MERSEYSIDE
**Arrowe Park**
Ivy Farm Visitor Centre

**Birkenhead**
Birkenhead Priory
Tam O'Shanter Wirral Urban Farm
Williamson Art Gallery
**Bromborough**
Dibbinsdale Local Nature Reserve
**Eastham**
Eastham Woods Country Park
**Frankby**
Royden Park & Thurmaston Common
**Halewood**
Halewood 'Triangle' Country Park
**Liverpool**
The Bluecoat
Liverpool City Libraries
Liverpool Museum
Museum of Labour History
Sudley Art Gallery
University of Liverpool Art Gallery
Walker Art Gallery
**Port Sunlight**
Lady Lever Art Gallery
**Prescot**
Museum of Clock and Watchmaking
**St Helens**
Pilkington Glass Museum
St Helens Museum
**Southport**
Atkinson Art Gallery
Botanic Gardens Museum
**Thurstaston**
Wirral Country Park
**Whiston**
Stadt Moers Country Park
**Widnes**
Pex Hill Country Park

*NORFOLK*
**Baconsthorpe**
Baconsthorpe Castle
**Binham**
Binham Priory
**Burgh Castle**
The Castle
**Burston**
Burston Strike School
**Caister-on-Sea**
Caister Roman Site
**Cromer**
Lifeboat Museum
**Diss**
100th Bomb Group Memorial Museum
**East Dereham**
Bishop Bonners Cottages Museum
**Erpingham**
Alby Crafts
**Heacham**
Norfolk Lavender
**Holt**
Picturecraft of Holt
**North Creake**
Creake Abbey

**North Walsham**
Cat Pottery
**Norwich**
City Hall
Guildhall
**St Olave's**
St Olave's Priory
**Seething**
Station 146 World War II Control Tower
**Sheringham**
Henry Ramey Upcher Lifeboat
**Sheringham, Upper**
Sheringham Park
**Snetterton**
Int. League for the Protection of Horses
**Starston**
Cranes Watering Farm & Shop
**Thetford**
Ancient House Museum
Thetford Castle
Warren Lodge
**Weeting**
Weeting Castle
**Yarmouth, Great**
Museum Exhibition Galleries
Tollhouse Museum & Brass Rubbing Centre

*NORTHAMPTONSHIRE*
**Brigstock**
Brigstock Country Park
**East Carlton**
East Carlton Countryside Park
**Ecton**
Sywell Country Park
**Irchester**
Irchester Country Park
**Kettering**
Alfred East Art Gallery
Manor House Museum
**Northampton**
Central Museum & Art Gallery
Delapre Abbey
Museum of Leathercraft
**Oundle**
Barnwell Country Park
**Pitsford**
Pitsford Water
**Salcey Forest**
**Wellingborough**
Wellingborough Heritage Centre

*NORTHUMBERLAND*
**Allen Banks**
**Bamburgh**
Grace Darling Museum
**Berwick-upon-Tweed**
Castle & Town Walls
Lindisfarne Wine & Spirit Museum
**Carrawburgh**
Temple of Mithras
**Craster**
Kipper Curing (L Robson & Sons Ltd)

**Hadrian's Wall**
**Holy Island (Lindisfarne)**
Lindisfarne Limited

## NOTTINGHAMSHIRE

**Calverton**
Patchings Farm Art Centre
**Creswell Crags**
Cresswell Crags Visitor Centre
**Edwinstowe**
Sherwood Forest & Visitor Centre
**Langold**
Langold Country Park
**Mansfield**
Museum & Art Gallery
**Newark-on-Trent**
Millgate Museum of Social & Folk Life
Newark Castle
**Nottingham**
Brewhouse Yard Museum
Canal Museum
Green's Science Centre, Mill Museum
Industrial Museum
The Lace Centre
Museum of Costume & Textiles
Natural History Museum
Nottingham Castle Museum
Nottingham Story
**Rufford**
Rufford Craft Centre & Country Park
**Worksop**
IBTE Museum of Telecommunications
Worksop Priory Church & Gatehouse

## OXFORDSHIRE

**Aston Rowant**
Nature Reserve
**Banbury**
. Banbury Museum
**Coxwell, Great**
Great Barn
**Deddington**
Deddington Castle
**Dorchester-on-Thames**
Dorchester Abbey & Museum
**Nuneham Courtenay**
John Mattock Rose Nurseries
Oxford University Arboretum
**Oxford**
Ashmolean Museum of Art & Archaeology
Museum of the History of Science
Museum of Oxford
St Edmund Hall
University Botanic Garden
**Uffington**
Castle & White Horse
**Wantage**
Vale & Downland Museum Centre
**Wayland's Smithy**
**Woodstock**
Oxfordshire County Museum

## SHROPSHIRE

**Acton Burnell**
Acton Burnell Castle
**Clun**
Clun Local History Museum
**Little Ness**
Adcote
**Moreton Corbet**
Moreton Corbet Castle
**Oswestry**
Old Oswestry Hill Fort
Oswestry Bicycle Museum
**Shrewsbury**
Bear Steps

## SOMERSET

**Axbridge**
King John's Hunting Lodge
**Bridgwater**
Admiral Blake Museum
**Castle Cary**
Castle Cary & District Museum
**Churchstanton**
Somerset Spring Water
**Dowlish Wake**
Perry's Cider Mills
**Glastonbury**
Glastonbury Tor
**Kingston St Mary**
Fyne Court
**Moorlynch**
Moorlynch Vineyard
**North Wootton**
Wootton Vineyard
**Nunney**
Nunney Castle
**Old Cleeve**
John Wood Sheepskins
**Stoke-sub-Hamdon**
Stoke-sub-Hamdon Priory
**Street**
The Shoe Museum (C & J Clark Ltd)
**Yeovil**
Museum of South Somerset

## STAFFORDSHIRE

**Cheddleton**
Flint Mill
**Hamstall Ridware**
Ridware Arts Centre
**Himley**
Himley Country Park
**Lichfield**
The Staffordshire Regiment Museum
**Newborough**
The Piano Workshop
**Stafford**
Art Gallery
Stafford Castle
**Stoke-on-Trent**
City Museum & Art Gallery
Coalport Craft Centre

Etruria Industrial Museum
Ford Green Hall
Minton Museum
Moorcroft Pottery
Sir Henry Doulton Gallery
**Tutbury**
Georgian Crystal
**Whittington**
Staffordshire Regiment Museum

## SUFFOLK

**Brandeston**
The Suffolk Cider Company
**Bury St Edmunds**
Abbey Gardens & Ruins
The Clock Museum
Moyse's Hall Museum
Suffolk Regiment Museum
**Dunwich**
Dunwich Museum
**Flixton**
Norfolk & Suffolk Aviation Museum
**Hadleigh**
Wolves Wood
**Halesworth**
The Halesworth Gallery
**Ipswich**
Christchurch Mansion
Ipswich Museum
**Laxfield**
Laxfield & District Museum
**Leiston**
Leiston Abbey
**Lindsey**
St James's Chapel
**Lowestoft**
Royal Naval Patrol Service Association
**Mildenhall**
Mildenhall & District Museum
**Parham**
300th Bomb Group Memorial Air Museum
**Sizewell B**
Sizewell Information Centre
**Southwold**
Southwold Museum
**Woodbridge**
Phoenix Trail

## SURREY

**Ash Vale**
RAMC Historical Museum
**Chertsey**
Chertsey Museum
**Compton**
The Pottery
**Farnham**
Alice Holt Forest Visitor Centre
Farnham Museum
New Ashgate Gallery
**Godalming**
Godalming Museum

**Guildford**
Gallery 90
Guildford Museum
The Guildhall
Women's Royal Army Corps Museum
**Leatherhead**
Fire & Iron Gallery
**Outwood**
Outwood Art Gallery
**Reigate**
Priory Museum
**Reigate Heath**
Old Windmill
**Shere**
Silent Pool
**Weybridge**
Weybridge Museum

## SUSSEX, EAST

**Blackboys**
Brownings Farm
**Brighton**
Booth Museum of Natural History
Museum & Art Gallery
**Eastbourne**
The Pier
Towner Art Gallery & Local History Museum
**East Hoathly**
Specially For You
**Hastings**
Fishermen's Museum
Hastings Country Park
**Hove**
Hove Museum & Art Gallery
**Seaford**
Seven Sisters Country Park
**Stanmer Park**
Stanmer Rural Museum
**Wilmington**
The Long Man

## SUSSEX, WEST

**Bramber**
Bramber Castle
**Chichester**
District Museum
Guildhall Museum
**Findon**
Cissbury Ring
**Halnaker**
Halnaker Mill
**Highdown**
Highdown Gardens
**Horsham**
Horsham Museum
**Littlehampton**
Littlehampton Museum
**Nutbourne**
Nutbourne Manor Vineyard
**Shoreham-by-Sea**
Marlipins Museum
**Washington**
Chanctonbury Ring

**Worthing**
Worthing Museum & Art Gallery

## TYNE & WEAR

**Newcastle-upon-Tyne**
John George Joicey Museum
Laing Art Gallery
Museum of Antiquities
Museum of Science & Engineering
Theatre Royal

**North Shields**
Stephenson Railway Museum

**South Shields**
Arbeia Roman Fort & Museum

**Sunderland**
Grindon Close Museum
Museum & Art Gallery
Monkswearmouth Station Museum

**Wallsend**
Wallsend Heritage Centre

## WARWICKSHIRE

**Hatton**
Hatton Craft Centre

**Leamington Spa**
Warwick District Council Art Gallery &
Museum

**Warwick**
St John's House
Warwickshire Museum
Warwickshire Yeomanry Museum

## WEST MIDLANDS

**Birmingham**
Aston Hall
Birmingham Nature Centre
Blakesley Hall
City Museum & Art Gallery
Museum of Science & Industry
Sarehole Mill
Selly Manor Museum & Minworth Greaves
Exhibition Hall
Weoley Castle

**Brierley Hill**
Royal Brierley Crystal

**Coventry**
Coombe Abbey Country Park
Herbert Art Gallery & Museum
Old Cathedral of St Michael
St Mary's Guildhall

**Dudley**
Museum & Art Gallery

**Kingswinford**
Broadfield House Glass Museum

**Rubery**
Waseley Hills Country Park

**Stourbridge**
Edinburgh Crystal Factory Shop & Museum
Royal Doulton Crystal (UK)

**Walsall**
Museum & Art Gallery
Walsall Leather Centre Museum

**Willenhall**
Willenhall Museum

**Wolverhampton**
Bantock House Museum
Central Art Gallery

**Wordsley**
Stuart Crystal

## WIGHT, ISLE OF

**Chilton Chine**
Isle of Wight Pearl

**Cowes**
Maritime Museum & Public Library
Sir Max Aitken Museum

**Sandown**
Museum of Isle of Wight Geology

**Ventnor**
Botanic Gardens

## WILTSHIRE

**Avebury**
Stone Circle

**Bedwyn, Great**
Bedwyn Stone Museum

**Chippenham**
Yelde Hall Museum

**Fovant**
Regimental Badges

**Ludgershall**
Ludgershall Castle

**Malmesbury**
Athelstan Museum

**Swindon**
Lydiard House
Museum & Art Gallery
Richard Jefferies Museum

**Woodhenge**

## YORKSHIRE, NORTH

**Aysgarth**
Yorkshire Dales National Park Centre

**Bedale**
Bedale Museum

**Clapham**
Yorkshire Dales National Park Centre

**Danby**
The Moors Centre

**Grassington**
Yorkshire Dales National Park Centre

**Hawes**
Yorkshire Dales National Park Centre &
Dales Countryside Museum
W R Outhwaite & Son, Ropemakers
The Wensleydale Pottery

**Malham**
Yorkshire Dales National Park Centre

**Richmond**
Swaledale Pottery

**Skipton**
Craven Museum

**Thirsk**
Treske Limited

**Whitby**
Whitby Archives
**York**
Borthwick Institute of Historical Research
City Art Gallery
King's Manor

*YORKSHIRE, SOUTH*
**Barnsley**
. Cooper Gallery
**Campsall**
Campsall Country Park
**Cawthorne**
Cannon Hall Museum & Country Park
**Crowtherwood**
Sandall Beat Nature Reserve
**Cusworth**
Cusworth Country Park
Museum of South Yorkshire Life
**Doncaster**
Museum & Art Gallery
**Rotherham**
Art Gallery
Clifton Park Museum
Rother Valley Country Park
**Sheffield**
City Museum
Shepherd Wheel

*YORKSHIRE, WEST*
**Batley**
Art Gallery
Bagshaw Museum
**Bingley**
Bingley Five Rise Locks
**Birstall**
Oakwell Hall & Country Park
**Bradford**
Bolling Hall
Cartwright Hall Art Gallery
Industrial Museum
National Museum of Photography, Film &
Television
**Brierley**
Howell Wood Country Park
**Brighouse**
Brighouse Art Gallery
**Dewsbury**
Dewsbury Museum
**Halifax**
Bankfield Museum & Art Gallery
Piece Hall
**Huddersfield**
Art Gallery
Castle Hill
Tolson Memorial Museum
**Ilkley**
Manor House Museum & Gallery
**Keighley**
Cliffe Castle Museum & Gallery
**Leeds**
Kirkstall Abbey
Leeds City Art Gallery

Leeds City Museum
Tropical World, Canal Gardens
**Lotherton Hall**
Lotherton Hall Bird Gardens
**Marsden**
Tunnel End Canal & Countryside Centre
**Pontefract**
Pontefract Castle & Visitor Centre
**Wakefield**
Wakefield Art Gallery
Wakefield Museum
**West Bretton**
Yorkshire Sculpture Park

# CHANNEL ISLANDS

*GUERNSEY*
**Catel**
Guernsey Telephone Museum
**St Peters**
Coach House Gallery
**St Sampson**
Oatlands Craft Centre

*JERSEY*
**Gorey Village**
Jersey Pottery
**St Helier**
Jersey Photographic Museum
**St Ouen**
Jersey Goldsmiths
Kempt Tower Interpretation Centre
Plemont Candlecraft
Sunset Carnation Nurseries

*ISLE OF MAN*
**Douglas**
Manx Museum

# SCOTLAND

*BORDERS*
**Broughton**
Broughton Gallery
**Galashiels**
Peter Anderson Cashmere Woollen Mill
Old Gala House
**Hawick**
Wrights of Trowmill
**Kelso**
Kelso Abbey
**Melrose**
Priorwood Garden
**St Abbs**
St Abbs Head Nature Reserve
**Selkirk**
Halliwells House Museum

## CENTRAL

**Bo'ness**
Kinneil Museum & Roman Fortlet
**Callander**
Kilmahog Woollen Mill
**Dunblane**
Dunblane Cathedral
**Falkirk**
Falkirk Museum
Rough Castle
**Grangemouth**
Grangemouth Museum
**Kilmahog**
Trossachs Woollen Mill
**Stirling**
Mar's Wark
Stirling Smith Art Gallery & Museum
**Tillicoultry**
Clock Mill Heritage Centre

## DUMFRIES & GALLOWAY

**Bladnoch**
Bladnoch Distillery
**Drumcoltran Tower**
**Dumfries**
Burns' Mausoleum
Robert Burns Centre
Dumfries Museum
Old Bridge House
**Moffat**
Ladyknowe Mill
**Newton Stewart**
Creebridge Weaving Mills
Kirroughtree Visitor Centre
**Palnackie**
Orchardton Tower
**Ruthwell**
Savings Bank Museum
Ruthwell Cross

## FIFE

**Balmerino**
Balmerino Abbey
**Burntisland**
Burntisland Edwardian Fair Museum
**Culross**
Culross Abbey
Little Houses
**Dunfermline**
Andrew Carnegie Birthplace Museum
Dunfermline Abbey
Dunfermline District Museum
Pittencrieff House Museum
**Inverkeithing**
Inverkeithing Museum
**Kirkcaldy**
Kirkcaldy Museum & Art Gallery
John McDouall Stuart Museum
**Leven**
Letham Glen
Silverburn Estate

**St Andrews**
Crawford Arts Centre

## GRAMPIAN

**Aberdeen**
Aberdeen Art Gallery
Cruickshank Botanic Garden
Duthie Park & Winter Gardens
James Dun's House
Kings College
Marischal College
Maritime Museum
Provost Skene's House
St Machar's Cathedral
**Banchory**
Banchory Museum
**Banff**
Banff Museum
**Buckie**
Buckie Maritime Museum
**Burghead**
Burghead Museum
**Collieston**
Slains Castle
**Crathie**
Royal Lochnagar Distillery
**Dufftown**
Dufftown Museum
Glenfiddich Distillery
**Duffus**
Duffus Castle
**Elgin**
Pluscarden Abbey
**Fochabers**
Baxters Visitor Centre
**Forres**
Falconer Museum
**Glendronach**
Glendronach Distillery
**Glenlivet**
The Glenlivet Distillery Visitor Centre
**Huntly**
Huntly Museum
**Inverurie**
Inverurie Museum
**Keith**
Strathisla Distillery
**Knockando**
Cardhu Distillery
Tamdhu Distillery Visitors Centre
**Mintlaw**
Aden Country Park
**Peterhead**
Arbuthnot Museum & Art Gallery
**Rothes**
Glen Grant Distillery
**Spey Bay**
Tugnet Ice House
**Stonehaven**
Stonehaven Tolbooth
**Tomintoul**
Tomintoul Museum

**Tomnavoulin**
Tomnavoulin-Glenlivet Distillery

*HIGHLAND*
**Achiltibuie**
The Smokehouse
**Auldearn**
Boath Doocot
**Aviemore**
Craigellachie National Nature Reserve
**Clava Cairns**
**Corrieshalloch Gorge**
**Dalwhinnie**
Dalwhinnie Distillery
**Dornoch**
Dornoch Cathedral
Dornoch Craft Centre
**Fortrose**
Fortrose Cathedral
**Fort William**
Inverlochy Castle
**Inverfarigaig**
Farigaig Forest Centre
**Inverness**
James Pringle Weavers
Museum & Art Gallery
**Kingussie**
Ruthven Barracks
**Kintail**
Kintail & Morvich Countryside Centre
**Kirkhill**
Highland Wineries
**Lochcarron**
Strome Castle
**Muir of Ord**
Glen Ord Distillery
**Newtonmore**
Clan MacPherson House & Museum
**Reay**
Dounreay Public Exhibition
**Spean Bridge**
Spean Bridge Woollen Mill
**Wick**
Castle of Old Wick

*LOTHIAN*
**East Fortune**
Museum of Flight
**Edinburgh**
Clan Tartan Centre
Fruit Market Gallery
General Register House
George Heriot's School
Huntly House
Lady Stair's House
Museum of Childhood
National Gallery of Scotland
National Library of Scotland
National Museum of Scotland
Parliament House
The People's Story
Royal Botanic Garden

Scottish National Gallery of Modern Art
Scottish National Portrait Gallery
South Queensferry Museum
Trinity Apse
West Register House
**Ingliston**
Scottish Agricultural Museum
**Livingston**
Almondell & Calderwood Country Park
**Musselburgh**
Pinkie House
**North Berwick**
North Berwick Law
North Berwick Museum
**Prestonpans**
Scottish Mining Museum
**Vogrie Country Park**

*STRATHCLYDE*
**Ayr**
Maclaurin Art Gallery & Rozelle House
**Balloch**
Balloch Castle Country Park
**Bearsden**
Roman Bath House
**Carnasserie Castle**
**Coatbridge**
Summerlee Heritage Trust
**Dunoon**
Scottish White Heather Farm
**Glasgow**
Bellahouston Park
Botanic Garden
The Burrell Collection
Cathedral
City Chambers
Collins Gallery
Glasgow Art Gallery & Museum
Haggs Castle
Hunterian Museum
Hutchesons's Hall
Mitchell Library
Museum of Transport
People's Palace Museum
Pollok Country Park
Pollok House
Provand's Lordship
Provan Hall
Regimental Museum of the Royal Highland
Fusiliers
Ross Hall Park
Rutherglen Museum
Victoria Park
**Greenock**
McLean Museum & Art Gallery
**Hamilton**
Hamilton District Museum
**Hunterston**
Hunterston Power Station
**Irvine**
Eglinton Park
Glasgow Vennel Museum

**Kilmarnock**
Dick Institute
Johnnie Walker Plant Tours
**Kilmartin**
Dunadd Fort
**Kilmun**
Kilmun Arboretum
**Kilsyth**
Colzium House & Estate
**Lochgilphead**
Kilmory Castle Gardens
**Milngavie**
Lillie Art Gallery
**Mugdock**
Mugdock Country Park
**Muirshiel**
Muirshiel Country Park
**Oban**
Oban Distillery
**Paisley**
Coats Observatory
**Saltcoats**
North Ayrshire Museum

*TAYSIDE*
**Aberfeldy**
Aberfeldy Distillery
**Bruar**
Clan Donnachaidh Museum
**Crieff**
Stuart Strathearn Glass
**Dundee**
Barrack Street Museum
Broughty Castle Museum
McManus Galleries
Mills Observatory
**Dunkeld**
Hermitage
Little Houses & The Ell Shop
Loch of the Lowes Visitor Centre
**Kinross**
Loch Leven Castle
**Milnathort**
Burleigh Castle
**Perth**
Black Watch Regimental Museum
Dewar's Scotch Whisky
Fair Maid's House
Perth Museum & Art Gallery
Quarrymill Woodland Park
**Pitlochry**
Blair Atholl Distillery
Faskally
**Queen's View**
Queen's View Centre

======= SCOTTISH ISLANDS =======

*BUTE*
**Rothesay**
Ardencraig

*COLONSAY*
**Kiloran**
Kiloran Woodland Garden
*GREAT CUMBRAE*
**Millport**
Museum of the Cumbraes
*IONA*
**Iona Abbey**
*LEWIS*
**Callanish**
Callanish Standing Stones
**Carloway**
Dun Carloway Broch
*ORKNEY*
**Birsay**
Earls Palace
**Dounby**
Click Mill
**Finstown**
Stennes Standing Stones
**Hoy**
Dwarfie Stane
**Kirkwall**
Highland Park Distillery
Rennibister Earth House
**Lamb Holm**
Italian Chapel
**Papa Westray**
Knap of Howar
**Rousay**
Midhowe Broch & Tombs
**Stromness**
Pier Arts Centre
**Westray**
Noltland Castle
*SHETLAND*
**Lerwick**
Clickheinen
Fort Charlotte
Shetland Museum
**Mousa Island**
Mousa Broch
**Scalloway**
Scalloway Castle

======= WALES =======

*CLWYD*
**Cerrigydrudion**
Llyn Brenig Centre & Welsh Water Estate
**Clawdd-Newydd**
Bod Petrual Visitor Centre
**Ewloe**
Ewloe Castle
**Flint**
Flint Castle
**Holywell**
Greenfield Valley Heritage Park

**Loggerheads**
  Loggerheads Country Park
**Moel Famau**
  Moel Famau Country Park
**Waen-y-Llyn**
  Waen-y-Llyn Country Park
**Wrexham**
  Bersham Industrial Heritage Centre
  Ty Mawr Country Park

## DYFED
**Aberystwyth**
  National Library of Wales
  Yr Hen Gapel
**Borth**
  Brynllys Farm
**Capel Dewi**
  Y Felin Wlan (Rock Mills)
**Cenarth**
  The National Coracle Centre
**Dryslwyn**
  Dryslwyn Castle
**Golden Grove**
  Gelli Aur Country Park
**Llanelli**
  Parc Howard Art Gallery & Museum
**Llansteffan**
  Llansteffan Castle
**Newport**
  Pentre Ifan Burial Chamber
**St Dogmaels**
  St Dogmaels Abbey
**St Nicholas**
  Tregwynt Woollen Mill
**Saundersfoot**
  Saundersfoot Pottery & Craft Shop
**Tenby**
  Tenby Pottery

## GLAMORGAN, MID
**Aberbargoed**
  Stuart Crystal
**Aberdare**
  Dare Valley Country Park
**Bridgend**
  Newcastle
**Merthyr Tydfil**
  Joseph Parry's Cottage
**Ogmore**
  Ogmore Castle
**Pontypridd**
  The Grogg Shop
**Tondu**
  Glamorgan Nature Centre

## GLAMORGAN, SOUTH
**Llantwit Major**
  Town Hall
**Penarth**
  Turner House
**St Hilary**
  Old Beaupre Castle

## GLAMORGAN, WEST
**Swansea**
  Glynn Vivian Art Gallery & Museum
  Maritime & Industrial Museum

## GWENT
**Caerwent**
  Roman Town
**Chepstow**
  Stuart Crystal
**Cwmcarn**
  Cwmcarn Forest Drive Visitor Centre
**Grosmont**
  Grosmont Castle
**Llanthony**
  Llanthony Priory
**Llantilio Crossenny**
  Hen Gwrt
**Monmouth**
  The Kymin
**Newport**
  Museum & Art Gallery
**Sirhowy Valley**
  Sirhowy Valley Country Park
**Skenfrith**
  Skenfrith Castle

## GWYNEDD
**Bangor**
  Bangor Museum & Art Gallery
**Bryn-Celli-Ddu**
  Bryn-Celli-Ddu Burial Chamber
**Caernarfon**
  Segontium Roman Fort & Museum
**Corris**
  Railway Museum
**Dinas Mawddwy**
  Meirion Mill
**Holyhead**
  South Stack RSPB Reserve
**Llanallgo**
  Din Lligwy Ancient Village
**Llanberis**
  Dolbadarn Castle
**Llandudno**
  Great Orme Country Park & Nature Reserve
**Llanfihangel-y-Pennant**
  Castell y Bere
**Llangybi**
  St Cybi's Well
**Maesgwm**
  Maesgwm Visitor Centre
**Menai Bridge**
  Tegfryn Art Gallery
**Penmachno**
  Penmachno Woollen Mill
**Penmon**
  Penmon Priory
**Pennarth Fawr**
**Porthmadog**
  Ffestiniog Railway Museum

**Trefriw**
Trefriw Woollen Mill

*POWYS*
**Brecon**
Brecknock Museum
**Lake Vyrnwy**
**Llandrindod Wells**
Llandrindod Wells Museum
Rock Park Spa
**Llanidloes**
Museum of Local History & Industry
**Llanwrtyd Wells**
The Cambrian Factory

**Mongomery**
Montgomery Castle
**Newtown**
Oriel 31 (Davies Memorial Gallery)
Robert Owen Memorial Museum
Textile Museum
W H Smith (1920s Replica Shop)
**Welshpool**
Cockpit
Oriel 31 Art Gallery
Powysland Museum & Montgomery Canal
Centre
Severn Farm Pond